Cover Illustration: 'Faces 12–24'
A series of 12 woodcuts by Kenyan artist Peterson Kamwathi. These 12 colour reduction woodcut prints on paper are part of a long-running series of 36 woodcuts on the theme of access, which concerns voter registration, photo ID records, individual choices and identities and the struggle of Kenyans to access their rights and opportunities among the complexities of modern life.

Peterson Kamwathi was born in Nairobi in 1980. He started practising art full-time in 1999 at the Kuona Trust Museum Art Studio where he was exposed to different techniques, including print-making. Since late 2002 he has been involved primarily in print-making, especially monotype and woodcut techniques. His work during this time represents his perspective on the social, environmental and political happenings in Kenya. Kamwathi has had two solo exhibitions and his work has been exhibited in Kenya, the UK, the USA, Holland and Denmark. He has participated in the Fontys Acadamie Kenya-Holland Exchange in 2003, the Wasanii International Artists 2004 Workshop in Lamu, Kenya, the Kenya Artists in Residence Program at the University of Kentucky in 2005, and print-making residencies at the London Print Studio and Bath Spa University College in 2006. He currently works from the Godown Art Centre in Nairobi, Kenya.

Public & Private Universities in Kenya

New Challenges, Issues & Achievements

Higher Education in Africa

All titles published in association with Partnership for Higher Education in Africa

Daniel Mkude, Brian Cooksey & Lisbeth Levey
Higher Education in Tanzania
A Case Study

Nakanyike B. Musisi
& Nansozi K. Muwanga
Makerere University in Transition 1993–2000
Opportunities & Challenges

Mouzinho Mário, Peter Fry, Lisbeth Levey
& Arlindo Chilundo
Higher Education in Mozambique
A Case Study

Nico Cloete, Pundy Pillay,
Saleem Badat & Teboho Moja
National Policy & a Regional Response
in South African Higher Education

Kilemi Mwiria, Njuguna Ng'ethe, Charles Ngome,
Douglas Ouma-Odero, Violet Wawire & Daniel Wesonga
Public & Private Universities in Kenya
New Challenges, Issues & Achievements

Charmaine Pereira
Gender in the Making of the Nigerian
University System

Takyiwaa Manuh, Salley Gariba & Joseph Budu
Change & Transformation in Ghana's
Publicly Funded Universities
A Study of Experiences, Lessons & Opportunities

Public & Private Universities in Kenya

New Challenges, Issues & Achievements

Kilemi Mwiria
Assistant Minister of Education
Republic of Kenya

Njuguna Ng'ethe
Associate Professor, Institute of Development Studies
University of Nairobi

Charles Ngome
Lecturer, Department of Educational Foundations
Kenyatta University

Douglas Ouma-Odero
Senior Programme Officer, Pact Kenya

Violet Wawire
Lecturer, Department of Educational Foundations
Kenyatta University

Daniel Wesonga
Lecturer, Educational Planning
Kenyatta University

Published in association with
Partnership for Higher Education in Africa

James Currey
OXFORD

East African Educational Publishers
NAIROBI

Partnership for Higher Education in Africa
IGEMS, New York University
The Steinhardt School of Education
726 Broadway, Room 532
New York, NY 10003

Published by

James Currey Ltd
73 Botley Road
Oxford
OX2 0BS, UK

East African Educational Publishers
P.O. Box 45314
Nairobi
Kenya

with the support of the Partnership for Higher Education in Africa, an initiative of Carnegie Corporation of New York, Ford Foundation, The John D. and Catherine T. MacArthur Foundation and The Rockefeller Foundation. The views expressed are those of the authors and not necessarily the foundations that funded this work.

1 2 3 4 5 11 10 09 08 07

British Library Cataloguing in Publication Data
Public & private universities in Kenya : new challenges,
    issues & achievements. - (Higher education in Africa)
    1. Universities and colleges - Kenya
    1. Mwiria, Kilemi II. Partnership for Higher Education in
    Africa
    378'.0096762

ISBN 978-0-85255-442-5 Paper

**Library of Congress Cataloging-in-Publication Data
is available**

Typeset in 10/11 pt Monotype Photina
by Long House Publishing Services, Cumbria, UK
Printed and bound in Malaysia

Contents

List of Figures, Tables & Boxes — xii
List of Acronyms — xiv
Preface to the Series — xvi

INTRODUCTION — 1
Kenyan Universities in the Coming Decades:
The Policy Intention
Kilemi Mwiria
    A new dawn — 1
    The inherited legacy — 1
    Governance & management — 4
    Quality & curriculum reform — 6
    Expansion & integration — 8
    Access & equity — 9
    Finance & financial management — 10
    Service outreach & engagement with society — 11

I

PUBLIC UNIVERSITY REFORM IN KENYA:
MAPPING THE KEY CHANGES OF THE LAST DECADE
Kilemi Mwiria & Njuguna Ng'ethe — 13
    Acknowledgements — 14

1

Kenyan Universities in the Coming Decades — 15
    Background to the study — 15
    Historical context — 18

2

Reforms Related to Access, Equity, Quality & Relevance — 23
    Access — 23
    Equity-related reforms — 32
    Reforms & the problem of quality — 37
    Relevance, research & community outreach programmes — 44
    New delivery mechanisms — 49
    ICT in public universities — 52

Contents

3

Reforms Related to Governance/Management & Planning

54

New structures of governance & management	54
Strategic planning	55
Staffing in public universities	56
The management of human resources	61
Health & recreation activities	62
Management of student needs/affairs	63
Strategies for managing HIV/AIDS	64

4

Reforms Related to University Financing

66

Cost-sharing & the unit-cost system	66
Income-generating activities & privately sponsored students	68
Cost-reduction measures & constraints	70
Financial enhancement & management measures	72

5

Motivation for & Management of Reforms

76

Motivation for reform	76
The role of intermediary bodies in mediating reforms	87
The management of reform initiatives	94

6

Impact of the Reform Process

99

Increased access	99
Equity	99
Quality	100
Relevance	102
Kenya's quest for industrialization	102
Planning & management of university programmes	103
Utilization of financial, human & physical resources	104
Challenging the relevance of the Joint Admissions Board	105
Cost-sharing measures & student welfare	105
Public perception of the public universities	107

7

Concluding Observations & Questions Raised

Concluding Observations & Questions Raised 108
Improving the reform process & winning support 110
Lessons learned & questions raised 112
Final thought: Are the reforms innovative or transformative? 116

Appendix Research Methodology 119

II

PRIVATE PROVISION OF HIGHER EDUCATION IN KENYA: TRENDS & ISSUES IN FOUR UNIVERSITIES

Daniel Wesonga, Charles Ngome,
Douglas Ouma-Odero & Violet Wawire

Daniel Wesonga, Charles Ngome, Douglas Ouma-Odero & Violet Wawire 121
Acknowledgements 122

1

Origins of Private Higher Education in Kenya

Origins of Private Higher Education in Kenya 123
The establishment & location of private universities 123
Rationale for the study 125
The four case studies 125

2

Accreditation, Governance & Management

Accreditation, Governance & Management 127
Accreditation status 127
Governance structures 128
Management of human resources 128
Inter-university networking & linkages 133
Management of student affairs 134
Strategies for the management of HIV/AIDS 136
Extension & community services 137

3

Issues of Access & Equity   139

Access to university education   140
Equity of access   145
Gender equity in administration, teaching & research   150
University policies & support systems   152

4

Curriculum & Learning Systems   156

Academic programmes   156
Curriculum delivery & teaching resources   160
Relevance & quality of new programmes   161
Student evaluation   163
Faculty/student ratios   163
Research   164
Library facilities   165
University physical facilities   167
Co-curricular activities   168

5

Information & Communication Technologies   169

ICT resources in the private universities   169
Strategic plans & policies   170
Utilization & management   171
Benefits & constraints   175

6

Financing of Private Universities in Kenya   177

Sources of university finance   177
Recurrent expenditure trends in the private universities   183
The cost of private university education   186
The financial status of private universities   189
Financial management strengths   190

7
Recommendations

Recommendations   192
    Accreditation, governance & management   192
    Financing   194

Appendix   196
Research methodology   196
Data collection   196
Dissemination seminars   197

References   199

List of Figures, Tables & Boxes

Figures

I.1	Location of public and private universities in Kenya, 2003	17
I.2	Distribution of Kenyan public university students by ethnic origin	33
I.3	Actual and intended capacities of public university libraries	41
I.4	Enrolment in Kenyatta University's AVU site, 1997–2001	50
I.5	KCSE candidates by sex, 1992–2001	79
II.1	Faculty salary structure at USIU and public universities, 2002	132
II.2	Students' region of origin (CUEA)	145
II.3	Students' region of origin (USIU)	145

Tables

I.1	Undergraduate enrolment in public universities by sex, 1990–2002	24
I.2	Undergraduate programmes for self-sponsored students by university, 1998–2002	26
I.3	Location of programmes by university	31
I.4	Change in enrolment by sex, 1990–2001	35
I.5	Enrolment by sex and degree programmes in public universities, 1990–95	37
I.6	Effectiveness of Kenyan universities in fostering attributes valued in management literature (%)	39
I.7	Staff/student ratios in public universities 1994–2002	57
I.8	Academic staff by university, rank and sex, 2000/01 academic year	58
I.9	Cumulative recurrent deficits for all public universities	67
I.10	Capitation vs. expenditure at Kenyatta University, 1995–9	77
I.11	Growth of secondary education in Kenya, 1963–2000	79
II.1	Staff/student ratios, 2001/02 academic year	129
II.2	Enrolment trends, 1997–2001: number of students enrolled	143
II.3	Average student enrolment per school/faculty/discipline, 1999–2000	144
II.4	Province of origin of private university students (%)	146
II.5	Regional distribution of poverty	147
II.6	Undergraduate enrolments by sex, 1998–2000	148
II.7	Enrolment by sex and area of specialization, 1999	149
II.8	USIU student enrolment trends by age and sex, 1996–6	149
II.9	Staff participation in teaching and administration by sex, 2000	150
II.10	UEAB academic staff distribution by subject and sex, 2001	151
II.11	Student levels of satisfaction with facilities and services	154
II.12	Courses offered at USIU, Daystar, UEAB and CUEA	157
II.13	Student levels of satisfaction with the curriculum	160
II.14	Full-time/part-time academic staff ratios, 2001	164

xii

II.15	Student levels of satisfaction with computer facilities	173
II.16	Tuition income as a proportion of university revenue, 1995–2000	178
II.17	Tuition and fees as % of total recurrent expenditure, 1994/95–1999/2000	179
II.18	Priority recurrent expenditure items, 1994/95–1999/2000	184
II.19	Cost per credit hour/unit for undergraduate programmes	187
II.20	Tuition charges per year for undergraduate programmes	187
II.21	Recurrent unit costs per student, 1997/98–1999/2000	188

Box

| II.1 | The long journey to my MBA: Stanley Mugwiria, financial accountant, USIU | 131 |

List of Acronyms

ACUs	AIDS control units
ADRA	Adventist Development and Relief Agency
AJOL	African Journals Online
AMECEA	Association of Member Episcopal Conferences in Eastern Africa
ANU	Africa Nazarene University
ASAL	Arid and Semi-arid Land
AUSI	Australian Studies Institute
AVU	African Virtual University
BTC	Bureau of Training and Consultancy
CARS	College Administration and Registration System
CCK	Communications Commission of Kenya
CCMB	Centre for Complementary Medicine and Biotechnology
CHE	Commission for Higher Education
CIP	Centre for Improvement and Protection
CODESRIA	Council for the Development of Social Science Research in Africa
CUEA	Catholic University of Eastern Africa
CUSO	Catholic University Students Organization
DAAD	German Academic Exchange Service
DUSA	Daystar University Students' Association
DVC	Deputy Vice-Chancellor
EFMD	European Foundation for Management Development
EUHCP	Egerton University Health Centre Project
FAWE	Forum for African Women Educationalists
FGD	Focus group discussion
FKE	Federation of Kenyan Employers
FM	Frequency Modulation radio station
FTSE	Full-Time Staff Equivalent
GoK	Government of Kenya
GPA	Grade point average
HELB	Higher Education Loans Board
IAVI	International AIDS Vaccine Initiative
ICIPE	International Centre for Insect Physiology and Ecology
ICT	Information and Communications Technologies
IFESH	International Foundation for Education and Self-Help
IGA	Income-generating activity
INASP	International Network for the Availability of Scientific Publications
ISSP	International Students Services and Programs
JAB	Joint Admissions Board
JICA	Japanese International Co-operation Agency
JKUAT	Jomo Kenyatta University of Agriculture and Technology
KCCT	Kenya College of Communication and Technology
KCPE	Kenya Certificate of Primary Education
KCSE	Kenya Certificate of Secondary Education

KEMRI	Kenya Medical Research Institute
KENET	Kenya Education Network
kg	kilogram(s)
km	kilometre(s)
KNEC	Kenya National Examination Council
Kshs.	Kenya shillings
KU	Kenyatta University
KUSA	Kenyatta University Students Association
KVU	Kenyatta Virtual University
LAN	Local Area Network
MBA	Master of Business Administration
MMS	Macro/Mini Systems, Inc.
MoEST	Ministry of Education, Science and Technology
MUSO	Moi University Students Organization
NGO	Non-governmental organization
NUSA	Nairobi University Students Association
OCLC	Online Computer Library Center
OKUO	Operation Kenyatta University Outreach
PAC	Project Appraisals Committee
PAYE	Pay-as-you-eat
PERI	Programme for the Enhancement of Research Information
PIMC	Project Monitoring and Incubation Committee
PMC	Production and Marketing Committee
PSSP	Privately-Sponsored Students Programmes
SAC	Student Affairs Council
SAP	Structural Adjustment Programme
SDA	Seventh-day Adventist
TAC	Tanzania Adventist College
TIVET	Technical, Industrial, Vocational and Entrepreneurship Training
UASU	Universities' Academic Staff Union
UEAB	University of Eastern Africa, Baraton
UoN	University of Nairobi
UNES	University of Nairobi Enterprise Services
UNESCO	United Nations Educational, Scientific and Cultural Organization
UNISA	University of South Africa
USIU	United States International University
VC	Vice-Chancellor
VCT	Voluntary Counselling and Testing Centre
VSAT	Very Small Aperture Terminal
WASC	Western Association of Schools and Colleges
WERK	Women Educational Researchers of Kenya

Preface to the Series

The Partnership for Higher Education in Africa began as an affirmation of the ability of African universities to transform themselves and promote national development. The presidents of the four founding Partnership foundations – Carnegie Corporation of New York, the Ford Foundation, the John D. and Catherine T. MacArthur Foundation and the Rockefeller Foundation – came together out of a common belief in the future of African universities. Interest in higher education proceeds from a simple faith that an independent scholarly community supported by strong universities goes hand-in-hand with a healthy, stable democracy. Universities are vitally important to Africa's development. Their crucial activities in research, intellectual leadership and developing successive generations of engaged citizens will nourish social, political and economic transformation in Africa. Through the pooling of resources, the foundations will help advance the reform of African universities and accelerate the development of their countries.

Much of sub-Saharan Africa has suffered deep stagnation over the last two decades, and is staggering under the weight of domestic and international conflict, disease (especially the plague of HIV/AIDS), poverty, corruption and natural disasters. Its universities—once shining lights of intellectual excitement and promise—suffered from an enormous decline in government resources for education. In the late 1990s, however, things began to change in a number of countries. Our interest was captured by the renewal and resurgence that we saw in several African nations and at their universities, brought about by stability, democratization, decentralization and economic liberalization. Within these universities a new generation of leadership has stepped forward to articulate a vision for their institutions, inspiring confidence among those who care about African higher education.

At the outset the Partnership foundations selected six countries on which to focus – Ghana, Mozambique, Nigeria, South Africa, Tanzania and Uganda – and supported in each one higher education case studies. The case studies found that while the universities represented in these volumes have widely varying contexts and traditions, they are all engaged in broad reform. They are examining and revising their planning processes, introducing new techniques of financial management, adopting new technologies, reshaping course structures and pedagogy, and demonstrating genuine commitment to national capacity-building in contexts of national reform.

Although both the Ford and Rockefeller Foundations have long-standing offices in Nairobi, Kenya, and active higher education grant-making programmes there, Kenya did not become a Partnership country until 2005 when political reform led to an environment conducive to innovation and transformation within the higher education system. However, in advance of this development, our two foundations decided to collaborate with Kenyan researchers to produce this two-part country case study *Public and Private Universities in Kenya; New Challenges, Issues and Achievements*. We believed that including Kenya in the ongoing case-study process would better inform our grantmaking and would dovetail with the major aims of the Partnership:

- generating and sharing information about African universities and higher education
- supporting universities seeking to transform themselves
- enhancing research capacity on higher education in Africa
- promoting collaboration among African researchers, academics and university administrators

Like the other case studies published in this series, the Kenya studies were carried out under the leadership of local scholars, using a methodology that incorporates feedback from the institutions under study and involving a broad range of stakeholders.

The Rockefeller Foundation supported the public universities study by Kilemi Mwiria, now Assistant Minister for Education, Science, and Technology, and Njuguna Ng'ethe, Professor at the Institute of Development Studies (IDS), University of Nairobi. Professor Mwiria also wrote an introduction to this volume: 'Kenyan Universities in the Coming Decades: the Policy Intention' as an update on developments in Kenya since January 2003 when a new government took power in a peaceful electoral transition that rejected one-party rule.

The public universities case study is similar to the other studies that the Partnership has commissioned in that well-known senior academics were selected for the research. The Ford Foundation took a different tack when it funded a group of young scholars to carry out a study of Kenya's private universities. We believe it important to nurture and mentor the next generation of scholars. The Ford Foundation used the private universities case study as a way of encouraging first-rate work from younger and less experienced researchers. The Ford Foundation grant covered support for the research and writing of the case study as well as the establishment of an advisory committee to work with and mentor the authors – Daniel Wesonga, Charles Ngome, Douglas Ouma-Odero and Violet Wawire.

All of the Partnership case studies are the product of the foundations' support for conceptual work that generates information about

African higher education and university issues. Through the case studies, the foundations hope to promote a wider recognition of the importance of universities to African development. Additional studies will be published in 2007.

When the Partnership was established in 2000 we pledged $100 million in support of higher education in Africa. Working together, the foundations exceeded that goal and contributed $150 million through September 2005 to fund higher education reform efforts in the targeted countries and institutions involved. The Partnership was relaunched for a second five-year period on 16 September 2005. Two additional foundations have joined the Partnership – the William and Flora Hewlett Foundation and the Andrew W. Mellon Foundation. Together, the six foundations have pledged a minimum of $200 million over the next five years.

We hope that the publication of these case studies will help advance the state of knowledge about higher education in Africa and support the movement for university reform on the continent. Equally significant, the process of our involvement in the case studies has enhanced our own understanding and helped the foundations focus future efforts of the Partnership. Interest in higher education in Africa has grown since the Partnership was launched in 2000. In this way, the Partnership not only uses its own resources but also acts as a catalyst to generate the support of others, on the continent and elsewhere, for African universities as vital instruments for development. We see these case studies as a critical step in the process of regeneration and transformation.

Susan Berresford, President
FORD FOUNDATION

Judith Rodin, President
THE ROCKEFELLER FOUNDATION

INTRODUCTION
Kenyan Universities in the Coming Decade:
The Policy Intention

KILEMI MWIRIA

A new dawn

In January 2003 a new government took over in Kenya in a peaceful electoral transition that reflected the ultimate popular rejection of 25 years of one-party autocratic rule. It came to power on the promise of creating a more open, less fearful society that would be transparent in its practice, decentralized in its style, accountable in its procedures, meritocratic in recruitment, efficient in the use of resources and relevant in objectives and outcomes – in short, a more democratic dispensation. The proposed less politicized context had immediate relevance to the management of Kenya's universities. Early evidence was provided by the removal of the requirement that the President be the titular head of all the public universities and more generally by the beginnings of a move towards greater autonomy for universities in the management of their internal affairs and the removal of the somewhat autocratic culture, which had mirrored that of society itself.

The analytical essays on the public and private universities in Kenya that make up this two-part volume were conceived and written before this change in political culture. Indeed, the section on public universities focuses on reforms that were possible in the interstices of official policy and despite government interventions. The private universities were less subject to government intrusion but nevertheless were bound by broad regulatory measures established by the Commission for Higher Education (CHE) and, while able to exercise relatively greater autonomy than their public colleagues, were not entirely immune to the surrounding official culture. Although we are in the early days of the new dispensation, it is important to place the current state of the public and private universities described in this volume in the context of the inherited legacy from the past and, more importantly, within a framework of policy intentions for the future, and to anticipate likely changes in university purposes, management and practice. This Introduction attempts to address these broad themes.

The inherited legacy

As I write, there are 6 public universities and 17 private universities in Kenya today. Two national polytechnics (Nairobi and Mombasa)

1

are soon to upgrade some of their academic programmes to university status. While enrolment in the public universities amounted to 31,600 in the 1990/91 academic year, there were some 77,000 students enrolled in the public universities in 2005, of whom roughly 33,000 were privately sponsored. The dramatic pace of increase is due largely to the abolition of the 'A' level in 1992,[1] as a result of which entry to university now occurs after eight years of primary and four years of secondary education. Expansion has also been fuelled by the opening of the public universities to privately sponsored students under the so-called 'parallel' degree programme. Since this expansion was not accompanied by a commensurate increase in government funding, the result has been a steady decline in quality and increasingly serious questions about relevance. Although fees from privately sponsored students have been used to expand facilities and improve staff remuneration, it is not clear whether major strides have been made in the area of quality enhancement. This expansion of student numbers also took place within a macroeconomic context of a declining growth rate and an absolute decline in wage employment between the years 1990 and 2001.

From a policy perspective, issues of quality, relevance and employment were compounded by the confused state of legislation governing universities. Each public university has its own act, dating back to its date of foundation, but they are also affected by numerous pieces of sectoral legislation that created a situation in which the Ministry of Education was not the sole institution of government responsible for all matters of higher education. This has led to different methods of accreditation and programme certification. Attempts by the Commission for Higher Education to rationalize post-secondary education – its central mandate – met with widespread resistance from the public universities, with the result that it tended to confine itself to the registration and certification of private ones. However, it is now accepted that the Commission will in the future subject the public universities to quality assessment. Moreover, the haphazard growth of branches of foreign universities in Kenya will be better co-ordinated

---

[1] After independence, the educational system in Kenya was structured on the British 7-4-2-3 model, with seven years of primary schooling, four years of secondary education and two years of advanced secondary education to be eligible for a 3-year university bachelors degree programme. Since the 1980s, following the Mackay Report (Republic of Kenya, 1981) there was a shift to the 8-4-4 model of the American system with eight years of primary schooling followed by four years of secondary education and a four-year bachelors degree programme. The shift to 8-4-4 was completed in 1992 with the abolition of the 'A' level.

2

and subjected to thorough assessments. Likewise, although middle colleges will be supported as a way of enhancing access and quality, a unit will be established within the Ministry of Education to co-ordinate the previously uncontrolled mushrooming of largely profit-oriented poor-quality institutions.

The large body of legislation that has grown up over the years in the field of university education has created numerous problems. The most serious are the following: (i) the absence of a mechanism for the determination and assessment of universal quality standards, (ii) chronic resource deficits for programme expansion, and research and staff development, and (iii) the lack of decision-making auton-omy for the universities and (iv) the absence of a clear mechanism for the opening of satellite public university campuses across the country.

Because each university derives its powers from its specific legal instrument, co-ordination even in the interest of standardization has not been possible. Even the limited powers granted to the CHE under the old Universities Act to co-ordinate certain aspects of education provided by the public universities cannot be effected. The existing legal framework is now being reviewed. This exercise addresses the challenges facing higher education in Kenya in the twenty-first century with a view to producing a system that is knowledge-driven and quality-assured, technologically informed, research-supported, democratically managed and globally marketable. This legal harmo-nization is being effected for all levels of education under a recently established task force to review all laws governing education provision in Kenya – a matter that is also being addressed by the Public Universities' Inspection Board.

In the face of this inherited challenge, the new government in Kenya promises significant changes in higher education and has appointed a team of experts to review the required changes. Accord-ing to the team's report, policy will target six key reform areas: (i) governance/management, (ii) quality/relevance, (iii) expansion/integration, (iv) access/equity, (v) finance/financial management and (vi) community service and engagement with society. In addition, the proposed reforms will promote the creation of a broader, national system that will integrate the increasing number of private institutions with the more established public ones. In this connection, recommendations have been made regarding the putting in place of appropriate incentives to support private-sector participation.

Governance & management

Governance is perhaps the most critically needed area of reform, because higher education in Kenya has been the subject of much political manipulation and intervention. Partly as a consequence, the public universities have experienced numerous strikes and closures over the past decade, prolonging the time required for graduation, disrupting academic life and driving prospective students and resident staff to private and overseas institutions. In the future the government will see its role more in terms of the provision of a regulatory framework than as an intervening force. This will require, as a first step, changes in the legislation govering the universities, providing a single integrated act to cover public and private universities, offering greater autonomy and replacing the current mixture of restrictive and inconsistent acts mentioned above. Draft legislation for this purpose is being prepared.

Governance is important too because it involves the recruitment of the individuals managing the higher education institutions and determines relevance and whether management structures are more or less open. Steps have already been taken to enhance the democratization of decision-making within the universities by promoting wider representation of staff and students in key university governing bodies and by allowing staff a greater say in selecting senior university administrators. Currently the position of Vice-Chancellor is filled through competitive bidding. Similarly, each public university has its own Chancellor as opposed to the previous situation where the country's President was Chancellor of all of them. These reforms have reduced the politicization of decision-making in the universities. With regard to councils, the system of identifying their membership is being reviewed with a view to rationalizing their numbers as well as promoting representative and relevant composition. These moves should enhance the accountability of these top administrators to the university community. In this regard, it is the intention of the government that other key administrative positions be advertised on the expiry of the current contracts, with more representative senates and university councils doing the short-listing of candidates and final appointment following consultations with Chancellors and government officials. Regrettably, recent advertisements of Vice-Chancellor positions have attracted few non-university personnel – a blow to the strengthening of management efficiency. An important policy of the new government is designed to ensure that universities and other public bodies be held to performance contracts, and requires that all such bodies have current strategic plans. As of 2005, all the public universities had prepared these plans.

In the area of student affairs, the position of dean of students has been strengthened by making the dean answerable to the Vice-Chancellor, and in some cases by creating the position of a Deputy Vice-Chancellor (Student Affairs). This new position will also be made financially attractive to potential aspirants. Making the positions of deans of faculties and heads of departments elective should further enhance accountability. Also important will be the promotion of regular formal and informal contacts and more consultations between the top university administrators and students and staff in order to improve relations. Informal and other contacts can play an important role in enabling university administrators to anticipate potentially explosive situations on campus by preparing possible solutions in advance of conflict. Also to be encouraged is a more regular and intensive information flow between university administration and staff and the use of in-house newsletters and policy briefing meetings on a regular basis to inform academics and students of policies arrived at by council or government, while at the same time allowing students and staff to shape some of these policies.

Still with regard to governance, staff and student associations are to be strengthened to enable them to play an enhanced role as buffers between staff and students, on the one hand, and the university administration, on the other. The new government recently re-registered the Universities Academic Staff Union (UASU), which had been closed down under the former regime. It will now be expected to play roles beyond simply pressing for salary rises, including checking the excesses of the administration with regard to management, monitoring the use of institutional resources and promoting improved quality. Likewise, through their associations, students will be expected to be responsible and committed to their studies and to project a good image of themselves in the eyes of the wider public.

The appointment of Chancellors for all the public universities, taking the place previously reserved for the country's head of state, should enhance university autonomy. These Chancellors can play an important mediation role in conflict situations and will spearhead institutional fund-raising campaigns. In this connection the sharing of personnel between government and universities (getting government people to work in universities and vice versa) will be encouraged in order to improve understanding between the government and members of the university community. Universities will accordingly be aware that the government is likely to appreciate and encourage their role in national development and be more sympathetic to their needs, if such links exist and autonomy is accompanied by responsible and imaginative outreach and service activities by both academics and students. With regard to Chancellors, an emerging question relates to how they should be identified. The current system of leaving it to the country's President is being questioned on the grounds that the best candidates may not be appointed while political manipulation cannot be ruled out. In this connection, the Public Universities Inspection Board has suggested that university councils be responsible for the identification of their respective Chancellors.

Finally with regard to governance, the CHE will be strengthened so that it can play a pro-active role in developing an integrated national system of higher education, explaining the needs of universities to government, and directing development through the planning, co-ordination and funding of tertiary education. The CHE will be staffed by qualified professionals and will attain a sufficiently powerful position within the government structure to maintain a measure of professional distance between itself and all the parties interested in university education. To promote access and integration, the CHE will also be encouraged to develop an appropriate regulatory framework to facilitate the setting up of private universities, including those which make particular or exclusive provision for women. The CHE's mandate will also be expanded to deal with the unchecked and unco-ordinated mushrooming of campuses of universities based in foreign countries that has become a feature of the higher education scene in Kenya. The CHE will further be expected to promote improved quality at the tertiary level by means of rigorous inspection of both public and private universities, and will no longer limit its attention to private institutions. Officers of these institutions will be expected to collaborate with distinguished professionals from the private sector, civil society and government who have knowledge and experience of, and belief in, what universities are about. Reform will draw on the experience of private institutions that, although relatively new in the Kenya higher education scene, can offer some useful lessons in efficiency, as is evidenced in this volume.

Quality & curriculum reform

In the area of curriculum reform and quality assurance, universities will increasingly be called upon to concentrate attention on the quality of the education they offer. They will need to become the most publicized custodians of the principle of meritocracy with regard to the recruitment and promotion of academic and support staff and in the allocation of fellowships, research grants and opportunities to participate in seminars and international conferences. In this connection, the government will work as a partner with other stakeholders to ensure the provision of adequate teaching and learning inputs. Areas of particular focus will include expanded access to the internet for strengthening research and teaching capacity; increased institutional funding for research; more intensive training programmes for academics and university administrators; strengthened linkages with the private sector, especially in the areas of research, training and curriculum design; and the encouragement of new service roles and ways of engaging with urgent national needs. New universities or university campuses will be encouraged to start innovative programmes, and existing universities will be expected to strengthen their niche areas.

In the interests of enhancing the quality of public university education, the government has already increased salaries by between 90 and 160 per cent for the most junior and most senior academics, respectively. Such a move is intended to promote competition and lead to the return of many academics from outside the country and from the private sector. Combined with other non-monetary benefits such as housing, health insurance, more time for research and the possibility for public university academics to consult and teach in private institutions, a case can be argued that Kenyan public universities are closing the gap with even the best-paying private institutions as far as faculty remuneration is concerned. This may have repercussions for private universities, which have been heavily dependent on the part-time employment of previously poorly remunerated public university academics. With improved remuneration in the public universities, academics will be required to devote more time to research and teaching; they will also be subjected to a mutually agreed code of conduct. The university system will be called upon to develop a system of peer accreditation on what the key elements of a desirable university education ought to be, as well as a common body of knowledge expected of all university graduates. In this connection, basic communication and computer skills as well as other broad knowledge of specific subjects will be required from all students and academics. Peer reviews of faculty members and the latter's evaluation by their students will be encouraged. Promotion criteria will be much more rigorous and objective.

Quality will also be enhanced by a system in which academics are held to performance contracts and are not given permanent positions until they prove themselves. In the long run, the Kenya government hopes that a more supportive work environment will accompany improved remuneration. Critical ingredients of such an environment include adequate and comfortable office space; appropriate infrastructure, computers and internet facilities; attractive teaching facilities including lecture theatres, laboratories and libraries; and opportunities for conference attendance and research.

Expansion & integration

Fewer than 2 per cent of the relevant age cohort join Kenya's higher education institutions. With the virtual achievement of universal primary education following the 2003 government declaration of free primary education, and the planned expansion of secondary education to support basic education reform, the higher education sub-sector equally requires expansion. In any case, sustained economic growth is very much dependent on the generation of middle- and high-level manpower. The private sector will be expected to play a more prominent role and will be encouraged through a variety of incentives including tax breaks on imports of educational materials, provision of land on which to set up institutions and bursary support for privately sponsored students in both private and public universities. In the public realm, measures to promote expansion of opportunity include the enhanced use of distance-learning, allowing a system of credit transfers across institutions, with the possibility of middle-level college students enrolling at university, and equipping national polytechnics to provide high-quality education. In contrast with previous practice, universities will be permitted to expand enrolments or open up new campuses only after it is clear that they have the capacity to accommodate increased student numbers. Also to be taken into account will be the need to ensure the appropriate ratio between the outputs of middle-level colleges and universities in order to avoid previous mistakes where a number of the middle-level colleges were converted into university campuses on the basis of politically motivated decisions.

Future expansion will also take account of geographical representation and the variety of Kenya's natural resource base in view of the learning potential of such diversity. Day universities will also be promoted so that socially and economically disadvantaged groups will have greater opportunities to enrol in the public universities. In the interests of supporting competitive institutions of higher learning, universities will be encouraged to recruit students individually so that those with more attractive programmes will draw more students than those regarded as providing a product of questionable value. This will require revision of the current centralized system under which the Joint Admissions Board allocates places to students. Also planned for revision is the current policy of tying admission to available bed capacity. The public universities will be encouraged to divert services such as catering and accommodation to the private sector, as one measure of improving the quality of instruction, efficiency of resource utilization and expansion as more students can enrol as day students.

Access & equity

To ensure that expansion also takes account of economically disadvantaged and other marginalized groups, affirmative action programmes will be strengthened. The government supports the current practice of permitting the admission to the public universities of female students, students from remote regions and disabled students with slightly lower grades than their more favoured counterparts. A proposal has been made to extend this reform to students from poorly endowed schools. Moreover, both the Higher Education Loans Board (HELB) and bursary programmes will be strengthened in order to benefit a larger body of needy students. The public universities will also be encouraged to support needy students through work-study programmes and merit-based scholarships, as is the case in some private universities. More students are likely to benefit from higher-education loan support if the system of evaluating who benefits from these loans is revised. This revision will lead to a situation in which students able to pay will pay more for their education, with the surplus income being used to benefit a greater number of economically disadvantaged students. Expansion will also be enhanced by supporting private universities opening up to more of the students who currently enrol in private programmes in the public universities, as they can afford private education.

The government will seek in particular to provide encouragement and incentives to the public universities to increase the proportion of women as students, faculty and administrators, so that they can approach the situation of near parity that exists in the private universities. With regard to students, a significant part of this challenge involves improving quality at the secondary level in order to enlarge

9

the pool of qualified boys and girls eligible for university admission, particularly in the fields of science and mathematics and especially for students enrolled in provincial and district secondary schools. At the same time, the government will watch with interest the private experiment of Kenya's first all-women's university in science and technology. Affirmative action reforms will also encourage the admission of more female students to science departments.

Finance & financial management

Because the proposed reforms have substantial monetary implications, in addition to the efficiency and cost-effective use of institutional resources, universities will have not only to diversify their sources but also to enhance their levels of income. They will be encouraged to intensify their income-generating activities by expanding programmes for fee-paying students, while paying attention to the implications for educational quality and equity; securing the support of the private sector through student and staff internship programmes, research support, student sponsorships and teaching support; introducing a private-sector training levy; involving alumni in fund-raising programmes; reaching out to individual benefactors of university education and generally utilizing all resources at their disposal more efficiently and effectively. The public universities can learn from their private counterparts, which benefit from endowments, gifts, trusts, alumni, friends' contributions and even church services.

The emergence of Kenyan Rockefellers, Fords and Carnegies as benefactors of higher education is long overdue. There undoubtedly are Kenyans who would be willing to fund a university library or laboratory if they were assured that the facility would be named after them and if the quality of the institution would bring renown to them as benefactors. The public universities could also benefit greatly from the more than Ksh.7 billion owed by their former students; in this regard, it may be necessary to contract the private sector to hasten the process of loan recovery. In addition, new and existing linkages with foreign universities would provide the source of many fellowships, joint research projects or exchange of visiting professors who may not require payment. There are also prospects for harnessing the potential of fee-paying programmes and increasing the fees of better-off students. The private universities are largely dependent on fees for their sustenance. To be able to attract more students, the public universities need to borrow ideas from their private counterparts, especially in the area of programmes, open days and graduation ceremonies.

In the future, the public universities will be expected to be more efficient and accountable managers of public resources. Efficiency should be manifested in the cost-effective use of available human and physical resources. University staff will thus be expected to devote more hours to teaching and research. In particular, more time will have to be spent on postgraduate supervision. It is an embarrassing fact that on average it takes four to six years for a Master of Arts or Master of Science student to complete his/her studies; a Ph.D. degree takes even longer. Cost-effective use of resources will further entail a reduction of support staffing and a more intensive use of available physical facilities through the full utilization of libraries, laboratories and lecture theatres and the rental of idle facilities such as hostels during the vacations and grounds for agriculture and livestock farming. Cost-effectiveness can be further enhanced by more economical use of water, electricity, telephones, institutional vehicles and stationery. In this regard, universities will be subjected to rigorous auditing procedures and the discretionary power of senior university administrators to spend on virtually anything will be curtailed.

Finally, future government support will be rationalized with a view to ensuring that funding for the universities is more closely tied to the cost of teaching programmes and academic performance and not just to student numbers. Needless to say, quality expansion will call for greater government and donor investments in higher education. Given that primary (and even secondary) education gives little guarantee of economic success to its beneficiaries and that most of the economic advancement witnessed in emerging economies and in the West is largely dependent on investment in higher education, the logic of donors focusing most of their education resources on basic education is hard to justify.

Service outreach & engagement with society

Accountability to the public will be reinforced by encouraging universities to become more market-oriented and generally more responsive to changing national development objectives as well as by enhancing outreach programmes for the wider public. The private universities tend to be stronger than their public counterparts in the area of outreach programmes. At United States International University, for example, student internships are an integral part of the

curriculum and often lead to longer-term employment after graduation. With the notable exceptions of Kenyatta University's response
to the HIV/AIDS crisis and the relationship of Jomo Kenyatta
University of Agriculture and Technology with small farmers, the
public universities have been slow to develop imaginative ways of
serving local communities and the national society. The government
will encourage research, pilot programmes and new thinking about
ways in which universities can more effectively engage with the
society in which they are located.

This volume illustrates both the contemporary situation and the
government's reformist intentions towards the public and private
universities in Kenya. What it shows above all is the extent to which
public and private universities can learn from and complement each
other. The Government of Kenya is committed to the support of this
learning process and the development of an integrated system that
can serve the interests and improve the well-being of all Kenyans.

Hon. Kilemi Mwiria
Assistant Minister of Education
Nairobi, March 2006

I Public University Reform in Kenya

Mapping the Key Changes of the Last Decade

KILEMI MWIRIA
& NJUGUNA NG'ETHE

Acknowledgements

This study would not have been possible without the support of the then Vice-Chancellors of the six public universities in Kenya: Professor Crispus Kiamba, University of Nairobi; Professor George Eshiwani, Kenyatta University; Professor Ratemo Michieka, Jomo Kenyatta University of Agriculture and Technology (JKUAT); Professor Ezra Maritim, Egerton University; Professor Raphael Munavu, Moi University and his successor Professor David K. Some, and Professor Fredrick Onyango of Maseno University. We would also like to express our gratitude to the lecturers, students and administrators at all the public universities for participating in this study in one way or another. The support extended to us by the Commission for Higher Education, the Higher Education Loans Board and the Joint Admissions Board is equally appreciated.

We also express our thanks to the team of researchers from the six public universities, namely, E. M. Standa and I. O. Ipara, Moi University; F. Mwaura, JKUAT; L. Othuon and L. Kiprop, Maseno University; J. Changeiywo and A. Oywaywa, Egerton University; the late A. Adala, University of Nairobi and C. K. Ngome, Kenyatta University. They all worked as a team to generate the information from which this report was written. In addition, we are grateful to Kibisu Kabatesi of the Institute for Development Studies at the University of Nairobi for the technical editing, to L. Kiiru for proofreading and to our colleague David Court for his commitment and support throughout.

Finally, we wish to thank the Rockefeller Foundation for funding this study. It would not have taken place without their generous grant, which made it possible for the principal researchers to put together excellent research teams at each of the six public universities.

Dr Kilemi Mwiria
Professor Njuguna Ng'ethe

1 Kenyan Universities in the Coming Decade

Background to the study

This is a study of significant changes and reforms in the Kenyan public university system since 1990. Within this context, the study seeks to document the motivation, management and, where possible, the impact of these reforms.

Since independence in 1963, the provision of higher education in Kenya, as in other African countries, has been subject to the dynamics of a fast-changing society. The government has had to demonstrate some commitment to the development of higher education, because of the latter's significance in the production of skilled manpower, including manpower for other levels of education. Society, for its part, has demonstrated a great appetite for university education. Government actions and societal demands combined have dictated that the entire public university system be reassessed in order to define its place in the country's socio–economic matrix. This reassessment has quite often adopted the twin reforms of creating new institutions and adding new activities to those existing in the already established institutions.

The result is a rapidly expanding and increasingly complex system, on the one hand, and institutional expansion and complexity, on the other. A further result is that each of the new institutions needs to strive to carve out its own niche, a task that has not been easy to accomplish. It is against this background that these institutions should be examined. In this regard, their greatest challenge is to provide high-quality education that is also relevant and accessible. This primary challenge has been compounded by the fact that, from the 1980s on, Kenya has experienced financial difficulties due to poor economic performance, rapid population growth and the burden of providing basic services such as primary education and health care, which has meant that university education has faced severe competition for limited government funds. Systemic, institutional, economic, social and political factors have therefore conspired to force the universities to reform. This study looks at what reforms have been effected, how they were carried out and why.

The study had the following broad objectives: (i) to document and understand the reforms that have taken place in the public universities over the last ten years or so; (ii) to assist the universities, where necessary, in the systematization of data storage and retrieval within the institutions; (iii) to persuade the universities to start studying themselves; (iv) to provide upcoming education researchers with an opportunity to conduct research under supervision; and (v) to increase public awareness of the changing role of universities.

This study is partly a response to a somewhat mistaken belief among some higher education researchers that the Kenyan public universities have little to show by way of reform when compared with universities in Uganda and Tanzania, If one interprets reform to mean departure from established past practices, however, the study shows that there are important reforms taking place in all the Kenyan universities. The issue, therefore, is to understand and explain these changes in a socio-political context that is quite different from that prevailing in neighbouring countries. The Kenyan context is one of reform under difficult (some would say adverse) university-state relations. Thus the general problem that the study seeks to highlight is how African universities, operating under less than optimal circumstances, have managed not to collapse. What explains their resilience? Perhaps the answer lies in understanding how universities that operate under adverse political and other difficult circumstances can still manage to effect some reforms, which is the Kenyan case. In this regard, the motivation for change becomes an issue worthy of systematic exploration.

The study was guided by a number of specific questions, including the following:

- In what areas have changes taken place in the public universities during the past decade?
- What has motivated the changes taking place? Have intermediate bodies and private universities played a role in motivating these changes?
- How have the public universities managed the change process and with what success?
- What has been the impact of the changes within the institutions?
- How could the implementation and management of change have been improved?
- How sustainable are these changes?
- Which of these changes could be said to be innovative or transformative?

There are currently six public universities in Kenya: Egerton University, Jomo Kenyatta University of Agriculture and Technology, Kenyatta University, Moi University, Maseno University and the University of Nairobi, the oldest. Each of them was established under

16

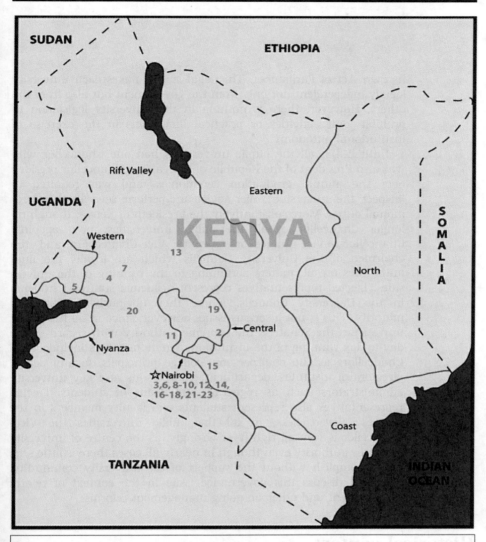

Figure 1.1: Location of public and private universities in Kenya, 2003

17

its own Act of Parliament. This legal status makes each university legally independent not only from the government but also from the others. However, there is nothing in the university legislation to prohibit joint activities or practical limitations in the exercise of institutional autonomy

Until 2003, all the public universities had one Chancellor who was also President of the Republic of Kenya. The Chancellor presided over the annual graduation ceremonies, and was required to 'inspect' the universities, offer advice and perform several other ceremonial duties. More substantively the President of Kenya, though no longer Chancellor of all the public universities, now appoints Chancellors, Vice-Chancellors, Deputy Vice-Chancellors and the chairmen of the University Councils which are legally the final authorities on all matters pertaining to the running of the universities. Elected representatives represent academic staff and students in the University Councils, where they obviously constitute a minority. This is not a serious issue, however, since in all the public universities the Senate is the supreme authority with regard to the day-to-day running of the institution. Senate members include Vice-Chancellors as the chairpersons, college principals, faculty deans, directors of institutes, department chairpersons and key university administrators such as registrars and deans of students. Elected representatives also represent students and faculty members in the senates. Nevertheless, in all the public universities the Vice-Chancellor is viewed, rightly or wrongly, as the centre of university power or authority even though in nearly all cases there is little s/he can accomplish without the support of the university community. We shall discuss this governance issue in the context of reform management and other on-going management reforms.

Historical context

The foundations of higher education in Kenya can be traced back to Makerere University in Uganda, founded in 1922 during British colonial rule as a technical college for African students from the East African countries of Uganda, Kenya and Tanganika. Although the college offered post-School Certificate courses in various fields including teacher training, carpentry, building technology, motor mechanics, medical care, agriculture and veterinary services, it was only after the publication of the Asquith Report in 1949 that the Makerere University Act was passed, giving the institution the legal status of a university. Makerere was thus established as the University of East Africa that was to offer degrees of the University of London, and admitted its first undergraduate students in 1950.

The first Kenyan higher-education institution was the Royal Technical College of East Africa, established in Nairobi in 1956 to provide instruction in courses leading to the Higher national certificate offered in Britain and to prepare matriculated students through full-time study for university degrees in engineering and commercial courses not offered by Makerere. As it admitted its first students, the need was felt for expert advice on the pattern of higher education in East Africa (Ngome, 2003: 360). This led to the appointment of a working party in 1958, which recommended that the Royal Technical College be transformed into an international university college in East Africa. In 1961, it was renamed the Royal College of Nairobi and turned into a university college, offering Bachelor of Arts and Bachelor of Science degrees in engineering of the University of London. In 1963, when Kenya attained its independence, Royal College became the University College of Nairobi and joined Makerere and Dar es Salaam Colleges to form the Federal University of East Africa.

Due to nationalist pressure mainly from Kenya and Tanzania, the University of East Africa was dissolved in 1970, with each of the three countries (Kenya, Uganda and Tanzania) establishing their own national universities under their respective Acts of Parliament. The University College of Nairobi was therefore renamed the University of Nairobi, and in the same year was expanded by the addition of new faculties and departments. The University of Nairobi has since grown to be the largest university in Eastern and Central Africa with over 30,000 students, the highest concentration of scholars and academic programmes housed in 14 faculties, 7 institutes, over 100 departments and one school, managed through 6 campus colleges headed by principals.

Since then, the government has established five other public universities. Moi University was the second public university to be established in Kenya following a recommendation by a presidential working committee – the Mackay Report (Republic of Kenya, 1981) – to develop degree programmes in vital scientific and technical fields and provide academic programmes with a practical orientation. The university has the distinction of being established on virgin farmland, a feature that contrasts it with the other public universities that inherited existing physical facilities from other institutions. Moi University is located 35 km from Eldoret town. It has three campuses: Main, Chepkoilel and Town campus and one constituent college – Western University College of Science and Technology. Moi is best known in the country for its forestry and wildlife conservation studies, although it also runs academic programmes in engineering, agriculture, physical sciences, medicine and social sciences.

Kenyatta University was inaugurated in 1985 as the third public university in Kenya. Its foundations were laid in 1965 when the British government handed over the Templer Barracks to the Kenyan government; it was converted into an institution of higher learning then known as Kenyatta College, located on the outskirts of Nairobi along Thika Road. The university offers degree courses in physical sciences, social sciences, business studies and environmental sciences. Notably, it is renowned for its programmes in education for which it is considered the leading education institution in Eastern and Central Africa.

Although Jomo Kenyatta University of Agriculture and Technology (JKUAT), situated 40 km northeast of Nairobi on the Thika/Nairobi highway in Central Province, became a fully-fledged university in 1994, its origin dates back to 1981 when it started as a middle-level technical college by means of assistance from the Japanese government over two decades (1981–2000). This assistance ended in 2000 after Japan had spent a total of Kshs8 billion in developing the institution. The Japanese government recently established a continent-wide research body at JKUAT known as the African Institute for Capacity Development to promote capacity-building in sub-Saharan Africa. The university offers a variety of degrees in engineering, computer science, food science and agriculture. While the University of Nairobi remains the institution preferred by Kenyans for most degree courses, it has recently started to lose ground to JKUAT in engineering and computer science programmes. This is perhaps a pointer to many of the problems that are afflicting the University of Nairobi, including the deterioration in the teaching of these degree programmes and the negative image its students have created by frequent riots in the city.

Egerton University, located close to the town of Nakuru, was the fourth public university to be established. While it was founded in 1987, its history dates back to 1939 when Lord Maurice Egerton of Tatton, a settler farmer, donated 300 hectares of land from his estate to found a school for training white settler youth for careers in agriculture. The mission of the university is to participate in the discovery, transmission and preservation of knowledge and to stimulate the intellectual life, the economy and the cultural development of Kenya. From a small school in the early 1940s, it grew into a college in 1950 and soon started offering certificate and diploma courses in agriculture and education. In 1979, the Government of Kenya and USAID funded the expansion of the college, and it was soon gazetted as a constituent college of the University of Nairobi, eventually rising to full university status in 1987. Apart from the main campus, Egerton has four other campuses, namely, Njoro, Laikipia, Kisii and Town campuses, and a student population of over 10,000. It offers various degree courses, but its best known programmes are in agriculture.

Although Maseno University in western Kenya was established in 2000, its history goes back to the first decade of the twentieth century, when a Church Missionary Society-established mission centre expanded to cater for learning and agricultural activities. Later, it became a teacher training college (Siriba Teacher Training College) and government training institute. These two institutions were handed over to Moi University in 1990. The process of upgrading these establishments at Maseno was triggered by the admissions crisis in 1990, when the public universities were unable to cope with the large numbers of students admitted for degree programmes. These students were from a combined admission of the former 7:4:2:3 and the later 8:4:4 education systems. Maseno remained a constituent college of Moi University until 2000 when it was elevated to the status of a fully-fledged university, with 3 faculties, 2 institutes and a student population of 4,300.

The most salient feature of university education in Kenya has been the rapid growth in the number of institutions and enrolments. The number of public universities increased from one in 1970 to six in 2000, with the student population rising to 42,193, excluding privately sponsored students. With the Kenyan economy experiencing negative growth for most of the 1980s and 1990s, the Government of Kenya found itself no longer able to sustain its previous levels of financial support to the public universities. This situation arose at the same time as the growth in student numbers that resulted from both the pressure exerted from the expanded lower levels of education as well as the fact that possession of higher-education qualifications was becoming more highly regarded as a ticket to formal sector employment. On the basis of policy statements by the relevant government authorities, there are strong indications that the government will no longer fully finance the public universities. Rather, the public universities have been advised to devise ways and means of raising additional funds to support their activities, which has provided the impetus for on-going reforms. Like

21

its public counterpart, the private university sector in Kenya has also grown tremendously. From one private university in 1970, the number has increased to 17, not including 4 offshore campuses.[1]

Technical, Industrial, Vocational and Entrepreneurship Training (TIVET) has become an important sub-sector of public higher education within the Ministry of Education, Science and Technology (MoEST). It has an enrolment of over 51,000 trainees in 4 national polytechnics, one technical teacher training college, 15 institutes of technology, 20 technical training institutes and 4 special vocational training centres. In the Ministry of Labour and Human Resources Development, there are 700 youth polytechnics, 3 industrial training centres, one vocational training centre and one textile training institute, with an enrolment of over 36,000 trainees. In addition, there are 40 other institutions spread over 13 ministries. Furthermore, private organizations, individuals, non-governmental organizations (NGOs) and religious organizations run TIVET programmes in about 700 training institutions. TIVET institutions provide a viable avenue for absorbing many primary and secondary school leavers.

[1] Part two of this volume is an in-depth examination of the situation of private universities in Kenya.

2 Reforms Related to Access, Equity, Quality & Relevance

Access

To evaluate student access to public university education in Kenya, this study focuses on undergraduate enrolments, self-sponsored students, postgraduate enrolments, bridging courses and the location of programmes.

Undergraduate enrolments

The total number of undergraduates enrolled in the six public universities in 2005, including privately sponsored students, stood at 77,000. Most of the growth in enrolment took place since the 1990s with the introduction of self-sponsored programmes and the establishment of several constituent colleges of the public universities, some of which were later converted into fully-fledged universities such as Maseno University and JKUAT.

In this regard, it should be noted that until Moi University was established in 1984, the University of Nairobi – as the only university in the country – was under constant pressure to expand its student intake. This pressure was the result of the massive expansion of primary and secondary education that took place throughout the 1960s. Whereas primary schools had a total enrolment in 1963 of 890,000 students (and secondary schools 31,000 students), by 2002 these figures had shot up to 5.9 million in primary (3.0 million boys and 2.9 million girls) and 650,000 in secondary (345,000 boys and 307,000 girls). The result is that currently all the public universities combined are able to admit only about 6 per cent of those who come through the pipeline. Viewed from this perspective, expansion as a form of reform of the university system, regardless of how it has been carried out, has been a logical outcome of pipeline pressure.

Table I.1 shows the regular trend in undergraduate enrolment between the 1990/91 and 2001/2 academic years, indicating that enrolments rose from 31,632 in the 1990/91 academic year to 42,193 in 2001/2, a 33 per cent increase. The table further shows that student enrolment in the public universities maintained a fairly steady level over the decade, except for a decrease during the 1992/3 academic year and a sharp increase in enrolment at Egerton University. Enrolment dropped by about 25 per cent in 1992/3, when Kenyatta University was closed for most of the academic year because of student disturbances. The enrolment at Egerton University between

23

Table I.1: Undergraduate enrolment in public universities by sex, 1990–2002

Academic	Nairobi		Kenyatta		Moi		Egerton	
	M	F	M	F	M	F	M	F
1990/91	8,504	2,597	5,153	3,522	4,684	1,666	2,917	927
1991/92	9,902	3,046	5,442	3,328	4,529	1,827	1,329	462
1992/93	9,961	2,868	–	–	4,702	1,869	1,707	545
1993/94	9,453	3,189	6,014	3,041	4,647	1,532	1,114	420
1994/95	9,697	2,866	5,781	2,671	3,866	1,368	1,442	491
1995/96	9,703	3,013	5,400	2,693	3,640	1,283	1,496	793
1996/97	9,853	3,165	5,304	2,976	3,416	1,149	5,445	2,340
1997/98	9,583	3,344	3,876	2,405	4,006	1,502	5,705	3,381
1998/99	9,192	3,121	3,686	2,540	3,650	1,410	5,654	2,519
1999/00	7,913	3,158	3,738	2,755	4,014	1,583	7,132	2,941
2000/01	7,381	3,095	3,716	3,044	4,537	1,900	6,089	1,997
2001/02	7,252	3,163	4,025	3,032	4,503	1,878	5,992	2,794
Total	108,394	36,625	52,135	32,007	50,194	18,967	46,022	19,610
	(75)	(25)	(62)	(38)	(73)	(27)	(70)	(30)
Grand Total	145,019		84,142		69,161		65,632	
	(34.5)		(20)		(16)		(15.6)	

Notes: 1) Figures in parentheses represent percentages; 2) Kenyatta University was closed for most of the 1992/93 academic year due to student disturbances; 3) JKUAT started admitting students through the Joint Admissions Board (JAB) in 1994.

1996/7 and 2001/2 rose from about 2,000 to over 7,000 students following the university's expansion of facilities at Njoro and Laikipia campuses.

Two factors help explain the relatively steady enrolment trend: the attachment of admission to accommodation facilities, and pressure from the World Bank not to exceed an annual intake of approximately 10,000 students in order to ensure the provision of quality education and to facilitate cost-cutting. Without both external and

Maseno		JKUAT		Total		Grand Total	Index	% Increase /Decrease
M	F	M	F	M	F			
50	610	–	–	22,308	9,322	31,630	100	–
20	720	–	–	22,422	9,383	31,805	100.6	+0.6
15	735	–	–	17,785	6,017	23,802	75.3	–24.7
56	871	–	–	22,884	9,053	31,937	101	+1.0
01	490	1,384	344	23,071	8,230	31,301	99	–1.0
67	562	1,583	329	22,889	8,673	31,562	99.8	–0.2
39	859	1,751	351	27,508	10,840	38,348	121.2	+21.2
15	896	1,843	371	26,728	10,899	38,627	122.1	+22.1
65	1,390	2,291	562	26,838	11,542	38,380	121.3	+21.3
47	1,732	2,256	598	27,800	12,767	40,567	128.3	+28.3
97	2,140	2,289	610	27,709	12,786	40,495	128.0	+28.0
23	2,342	2,665	624	28,360	13,833	42,193	133.4	+33.4
95	13,347	16,062	3,789	296,302	124,345			
4)	(36)	(81)	(19)	(70)	(30)			
	36,842	19,851		420,647				
	(8.8)	(4.7)		(99.6)				

Source: Computed from admissions records in Academic Registrars' office.

institutional pressures to stabilize enrolment, it is likely that the rate of growth would have been much higher. As the longest-established institution of higher learning in Kenya, the University of Nairobi accounted for some 34.5 per cent (145,019) of the student population between 1990 and 2001; Kenyatta took up 20 per cent (84,142); Moi, 16 per cent (69,161); Egerton, 15.6 per cent (65,632); Maseno, 9 per cent (36,842) and JKUAT, 4.7 per cent (19,851).

Table I.2: Undergraduate programmes for self-sponsored students by university, 1998–2002

Institution	Programme	1998/9 M	1998/9 F	1999/2000 M	1999/2000 F	2000/01 M	2000/01 F	2001/02 M	2001/02 F	Total M	Total F	Total
Nairobi	Architecture, Building Economics, Land Economics	25	14	32	17	15	8	–	–	72	39	111
	Engineering	63	4	46	3	91	6	3	1	203	14	217
	Agriculture	1		2	1					3	1	4
	Veterinary medicine	37	14	35	13	10	–	12	5	94	32	126
	Computer Science	12	7	6	4	5	3	–	–	23	14	37
	Natural Science Education (Arts)	47	16	47	15	29	10	–	–	123	41	164
	Distance Studies Education Arts Intergraded/Out	31	18	224	126	160	90	243	137	658	371	1029
	Evening	225	97	104	45	34	15	48	21	411	178	589
	Psychology	23	7	49	14	16	5	44	13	132	39	171
	Medicine	126	62	88	44	69	34	23	11	306	151	457
	BSc (Nursing)	10	10	4	4	1	1	3	3	18	18	36
	Dental Science	8	3	11	3	6	2	2	1	27	9	36
	Pharmacy	38	19	27	16	14	9	4	2	83	46	129
	Law	107	94	71	63	65	57	129	115	372	329	701
	Commerce/Business Management	416	138	116	38	63	21	307	102	902	299	1,201
	Arts	290	177	234	143	205	126	130	80	859	526	1385
	African Studies	3	3	3	1			4	3	10	7	17
	Total	1462	683	1099	550	783	387	952	494	4296	2114	6410
Moi	Education	67	63	101	109	234	203	298	239	700	614	1314
	Law	66	40	189	155	318	208	433	286	1006	689	1695
	Technology	3	–	10	–	93	13	145	19	251	32	283
	Business Management	22	9	44	32	107	28	119	47	292	116	408
	Information Science	–	–	–	–	–	–	25	23	25	23	48
	Natural Sciences	–	–	1	–	4	1	10	2	15	3	18
	Forest Resources	–	–	–	–	1	–	4	1	5	1	6
	Health Sciences	–	–	–	–	–	–	5	7	5	7	12
	Agriculture	–	–	–	–	–	–	3	1	3	1	4
	Social Cultural	–	–	–	–	–	–	5	6	5	6	11
	Total	158	112	345	296	757	453	1047	631	2307	1492	3799
Kenyatta	Education (Secondary)	328	180	269	164	131	104	223	188	951	636	1587
	Education (Primary)	466	181	226	87	66	39	–	–	758	307	1065
	Education (EGE)	16	16	25	23	17	32	17	34	75	105	180
	Education (Special)	66	48	107	78	141	114	115	92	429	332	761
	Total	876	425	627	352	355	289	355	314	2213	1380	3593

26

Table I.2: cont.

Institution	Programme	1998/9		1999/2000		2000/01		2001/02		Total		Total
		M	F	M	F	M	F	M	F	M	F	
JKUAT	SABS	–	–	–	–	25	3	–	–	25	3	28
	Engineering	–	–	–	–	84	13	–	–	84	13	97
	Natural Science	61	120	72	46	120	61	–	–	253	227	480
	Total	61	120	72	46	229	77	–	–	362	243	605
Egerton	Education	–	–	14	4	14	5	22	12	50	21	71
	Agriculture	–	–	–	–	5	2	1	5	6	2	8
	Food Science	–	–	–	–	–	4	5	1	5	5	10
	Arts	–	–	–	–	5	3	1	2	6	4	10
	Natural Science	–	–	–	–	8	–	4	1	12	2	14
	Computer Science	–	–	–	–	6	2	5	5	11	3	14
	Clinical Medicine (Diploma)	–	–	–	–	–	–	12	2	12	5	17
	Environment	–	–	–	–	–	–	5	24	5	2	7
	Commerce/Business Management	–	–	33	34	–	–	30	52	63	58	121
	Totals	–	–	47	38	38	16	85	104	170	158	328
Maseno	Education	150	110	128	121	116	98	107	63	501	392	893
	Arts	34	30	18	26	19	14	14	8	85	78	163
	Natural Sciences	15	5	20	8	16	11	8	11	59	35	94
	Health Sciences	26	6	23	12	33	12	14	5	95	35	130
	Totals	224	151	189	167	184	135	143	87	740	540	1280
Grand Total		2,781	1,491	2,379	1,449	2,346	1,357	2,582	1,630	10,088	5,927	16,015

Source: Generated from university admissions records.

Self-sponsored students

One way in which the public universities have responded to deficits in their financial support from the government is by introducing self-sponsored degree programmes. Most of these programmes were started in 1998 following the experience of Makerere University.[2] Currently, a total of 14,963 students (9,019 male and 5,944 female) are enrolled in these programmes. The University of Nairobi accounts for about 32 per cent, the largest share of this group. Student enrolment in the programme at Moi University increased from 370 in the 1998/9 academic year to 1,678 in 2001/2, a rise of 354 per cent. Currently, self-sponsored students represent about 26 per cent of the total enrolment in the public universities. Female students comprise some 37 per cent of the self-sponsored students, a somewhat higher percentage than their 29 per cent in the regular group.

Between the 1998/9 and 2000/01 academic years, Kenyatta University admitted a total of 2,531 teachers to its programme of continuing education, while about 2,000 untrained graduate teachers had already benefited from the institution's postgraduate Diploma in Education Programme started in the 1995/6 academic year. At Egerton University, the number of students enrolled in self-sponsored programmes has grown slowly. When the programme was started in 1999, it attracted only 51 students; by 2001, the number had risen to 264. It is expected that the programme will attract more students following the recent establishment of an urban campus in nearby Nakuru. Enrolment by fee-paying students at JKUAT rose from 181 in 1998/9 to 306 students in 2000/01. This enrolment will rise as soon as the 18 middle-level tertiary institutions accredited by the university through its Continuous Education Programme become fully operational. Although Maseno University has one of the lowest enrolments of self-sponsored students at present, it is expected that the situation will soon change, given its proximity to Kisumu, Kenya's third-largest town.

An analysis of these programmes shows that certain programmes such as business administration, medicine, pharmacy, law, accountancy, marketing, computer science and gender-related studies are the most popular. Other courses such as history, religious studies and philosophy attract very few students. One implication of this

---

[2] This experience is documented in another volume in the Partnership for Higher Education in Africa series on reform at African universities: Nakanyike B. Musisi and Nansozi K. Muwanga, *Makerere University in Transition, 1993–2000.* Oxford, UK: James Currey, 2003.

trend is that the disciplines which are less popular with students contribute less income to support improvements in teaching and reform. According to some of those interviewed, a further implication is that these disciplines could easily 'wither away' in the not too distant future if current trends continue.

Postgraduate enrolments

The enrolment of postgraduate students has also increased, though less dramatically than that of undergraduates. Postgraduate enrolment at the University of Nairobi rose from 1,000 students in 1990 to 1,500 in 2001. In the parallel degree programmes initiated at the university in 1998, the number now stands at approximately 800, bringing the total to 2,300 students. The total, against an undergraduate population of 14,415, represents a ratio of 1:6.

At Kenyatta University, the number of postgraduate students rose from 67 (38 male and 29 female) in 1990 to 564 in 2001. The parallel postgraduate programme (commonly referred to as the part-time category) attracted 434 students (262 male and 172 female) when it was launched in 1998. By late 2001 the programme had a student population of 832 (509 male and 323 female), putting the total number of postgraduate students at 1,396. Given the university's undergraduate enrolment of 10,978 students, this gives Kenyatta University a postgraduate to undergraduate ratio of 1:8.

Maseno University had only one (male) postgraduate student in 1994. This figure rose to 193 in the 2001/2 academic year, with female students comprising 25 per cent. Set against an undergraduate enrolment of 6,265, this gives the institution a postgraduate-undergraduate ratio of 1:33. Beginning from a total of 70 students in 1990 (43 male and 27 female), Moi University had 266 postgraduate students in 2002, 30 per cent of them female. With an undergraduate population of 10,188, Moi's postgraduate to undergraduate ratio is 1:38. At JKUAT the postgraduate programme was started with 10 students in 1994 (4 male and 6 female). In the 2001/2 academic year, the enrolment was 70 (48 male and 22 female). With an undergraduate student population standing at 3,289, the institution posts a 1:47 postgraduate to undergraduate ratio. Egerton University initiated its postgraduate programme in 1994 with only two male students. By the 2001/2 academic year, the programme had a total of 128 students (97 male and 31 female). With an undergraduate enrolment of 9,050 students in 2001/2, the university recorded a postgraduate to undergraduate ratio of 1:71.

Except for Nairobi and Kenyatta Universities, where postgraduate enrolments amount to more than 10 per cent of the undergraduate population, the enrolments at the remaining four public universities are dishearteningly low despite the expansion. These enrolments should be seen in the context of the official policy to strengthen post-graduate enrolment to at least 10 per cent of total undergraduate enrolment, thereby enhancing research output as well as training new faculty members.

Bridging courses

Access to university education has also been enhanced by the introduction of bridging courses. Kenyatta, JKUAT, Egerton and Nairobi Universities have ventured into pre-university training courses for potential university students who fail to meet the cut-off admission requirement but attain the acceptable minimum require-ment and are keen on university education. These programmes provide remedial instruction in mathematics, science, languages and other critical subjects for students who need them to gain access to the mainstream university system. Some 36 students who undertook their pre-university course at the African Virtual University pro-gramme at Kenyatta University in 1998/9 were admitted to the university's degree programme in January 2000.

Location of programmes

The public universities have worked to make university education more accessible by locating campuses near their target populations. JKUAT has done this through its Continuous Education Programme (CEP), which involves accrediting tertiary institutions located in various parts of the country to run its courses under the supervision of the university.

The University of Nairobi's College of Education and External Studies offers programmes through its regional Extra-Mural Centres in Mombasa, Kisumu, Kakamega, Nyeri and Nakuru. Kenyatta University has also set up regional centres in all eight provinces of the country to manage its distance-education programmes. Similarly, universities that are located far from urban areas (such as Egerton and Moi Universities) have been compelled to set up campus centres in the nearest towns, including Nakuru and Eldoret. Details of the courses offered are shown in Table 1.3.

Table I.3: Location of programmes by university

Regional university centres	Programmes offered
JKUAT has 18 centres: JKUAT-MMS Juja; Loreto Msongari, Nairobi; Kenya School of Professional Studies, Nairobi; Diamond Systems, Nairobi; Gitwe Technical College, Murang'a; Nyandarua Adventist Technical College, Kisii; Lamu Polytechnic, Lamu; Kenya College of Accountancy, Nairobi & Kisumu; Strathmore College of Accountancy, Nairobi; Jaffrey Institute of Professional Studies, Mombasa; Bandari College, Mombasa; Kenya Air Force Technical College, Nairobi; Kenya College of Communications Technology, Nairobi; Holy Rosary and Tala, Machakos; Regional Centre for Mapping of Resources for Development, Nairobi; Institute for Advanced Technology (Symphony Ltd), Nairobi.	B.Sc. in information technology Diploma in information technology Certificate in information technology Bridging course in mathematics Bachelor of commerce Bachelor of business management B.Sc. in computer technology M.Sc. in entrepreneurship B.Sc. in electrical & electronic engineering B.Sc. in telecommunications engineering
Kenyatta University regional centres: St. Ann's Junior Academy, Nairobi; Nakuru High, Nakuru; Kakamega High, Kakamega; Kimathi Institute, Nyeri; Todor Day Secondary School, Mombasa; Kangaru High School, Embu and Kisumu Day Secondary School, Kisumu.	Certificate diploma and bachelor's degree courses in: computing, laboratory techniques, forest management, disaster management, participatory project planning, health and environment, foods and nutrition, HIV and family education. Early childhood education, public relations, tourism, commerce, human resource development, marketing, ICT. Postgraduate diploma and Master's and Ph.D. programmes in: education, journalism, distance education in school management.
University of Nairobi has 7 regional centres: Mombasa, Nairobi, Nakuru, Nyeri, Kisimu, Kakamega, Embu.	B.Ed. Arts, B.Ed. (Science), M.Ed.
Moi University has 3 centres; Town Campus, Eldoret; Kenya Ports Authority Depot, Eldoret and Mombasa.	B.Ed.(Arts), B.Ed. B.Com.(Science), M.Ed., M.B.A., bachelor of business management; M.B.A. in ICT; bachelor of medicine.

31

Table I.3 cont.

Regional university centres	Programmes offered
University of Nairobi has 7 regional centres: Mombasa, Nairobi, Nakuru, Nyeri, Kisimu, Kakamega, Embu.	B.Ed. Arts, B.Ed. (Science), M.Ed
Egerton University has one centre, in Nakuru town.	B.Com., business management, information technology; B.Ed. (Arts), B.Ed. (Science)
Maseno University has one centre, in Kisumu.	B.Com. and business management

Source: Generated from relevant offices of the universities surveyed.

Equity-related reforms

Regional imbalances & admission policy

Members of those communities that made the earliest and more stable contacts with the European settlers, missionaries and colonial authorities have tended to enjoy greater access to formal higher educational opportunities than their counterparts in other regions, with students from the arid and semi-arid land (ASAL) zones of the country being the most under-represented in the public universities. The problem of under-participation in education among the youth of nomadic communities has a historical dimension. From the inception of Western education, schooling in ASAL areas of the country was treated less seriously than in high-potential agricultural areas. Neither outside religion nor formal education was adapted to the nomadic existence because the acceptance of either without adjustments would have required major changes in the nomads' way of life. Following independence in 1963, as in the colonial era, the ASAL districts have not yet been integrated into the mainstream socio-economic development agenda.

This massive neglect, coupled with insecurity, banditry and the nomadic nature of the indigenous populace, appears to have prolonged the underdevelopment that has, in turn, limited the provision of education to pastoral communities, especially the education of girls. An analysis by the British Council (Figure I.2) of the ethnic composition of students in the public universities indicates a heavy

32

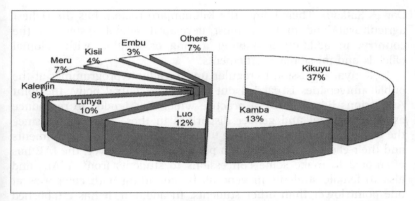

Figure I.2: Distribution of Kenyan public university students by ethnic origin

Source: British Council (1996).

representation of the Kikuyu ethnic group, which makes up 37.8 per cent of all students enrolled in the public universities. In a descending order of representation, the Kamba follow with 13 per cent, Luo (12 per cent), Luhya (10 per cent), Kalenjin (8 per cent), Meru (7 per cent), Kisii (4 per cent) and Embu (3 per cent). Only 6.7 per cent of all students originate from the remaining ethnic groups in Kenya such as the Teso, Mijikenda, Maasai, Samburu, Turkana, Boran and Somali. These other groups individually account for no more than 1.4 per cent of the students in the public universities.

Apart from their early contacts with Europeans, the large presence of the Kikuyu group in the public university system reflects their numerical strength in the country; they are the largest single ethnic group, at 24 per cent of the population. In addition, there are geographical, regional and developmental factors that selectively promote higher education among the Kikuyu community, so that they are over-represented in the university system compared with other large ethnic groups such as the Kamba, Luo, Luhya and Kalenjin, who are under-represented in relation to their demographic numbers. For example, the University of Nairobi is situated in the heartland of the Kikuyu community, and the community is, comparatively speaking, economically advantaged, hence its big numerical student presence at the university. This situation is not unique to Kenya. Near the Kenyan border, the populous Chagga who hail from the Kilimanjaro region in northern Tanzania are disproportionately represented among students at the University of

33

Dar es Salaam. Their home, the Kilimanjaro region, has the richest agricultural land and the most developed school system in the country, in addition to having a long association with colonial officials and missionary settlements.

In Kenya, admission to regular undergraduate programmes at the public universities is carried out through a central body, the Joint Admissions Board (JAB), a practice which has tended to reproduce existing regional and gender disparities in these institutions, since the board has not been sensitive to specific educational environments and their effects on examination performance. However, the JAB has attempted to make some concessions to students from ASALs and also to female students in general, by admitting both categories at one point lower than other students. In addition, it has established a quota system for students from the most disadvantaged districts.

Nevertheless, these measures do not seem to have helped much. One possible solution is the decentralization of admissions to the university level, but even here there is a danger of favouritism. This is illustrated by the Egerton University diploma programmes, which admit at the university level. Here the locally dominant ethnic group is over-represented, but perhaps this simply reflects the fact that many more local people apply for the programmes because they are being offered near home.

To compound the problem of equity, the existing trend towards the privatization of higher education might exacerbate inequality in access by excluding those who cannot afford to pay. Kenyatta University has been at the forefront of decentralizing admissions to the university and therefore doing away with the JAB. It has begun to admit students on a semester basis, as opposed to the JAB practice of admitting once a year. Students can now take any courses offered during any semester provided that they satisfy the course require-ments. One consequence of this reform is the gradual abolition of the traditional academic year, an important reform about which more will be said later.

Gender imbalances

In Kenya, as in other African countries, the proportion of female enrolment declines as females move up the educational ladder. As a result, slightly less than one-third of the 6 per cent of secondary school students who secure admission to public universities on government sponsorship are female. A look at female and male enrol-ment in the public universities reveals that female students represent only 30 per cent of the students in the public universities (124,345).

Table I.4: Change in enrolment by sex in public universities, 1990–2001

Year	Female enrolment			Male enrolment		
	Number	Index	% Increase or decrease	Number	Index	% Increase or decrease
90/91	9,324	100	–	22,308	100	–
91/92	9,383	100.6	+0.6	22,422	100.5	+0.5
92/93	6,017	64.5	−35.6	17,785	79.7	−20.3
93/94	9,053	97.1	−3.0	22,084	98.9	−1
94/95	8,230	88.3	−11.7	23,074	103.4	+3.4
1995/96	8,673	93.0	−7	22,889	102.6	+2.6
1996/97	10,840	116.3	+16.3	27,508	123.3	+23.3
1997/98	10,849	116.4	+16.4	26,728	119.8	+19.8
1998/99	11,542	123.8	+23.8	26,838	120.3	+20.3
1999/2000	12,667	135.9	+35.9	28,800	129.1	+29.1
2000/2001	12,789	137.2	+37.2	27,709	124.2	+24.2
2001/2002	13,833	148.4	+48.4	28,360	127.1	+27.1

Source: Generated from enrolment records in public universities (Registrars' offices).

JKUAT has the lowest enrolment of female students at 19 per cent. In ascending order, the University of Nairobi has 25 per cent female students; Moi, 27 per cent; Egerton, 30 per cent; Maseno, 36 per cent and Kenyatta University, 38 per cent. Kenyatta deviates from the gender enrolment norm in the public universities partly because most of its courses are in social sciences, arts, education and home economics, courses in which many female students enrol.

At the other end, JKUAT deviates from the mean because nearly all its courses are science-based. Despite this general under-representation at the public universities, female enrolment has been growing during the last decade. The number of female students increased by 4,509 from 9,324 in 1990 to 13,833 in 2001, a rise of 48.4 per cent. Male enrolment rose by 6,052 from 22,308 to 28,360, a 27.1 per cent increase during the same period (Table I.4). While the general representation of women in the public universities is low, gender parity is evident in all the accredited private universities, where female students comprised 54.5 per cent of those enrolled in the 1999/2000 academic year. (The sex distribution at private universities is discussed at length in Part II of this volume.)

Although the enrolment rates for both sexes registered some noticeable gains over the period under study, some academic years

35

(1992/3, 1993/4, 1994/5 and 1995/6) were characterized by declines, with 1992/3 recording the steepest fall (–35.6 per cent for females and –20.3 per cent for males). The closure of Kenyatta University in the 1992/3 academic year was instrumental in this sharp drop.

Female students' under-representation is more pronounced in medicine, pharmacy, engineering and technical-based degree programmes. Table I.5 indicates the sex distribution of enrolment by degree programmes from 1990 to 1995. The degree programmes that attracted most women were: education (52.2 per cent of all women enrolled in education), humanities and social sciences (30.8 per cent), natural sciences (6.7 per cent), agriculture and veterinary medicine (5.0 per cent), engineering and architecture (3.1 per cent) and medicine and pharmacy (2.3 per cent). The same order applied to male students, but with numbers almost equally divided between education and humanities and social sciences (33.1 per cent and 32.7 per cent respectively). The rest of the male students enrolled in natural sciences (13.1 per cent), agriculture and veterinary science (11.2 per cent), engineering and architecture (7.0 per cent) and medicine and pharmacy (3.0 per cent).

The need to increase enrolment in medicine, pharmacy, engineering and technical-based programmes of men and women alike cannot be over-emphasized, since there remains a shortage of these professionals in the country. Despite both male and female under-enrolment in these programmes, the case for enhancing the enrolment of female students is more compelling. Persistent gender imbalances at the tertiary level of education are a reflection of gender bias and structural differences in access to education.

The under-representation of female students cuts across all the public universities, despite the application of affirmative action by the JAB. This problem has roots in the country's education system as a whole. Although educational programmes in primary and secondary education are outside the realm of university education, public universities can make a substantive contribution to alleviating gender imbalance by encouraging women and girls to venture into the traditionally male-dominated fields of science and technology.

The first step is research to find out the underlying causes of the problem, with a view to devising appropriate strategies for tackling it. This is the main objective of the Female Education in Mathematics and Science in Africa project, a collaborative effort between the Ministry of Education, Science and Technology, the Forum for African Women Educationalists (Kenya Chapter) and JKUAT, which is funding projects in primary and secondary schools to promote

Table I.5: Enrolment by sex and degree programmes in public universities, 1990–95

Degree programmes	Number of students		Male/female as % of male/female enrolment	
	Male	Female	Male	Female
Education	37,932	19,320	66.3	33.7
Humanities and social sciences	37,488	11,405	76.7	23.3
Natural sciences	15,037	2,466	85.9	14.1
Agriculture and veterinary medicine	12,875	1,851	87.4	12.6
Engineering and architecture	7,974	1,139	87.5	12.5
Medicine and pharmacy	3,416	837	80.3	19.7
Total	114,722	37,018	75.6	24.4

Source: Generated from Joint Admissions Board records, 2002.

science subjects among girls. Egerton University has also given special attention to gender-related concerns through the Centre for Women Studies and Gender Analysis. The centre was the first of its kind in a public university in Kenya, established in 1991 in response to female students' demands to address concerns such as sexual harassment and unwanted pregnancies that have a negative impact on their academic performance. If implemented properly, this reform initiative could enhance the quality of the learning environment for female students. These and similar efforts could also result in better participation and performance of females in science subjects at all levels of the education system. As a matter of necessity, this kind of reform should be scaled up by initiating additional gender-responsive programmes in addition to those already in place in all the public universities.

Reforms & the problem of quality

Quality of academic programmes

Further studies need to be undertaken to assess the quality of graduates from the public universities. In the meantime, Kenyan employers have expressed their concerns about the ability of university graduates to respond flexibly and competently to the responsibilities with which they are entrusted. A 1994 study (Deloitte and Touche) asked employers how effective they thought public, private and

37

foreign university programmes were in fostering general competence, initiative, discipline, creativity, leadership, adaptability and responsibility. Except for adaptability, private universities scored much higher than their public counterparts in nearly all aspects (see Table I.6).

It is apparent that many lecturers are aware of the quality problem and of the many challenges that their graduates face. Hampered by a broad lack of resources and, sometimes, by students' attitudes to education, they fear that they cannot adequately prepare students for their future responsibilities. It is common knowledge, for example, that students prefer the familiar expository method of teaching; they perceive university education as consisting primarily of the reproduction of assimilated lecture materials for the purpose of passing examinations. This attitude is reinforced by the fact that teaching resources are so scarce that the 'talk-and-chalk' methodology is the only viable option. Even then, at least before universities embarked on their own income-generating activities, the chalk might not always be available.

Little emphasized but very clear from observation is the inefficient use of time imposed by the semester system. An academic year in the semester system consists of two semesters of 14 weeks each. Before the semester system, the university session (in one academic year) consisted of three terms, each of which lasted 11 weeks. Considering that two weeks are spent on examinations, one week is used for revision and one week is normally lost at the beginning of every semester due to slow take-off of the learning-teaching exercises, the effective teaching time per semester becomes 10 weeks; thus 20 weeks per year compared with the calendar time of 29 weeks. A loss of 4 weeks in a semester translates into 32 weeks – equivalent to two semesters or a whole academic year – in the four-year degree programme. This situation has not been helped by the lateness of most lecturers in commencing their lectures, partly because a substantial number of them spend a lot of time shuttling between different universities or different campuses of the same institution, doing extra teaching for extra money. The toll on their capacities is significant, especially for those lecturers who do not have personal vehicles. As a result, lecturers sometimes resort to poor methods of content coverage, such as focusing only on areas in which they intend to examine at the end of the semester.

Particularly distressing are the standards of the English language, which are at an all-time low. One literature professor has observed that it would be better if students learned no English at all in primary and secondary school, because they are taught so badly that

Table I.6: Effectiveness of Kenyan universities in fostering attributes valued in management literature (%)

Attributes Effectiveness	Public universities			Private universities			Foreign universities		
	VE*	ME*	NVE*	VE	ME	NVE	VE	ME	NVE
General competence	17	73	10	28	72	0	57	39	4
Initiative	10	52	38	33	72	6	57	39	4
Discipline	7	48	45	33	56	11	35	61	4
Creativity	10	62	38	17	61	22	48	48	4
Leadership	14	52	34	11	78	11	48	52	0
Adaptability	66	7	27	17	72	11	43	48	9
Responsibility	7	41	52	17	67	16	35	61	4

Source: Deloitte and Touche, 1994.
Key: *VE = very effective; * ME = moderately effective; *NVE = not very effective.

much of the time at the university is spent in re-teaching them the foundations of the language (Indangasi, 1991). Thus even literature students sometimes lack knowledge of such basics as the rules governing the use of capital letters and are unable to analyze the grammatical structure of simple sentences. A *Kenya Times* correspondent humorously captured this situation by observing that it is common to hear questions such as 'You, you, you, are going where?' instead of 'Where are you going?' being asked along university corridors (Mugonyi, 1996:15).

There is little consolation in the knowledge that the situation is no better in some of the other public universities in East Africa. Colleagues from the University of Dar es Salaam in Tanzania, for example, have identified some of the common grammatical mistakes made by their students. These include the use of 'doesn't' instead of 'do not', 'choosed' instead of 'chosen', 'gotten' instead of 'got', plural forms where the singular is appropriate and vice versa, capital instead of lower-case letters and so on. In addition, poor sentence construction, lack of paragraphing and lack of full stops are quite common, all indicating a below-average mastery of English grammar. The negative consequences of poor mastery of a language that is the medium of instruction can be far-reaching.

A problematic trend in current reforms is the tendency on the part of some universities to offer courses in their self-sponsored programmes, which they are, arguably, not fully qualified to offer. Kenyatta University has launched several courses in pharmacy-related subjects and medicine, while Egerton University is in the

39

process of embarking on similar programmes. Expressing his fears about the proliferation of such courses in Kenya, the executive secretary of the Kampala-based Inter-University Council of East Africa recently urged the Council on Higher Education to vet new degree programmes in order to ensure the delivery of high-quality education (Onyango, 2002).

Inadequate space & teaching materials

The teaching facilities and physical infrastructure of the public universities are the most wanting, being ranked very low in the institutions' planning priorities. Yet increasing student enrolment has overstretched the capacity of libraries, lecture theatres, laboratories, residential accommodation and dining halls. This is true of all the public universities with the possible exception of JKUAT, which enjoys significant support from the Japanese government and the World Bank. Research in 1990 revealed that lecturers in the Faculty of Education at Kenyatta University were forced to repeat the same lectures to as many as three or four groups of students because of the lack of adequate lecture theatres, while in other cases some students listened to their lecturers through the windows (Hughes and Mwiria, 1990: 228). Little has changed since then. At Moi University, students in Bachelor of Education (Arts) courses, often numbering about 1,800 in one class, take their notes from outside the lecture theatre through a public address system. Staff accommodation is an additional problem. On top of inadequate physical facilities, teaching materials are also woefully inadequate in all the public universities as a result of budgetary constraints. On average, teaching and learning materials are usually allocated around 6 per cent of the university's annual budget.

Inadequate library services

Libraries are among the worst hit facilities in public universities. In all the universities, both self-sponsored and regular students complain that the universities have not invested much in the acquisition of textbooks to cope with the increased student intakes. Although the Jomo Kenyatta Memorial Library of the University of Nairobi has a book capacity of 2.5 million volumes, it holds only about 750,000 volumes, many of which are quite old (Onyango, 2002). This library, originally meant for 6,000 readers, now caters for 16,715 students. At Moi University, 400 students sometimes chase one or two books (Rosenberg 1997:197). With a seating capacity of 2,500, the Moi University Library now serves 10,454

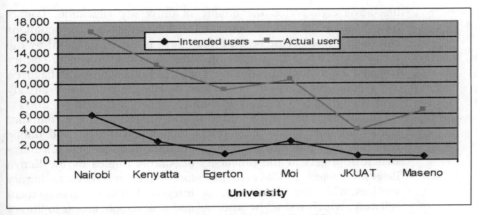

Figure I.3: Actual and intended capacities of public university libraries

Source: Public university libraries, 2002.

students. At Kenyatta University, the capacity of the University Library is about 2,500 students but the same library has over the last decade served a student population of between 8,000 and 12,400. An extension to that library, which will increase its size by one-third, was started in 1991 but has been stalled since 1993. With an enrolment of approximately 9,170 students, Egerton University has a library that was designed for only 1,600. JKUAT's library (designed for 600 users) currently has 3,964 students, while Maseno University's two libraries (with space for 600 students) host 6,458 undergraduate and postgraduate students (Figure I.3).

Apart from inadequate space, most libraries have no holding lists of their journals. Furthermore, entries in the existing catalogues generally do not match what is on the shelves. Shelving also leaves a great deal to be desired, partly as a result of too few library staff and partly because selfish students deliberately mix up textbooks of different disciplines so that they are the only ones who know where to find them. Scarcity of relevant reference materials has also led to the rise of vandalism in libraries. Due to financial constraints, most students are unable to photocopy the required chapters or pages from reference books. They therefore simply tear the pages out.

This situation is made worse by the fact that many lecturers in public universities use old material, which means that the courses they teach are also out of date (Rosenberg, 1997). Coupled with the flight of the best lecturers from the public universities, this situation

41

has adversely affected the quality of university education. Donors have occasionally donated books to the universities, but the donations can be of limited value because they have not been informed by the recipients' needs. For instance, in 1999 Kenyatta University Library received a donation of additional copies of Robinson and Gallagher's 1961 book, *Africa and the Victorians*, despite the fact that it already held enough copies of this particular publication (Murunga, 2001).

The libraries at Nairobi and Kenyatta Universities have computer units that offer electronic services including CD-ROM and online searches. In addition, the University Communication Network Infrastructure project at the University of Nairobi funded by the Kenya Belgium Project is likely to introduce major advances to library services with the installation of integrated library management software, which will allow students and staff remote access to library catalogues and to ask for books.

Quality-enhancement reforms

The universities have responded to the quality problem by instituting a variety of related measures which include boosting the quality of the teaching staff, broadening student assessment mechanisms, initiating students' appraisal of academic staff, introducing common units of study and adopting new delivery mechanisms.

Strengthening the quality of teaching staff. Between 1987 and 1990, there was great demand for more academic staff as a result of increased student intakes occasioned by two particular incidents. Two batches of students were admitted in 1987 in order to clear a backlog that had built up when the University of Nairobi and its constituent college, Kenyatta University College, were closed in the aftermath of the failed 1982 coup d'état. 1990 saw the implementation of both the new 8:4:4 structure of primary- and secondary-level education and admission of the last group of students from the previous system, resulting in the double intake. As a result, the public universities recruited master's degree graduates to teach and elevated them into lectureship positions. By the mid-1990s the universities had begun to stabilize their staff recruitments and were in a position to revise their promotion criteria in a bid to compel the majority of teaching staff to pursue doctorates. At Kenyatta and Egerton Universities, it has become university policy that no member of the teaching staff will be promoted to the lecturer grade without a Ph.D. This development has seen many tutorial fellows/ graduate assistants and assistant lecturers enrol for doctoral studies either

locally or abroad. The number of teaching staff in the public universities pursuing Ph.D. degrees is currently about 1,000, out of a total
teaching staff of 3,536, which means there is still some way to go
before Ph.Ds become the norm. (This subject is discussed further in
Chapter 3).

Broadening student assessment mechanisms. Some public
universities have taken steps to strengthen the evaluation of students
by including scores from two continuous assessment tests in summa-
tive examinations. As well as this initiative, at Egerton and Kenyatta
Universities, retakes in failed units have replaced supplementary
examinations. In addition, students who fail more than half of the
units in a semester are expelled. Furthermore, honoraria for external
examiners have been improved in order to attract competent and
unbiased examiners.

Students' appraisal of academic staff. In view of the increasing
numbers of fee-paying students who want value for their money,
some public universities have started initiatives that allow students
to appraise their teachers at the end of every unit or semester. Kenyatta University has introduced staff appraisal carried out by students
and peers. It is expected that, once this initiative is fully operational,
it will not only help assess the productivity of staff but will also
motivate performance and identify areas that need improvement.
Other public universities including Moi are thinking of launching
similar initiatives.

Common units of study. Most public universities have introduced
common units of study intended to produce balanced graduates with
interdisciplinary knowledge beyond their areas of specialization. At
JKUAT, two courses – communication skills and computer literacy –
are compulsory for all undergraduate students. Over the past decade
Kenyatta University has developed six common courses in its
undergraduate academic programmes: HIV/AIDS and drugs, introduction to computing, development studies, communication skills,
introduction to critical and creative thinking and entrepreneurship.
The University of Nairobi has for some time had development studies
and communication skills as compulsory undergraduate courses.

Teaching/learning strategies. Led by Kenyatta University, some
institutions are making efforts to address the quality of the teaching.
First, the allocation of courses for most of the programmes housed at

43

the main campuses of the public universities is now done in such a way as to ensure that whoever teaches a unit to the regular students also teaches the same unit to the self-sponsored group. Second, the tutorial system that collapsed more than ten years ago in the public university sector has been revived at Kenyatta University. Third, Kenyatta University is discouraging the 'talk and chalk' method of teaching in favour of the use of transparencies and overhead projectors. Fourth, the same institution is encouraging lecturers to post their lecture notes and other supplementary material on the Kenyatta University website. It is hoped that if and when these initiatives come to fruition, other public universities will emulate them.

Relevance, research & community outreach programmes

In the past, university education was characterized by concentration on only a few disciplines. Between 1985 and 1993, more than 69 per cent of graduates studied only four degree courses: Bachelor of Education, Bachelor of Arts, Bachelor of Science and Bachelor of Commerce (Deloitte and Touche, 1994). However, the last ten years or so have witnessed the expansion of university education concurrently with curricular growth. This has involved venturing into non-traditional disciplines that reflect perceived national manpower needs and student demands. The growth of new programmes and courses has been the result of splitting, collapsing, merging, modifying and redefining courses in order to meet different academic demands and interests. Thus most universities now offer a wide range of academic and professional programmes that focus on both theoretical and practical issues and concerns. Between them, the six public universities now have over 100 academic disciplines housed in nearly 200 different departments.

The latest to reorganize its programmes is Kenyatta University, with the transformation of faculties into schools in 2002. Under the new institutional restructuring, the former Faculty of Commerce (now part of the School of Humanities and Social Sciences) has set up a Centre for Entrepreneurship and Enterprise Development. The School of Education and Human Resource Development now offers new courses for teachers during school holidays including Special Education, Early Childhood Education and School-Based Continuing Education. The new programmes at KU provide additional training to both non-graduate and graduate teachers from primary and secondary schools and teacher training colleges in response to the changing demands of the profession.

Equally significant is the establishment of the Centre for Complementary Medicine and Biotechnology (CCMB) and the Centre for Improvement and Protection (CIP). Their objective is to generate and transmit research-derived knowledge for product development and alleviation of human suffering through disease control and management, enhanced food production, capacity-building and appropriate technology transfer. True to its objective of enhancing the accessibility of herbal medicine, which is affordable to the majority of Kenyans, the CCMB has already embarked on serious research on alternative medicine. Indeed, one drug – KU Superman, a drug to boost virility – is already on the market and is said to be showing good results. Another innovative programme started at KU is the International Students Services and Programs (ISSP) summer programme, established in 1998, which targets foreign students willing to extend their experiences beyond their home countries. The programme also targets Kenyan students studying in overseas universities. The participation of the latter in the programme enables them to earn credits, as the foreign students do, while at the same time enjoying a holiday at home. So far about 200 students from the United States, including three Kenyans, have benefited from this programme.

Efforts to enhance relevance at the University of Nairobi have entailed the undertaking of research that is useful in dealing with pressing development concerns. The university's Department of Medical Microbiology, in collaboration with the University of Manitoba and the University of Oxford under the auspices of the International AIDS Vaccine Initiative (IAVI), has been involved in HIV research for the past fifteen or so years with a segment of commercial sex workers in Nairobi who seem to have developed resistance to HIV. This research has generated an enormous body of information on the virology and immunology of HIV infection. A significant finding has been the phenomenon of HIV resistance and long-time survival following infection. The body of information gathered during the research has resulted in a unique and promising approach to the development of a HIV vaccine, which is already being tested on humans in the United Kingdom, Uganda and Kenya. During this trial phase, the University of Nairobi will investigate the size of the dosage and the frequency and method of administration (oral or injection) of the vaccine required to produce immunity. Uganda is conducting trials on the number of vaccine injections

45

required to produce the desired immunity, whereas the London researchers are conducting trials on dosage and intervals. In 1989, the Faculty of Education at the University of Nairobi launched the Home Science and Technology Education degree programme in order to respond to the scarcity of teachers in technology and domestic science. Five years later, the Bachelor of Education Science degree programme was established to alleviate the shortage of science teachers in secondary schools. The newest degree programmes at the University of Nairobi are the M.A. and Ph.D. in development studies.

At Moi University various disciplines in the School of Social, Cultural and Development Studies were repackaged in 1996 to constitute seven inter-related Bachelor of Arts degree programmes: in Cultural Studies (for majors in Anthropology, Religion and History), Social Studies (for majors in Sociology, Philosophy and Geography), Language and Literary Studies (English, Kiswahili, French and Arabic) and Theatre Arts. The uniqueness of this arrangement lies in the way its programmes are linked in an inter- and multi-disciplinary fashion through common faculty-based courses.

Moi University's newly launched programmes are also unique in that nearly all the degree programmes have in-built practical components in order to expose students to the environments in which they will find themselves. The programme at the Faculty of Human Medicine at Moi illustrates this approach. Using the Problem-Based-Learning pedagogy (which is also used in other East African universities, such as Mbarara in Uganda), the programme's mission is to train doctors acquainted with rural conditions and the health needs of Kenya's rural society. To achieve this goal, medical students are required to interact with the community during their training and to familiarize themselves with the health and socio-economic conditions of the people in rural surroundings.

Over the past ten years or so JKUAT has developed programmes jointly with experts from industry. This collaboration has helped the institution to offer courses in electronics, information technology and business management at its main campus as well as in numerous middle-level colleges that are accredited to it throughout the country.

Although it originally started as an agricultural college, Egerton University has diversified its programmes to include non-agricultural courses in science, arts and medicine. Most of its diploma courses in the Faculty of Agriculture have been replaced with new degree programmes. In addition, masters' and doctoral programmes are offered. The Egerton Faculty of Education has expanded from two departments in 1990 to eight departments. New programmes include the Faculty of Environmental Science and Natural Resources established in 1999, which has two departments. The newest programme is the Faculty of Health Sciences, which was established in 2002 in response to student demand. This course is in line with the government's health policy, which emphasizes the need to train more medical personnel to increase the population's access to health care. Egerton has also pioneered the introduction of a degree programme in military science. Although this programme has been temporarily suspended, it will be the first of its kind in the region.

Maseno University has also responded to market demand by launching new departments and programmes. In 1998, the Department of Hotel and Institutional Management was established – the only one of its kind at this level in the country – offering undergraduate and postgraduate degree courses. Other new units include the School of Public Health and Community Development (2001) and the Departments of Special Education, Media Technology (2001) and Information and Communication Technology (ICT).

It is worth noting here that, although new programmes have been initiated during the past decade, other programmes were envisioned but never developed while yet others are being proposed and may be offered in future. The reform process is therefore continuing. For example, 12 courses have been proposed but have yet to be approved by the Senate of Egerton University. The Faculty of Veterinary Medicine was part of the 1987 Moi University master plan but failed to take off, perhaps due to declining job opportunities for veterinary graduates. At Kenyatta, the Environmental Studies Department plans to launch new programmes in environmental toxicology, environmental law and policy analysis and environmental health.

Some public universities have always worked to translate their research programmes and findings into community development components. This is epitomized by the numerous community outreach projects in which the public universities have been involved over the years. Since the mid-1990s, farmers around JKUAT in Juja and Thika have benefited from the university's new banana variety that is produced at its Biotechnology Centre Laboratory. JKUAT has been producing 100,000 to 150,000 seedlings annually for farmers. Farmers who grow the old banana strains produce 15 to 20 tonnes of the crop per hectare, while those growing JKUAT's strain harvest about 130 tonnes per hectare.

The University of Nairobi's Nutribusiness Project benefits women's groups and co-operative societies in Ndanai (in Bomet District) and

47

Gatanga (in Murang'a District). This project is funded by USAID, the Self-Help Fund of the US Ambassador to Kenya and the International Foundation for Education and Self-Help (IFESH). It developed out of a linkage programme between Pennsylvania State and Tuskegee universities in the US and the University of Nairobi. Between 1992 and 1999, the three institutions worked with 88 Kenyan women's groups representing smallholder farmers, in an effort to increase the commercialization of their agricultural products. The aim of the project was to create an opportunity for women in Bomet and Murang'a districts to process some proportion of their commodities into supplemental weaning mixtures for young children, which would be marketed in district urban centres via Nutribusiness Co-operatives to which the women growers would sell their crops. Each co-operative has a solar dryer, a machine to de-hull maize, a posho mill (to grind maize into flour) and a pick-up truck. Crops sold to the co-operatives are dried, milled and mixed into a single, nutritious easy-to-cook weaning food for young children, which is sold in 500 gram and 1 kg packages, with the profits being distributed to individual members of the co-operative on the basis of the shares they hold. University of Nairobi researchers and students tested the weaning foods to be sure they contained enough vitamins, minerals and protein to be healthful foods for young children. In collaboration with the Kenya Industrial Research and Development Institute, the university designed the equipment needed to process the products.

The Nutribusiness Project also relates to the goal of building democracy by involving women from politically opposed ethnic groups in a common activity. The project was launched during a period of tribal unrest in 1992 with memorable exchange visits between women from Bomet and Murang'a. These visits established bonds of friendship and mutual respect between women with shared concerns about the development of their communities and the health of their children. Subsequently, the women have learnt many lessons about participation in a democratic society by electing their peers to positions of authority on sub-location Nutribusiness Councils. The council officers in turn elect the office bearers to their district's Nutribusiness Co-operative board of directors, who establish policies that will be binding upon the members of the participating women's groups. Although the University of Nairobi handed this project over to women's groups in Bomet and Murang'a Districts in 1999, the concepts of income generation and the joint ownership of property and management of resources by women from different locations are still going strong. This sort of grassroots-level organization helps women internalize the goals of civil society based on democratic principles.

In 1994 Kenyattta University set up the Operation Kenyatta University Outreach (OKUO). The programme has provided various services to the surrounding community, including the provision of piped water, access roads, foodstuffs and clothing. OKUO also offers education and training in personal and environmental hygiene, family relations, and laundry, dressmaking, tailoring and knitting. The impact of OKUO's training has been visible in a neighbouring village and slum. During the 2000/01 academic year, 45 students were enrolled out of the 70 who applied for admission to the tailoring and knitting programmes that OKUO offers. According to OKUO's co-ordinator (who is also the university's Vice-Chancellor for finance and planning) the most striking achievement of OKUO is the excellent performance by students in government Trade Test III where 12 out of 13 registered for the examination passed.

Although the other public universities also have outreach programmes through which they interact with their surrounding communities, they are less elaborate than those of Nairobi and Kenyatta Universities. Nonetheless, interacting with local communities is becoming an integral element of university culture.

New delivery mechanisms

The African Virtual University

With headquarters in Nairobi, the African Virtual University (AVU) is a distance-learning network with 25 centres distributed across the African continent. Also popularly known as the 'University Without Walls', the AVU prefers to define itself not by the technology it uses, but rather by the quality of the educational material that it delivers. Its courses connect African students and professors with advanced pedagogy and content across the globe, using digital satellite technology and the internet to deliver instruction to various sites within Africa. The AVU's mission is to promote sustainable economic development, maximize the profitability of African enterprises, improve the quality and relevance of science, engineering and business instruction in sub-Saharan Africa and support African universities in developing curricula which are then broadcast to other African countries.

The AVU has two main programmes: the Academic Channel, launched in 2001, which offers undergraduate degrees in computer

49

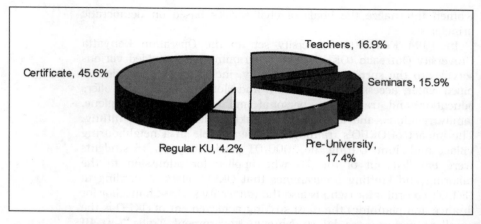

Certificate, 45.6%

Teachers, 16.9%

Seminars, 15.9%

Regular KU, 4.2%

Pre-University,
17.4%

Figure I.4: Enrolment at Kenyatta University's AVU Site, 1997–2001
Source: Data from Kenyatta Virtual University, Incorporated, 2002.

science and electrical and computer science engineering, and the Business and Technology Channel, which is responsible for offering non-credit courses in management and information technology and foreign languages. There are two AVU sites in public universities in Kenya: AVU–Kenyatta University and AVU–Egerton University. Established in 1997, Kenyatta University's site is one of the AVU's pioneering centres in sub-Saharan Africa. Since its inception, the centre has offered many programmes including certificate computer courses, pre-university programmes and executive seminars as shown in Figure 1.4. More than 10,000 students in Kenya from diverse professional areas have benefited from these programmes aimed at overcoming time, place and curriculum constraints to higher education.

During the 2001/2 academic year, Kenyatta University launched Kenyatta Virtual University Incorporated (KVU) after the end of the AVU pilot phase. Egerton University's AVU centre started in October 2000, with the launching of the Business and Technology Channel. The Academic Channel was launched at Egerton in 2001. The centre offers courses via satellite at one of the campuses and video-based courses at another campus. Since its inception, about 1,400 people have been trained despite the fact that the Egerton AVU programme initially experienced a poor response from students, staff and the general public at one of its campuses. The centre offers a wide range of courses including conflict resolution, performance

50

appraisal, teaching of English as a foreign language (TOEFL), entrepreneurship, precision management, French, computer literacy and
journalism.

Distance-education modes

Of the six public universities, the University of Nairobi has the oldest
distance-delivery mechanism. Based in the Faculty of Education and
External Studies, the programme has developed over the years
pioneering audio and print materials, some of which have been used
extensively by other universities in the region, including the Open
University in Tanzania. Kenyatta University's School of Education
and Human Resources Institute for Continuing Development offers
university education to primary and secondary school teachers who
are keen to upgrade their qualifications. JKUAT runs distance-education programmes through the accredited centres it has established,
thus reaching a wider population. At Egerton University, a military
science programme conducted by distance learning was suspended in
2001 by the Department of Defence, although there are indications
that the course will be reinstated.

Kenyatta University FM radio service

Kenyatta University will be the first of the public universities to
operate a frequency modulation (FM) radio station. The FM radio
station project will be part of the Institute of Distance Learning, which
will offer certificates, diplomas and degrees to students nationwide.
The KU media strategy will not only facilitate distance-learning
programmes, but will also raise awareness about the university's
strength, market its programmes in a highly competitive environment, keep staff and students informed about its activities, communi-
cate the research undertaken to the public, market university
facilities such as conference and catering services, run alumni programmes, build good will with the local community, enhance
corporate links and fund-raising and promote student recruitment.

The semester system & online registration

Before 1987, students in the public universities followed the quarter
system (the traditional first, second and third years and so on) of
study in which students registered for course units prescribed for
their respective year of study. The quarter system has now been
replaced with a semester system that allows students to take course
units per semester. In addition, they can now take any courses being
offered in the semester irrespective of their year of study, on

51

condition that they meet specified conditions set by the respective departments. These changes have essentially resulted in the abolition of the traditional academic year. Although the semester system has its own drawbacks (see below), it has two main advantages. First, compared with the previous system, it is flexible, and permits enterprising students to graduate in fewer years (three instead of four) by registering for trimester sessions. Secondly, students are examined on fresh material each semester, which, at least in theory, makes assessment more comprehensive and rigorous. A related reform is the introduction of online registration by Kenyatta University in 2001, the first public university in Kenya to introduce this mode of registration. Students can now register remotely from any part of the world.

Information & communication technologies (ICT) in public universities

If universities are to serve more students and meet their stated objectives in a context of limited resources, they must become more innovative with regard to teaching approaches, especially in the use of information technology (Mwiria, 2002). Even in a poor country such as Kenya, information technologies are increasingly changing the way Kenyans work and go about their daily business. The public universities have no choice but to embrace ICT and take the lead in spreading familiarity with and access to it.

Most of the universities lack adequate computer facilities; thus the level of computer literacy is generally low. One exception is JKUAT, which runs compulsory computer units for all its students. Even there, the small number of computers available limits student use. All the public universities now have their own websites. While some of the older universities, for example the University of Nairobi, have had departments of computer science for a long time, it is not evident that ICT literacy is an integral element of the institution's learning culture and environment. To raise the level of computer literacy among its students, Kenyatta University has made computer courses compulsory for all undergraduates and has organized computer literacy courses for its staff. Further systematic research is needed on the status of ICT in all the public universities.

It is too much to expect comprehensive internet access by university staff and students in the face of a severe shortage of computer equipment. However, Kenyatta and Egerton Universities should have better internet access since they are AVU sites. Among other things, the AVU provides over 10,000 free e-mail accounts and telephone services to facilitate interaction between AVU students and their instructors. The AVU centres at Kenyatta and Egerton universities also provide students with access to an online digital library with over 1,000 full-text journals. At Maseno University, concern has been raised about internet congestion leading to scrambling for the few available sites. For its part, the University of Nairobi completed a four-phase project in August 2002 that established a high-speed network infrastructure to link all its campuses as well as providing free internet access to staff and students. Students on distance-learning programmes will be the biggest beneficiaries of the new electronic infrastructure now fully operational in the UoN's four campuses.

Over time the prevailing ICT situation in the public universities will change with the completion of the Kenya Education Network (KENET) connectivity project launched in 2001 through the Leland Initiative of the US government. KENET helps local educational institutions obtain affordable high-speed internet connectivity, facilitate electronic communication and support teaching and learning. Some 22 institutions, including all the public universities, have been selected as sites for the first phase of the project.

3 Reforms Related to Governance/Management & Planning

New structures of governance & management

The reform process has led to radical changes in the administrative structures of some public universities. Notable among these is Kenyatta University, where the six existing faculties were dismantled and merged into three schools in March 2002. The Faculty of Education became the School of Education and Human Resource Development, the Faculties of Science, Environment and Home Economics were merged into the School of Pure and Applied Science, while the Faculties of Arts and Commerce were converted into the School of Humanities and Social Sciences. The three schools are under separate management boards, headed by executive deans appointed by the University Council – an authority structure that is expected to lead to better governance of teaching programmes, resulting in better and more innovative teaching and a more diversified and flexible curriculum.

In theory, this new management structure offers a number of advantages. It should encourage interdisciplinary collaboration and research networking, the collective sourcing of funds and other resources, the monitoring of programme harmonization, the effective utilization of resources, the reduction of current inter-faculty transfers among undergraduate students, the decentralization of the process of decision-making, including the establishment of a reformed, leaner administration, and the devolution of financial control. If the devolved system is allowed to operate independently, the three schools will establish their own admission criteria, examination standards, curricula, research goals and fund-raising activities. The Senate will address policy issues and rules, with the University Council acting as supervisor.

Administrative and academic structures have also been reconstituted with the purpose of streamlining the chain of command between school deans, Vice-Chancellors, Deputy Vice-Chancellors, associate deans and departmental heads. Administrative-related innovations also focus on reducing the numerous protocols that have to be followed. This reform is also meant to democratize management by creating more avenues for more people to participate in the running of the universities. If the restructuring is taken to its logical conclusion, the positions of Vice–Chancellor and Deputy Vice-Chancellor may be filled through a competitive recruitment process.

Search committees will be created that include representatives of staff, students, the government and members of the public. This system would be in stark contrast to the current one and, if it works, other public universities should feel substantial internal pressure to institute similar reforms with regard to the devolution of power.

Strategic planning

Although all the public universities have instituted reforms, some have done so without benefit of a planning unit or section to plan and co-ordinate these activities. Kenyatta University, for example, does not have a planning unit. In this case, the annual senior management seminars that had become an established event in the university calendar were used to reflect on the changes to be initiated. During these seminars, senior academic staff had the opportunity to review university performance in administrative, academic and developmental programmes. In 1995 the idea of coming up with a management structure for income-generation units was mooted. At its base the proposed management structure would comprise project managers answerable to the Income-Generating Activities Board. It was further proposed that the board should set up separate committees such as a projects appraisal committee, a project monitoring and incubation committee and a production and marketing committee (Ndiritu et al., 1995). The proposed structure has not yet been developed, although it is expected that the strategic planning committee formed in 2002 to implement the ten-year strategic plan to decentralize KU's operations will carry it out. The strategic planning committee represents a departure from the previous practice of most initiatives emanating from the Vice-Chancellor.

Moi University has had a master plan since 1984 but it has not been implemented. A new direction was imperative to signal the way forward. This came in 1991 when all the public universities were required to submit ten-year development plans, under the Universities Investment Project introduced by the World Bank. The Moi University Ten-Year Development Plan (1993–2003/4) was drawn up, but failed to meet the intended implementation deadline. Soon thereafter, the Commission for Higher Education advised all the public universities to draft three-year financial investment plans, which were also re-organized on the basis of the World Bank guidelines. The Moi University six-year development plan 1994/95–1999/2000 was formulated. The question of dwindling government revenue and the need for alternative sources of income to achieve set targets were factored into the plan. One of its major tasks was to review and revise the university mission, vision and objectives to make them more specific. The revised mission statement is: 'To contribute to knowledge and produce graduates that are all-round individuals, capable of functioning and contributing with maximum efficiency, cost benefit and cost effectiveness in the changing environment' (Moi University, 1994: 27).

The need to translate this mission into concrete terms was the driving force behind the plan. Guided by the master plan, it undertook a critical examination of academic programmes and proposed changes to address elements of relevance, marketability and flexibility. Since 1996, academic programmes have been reviewed as specified in the master plan, and several projects have been accomplished, including the creation of directorates in the university and the establishment of field stations used for research and generation of data. The document built in specific targets for the measurement of performance to ensure that plans are implemented in all aspects of development including academic programmes, physical facilities, and administrative and financial management.

The development plan also proposed the establishment and revamping of a planning and development unit headed by a principal administrative officer whose main function would be to design and implement development plans on a continuous basis as well as to monitor and evaluate their progress. The unit exists, but its impact is slight. Its major weakness is that it failed to resolve the issue of accommodation for students even when, in most cases, the increase in the number of students was well known in advance. Furthermore, appraisal of staff performance has not taken place because an evaluation instrument developed in 1997 for students to rate their lecturers failed to work for a number of reasons, one of them being the absence of an appraisal culture in public universities.

Other public universities have accepted, at least in principle, the need for strategic planning. The University of Nairobi, for example, is in the advanced stage of producing its strategic plan. Nevertheless, it will be interesting to see whether resources will be available to allow implementation of the plans. In this regard, Moi University is a case in point.

Staffing in public universities

Currently, non-academic staff represent 74 per cent of the total number of staff in the public universities while the academic staff

Table I.7: Staff/student ratios in public universities, 1994–2002

University	Teaching Staff/Student Ratio				Non-Teaching Staff/Student Ratio			
	1994/ 95	1995/ 96	1996/ 97	2001/2	1994/ 95	1995/ 96	1996/ 97	2001/2
Kenyatta	1:16	1:14	1:14	1:18	1:4	1:5	1:5	1:7
Nairobi	1:9	1:9	1:9	1:12	1:3	1:3	1:3	1:5
Egerton	1:14	1:14	1:14	1:23	1:4	1:3	1:3	1:5
Moi	1:12	1:6	1:6	1:17	1:4	1:3	1:3	1:5
JKUAT	1:9	1:9	1:9	1:15	1:3	1:3	1:3	1:5
Maseno	1:18	1:12	1:12	1:33	1:3	1:3	1:3	1:12
Average	1:13	1:12	1:12	1:20	1:3	1:3	1:3	1:6

Source: Generated from enrolment and staffing records of CHE and public universities, 2002.

make up 26 per cent (3,536). Since government funding of the public universities is based on the number of students and not the total number of staff, institutions that are overstaffed tend to spend most of their funds on emoluments and less on operations and maintenance. To avoid this situation, it is necessary to generate a model for determining optimal size. Towards this end, the Kenya government required the public universities to downsize their staff during the 2000/01 academic year. The first phase of this imposed reform was concluded in April 2001 and saw the retrenchment of 3,203 employees in the lower cadres, cutting the non-academic staff from a total of 13,420 to the current level of 10,217. The University of Nairobi had an excess of about 2,517 support staff and retrenched 1,838, followed by retrenchments at Egerton (502), Kenyatta (378), Maseno (243), Moi (200) and JKUAT (42).

The situation of the teaching staff in the public universities is somewhat better than that of non-academic staff, as shown in Table I.7. However, based on full-time staff equivalents (FTSE) computed by the CHE, the average staff-student ratio was a generous 1:12 (for academic staff) and 1:3 (for non-academic staff). In industrialized countries, staff-student ratios are generally much higher than this. Applying a ratio of 1:18, which is the average in universities in Commonwealth countries, reveals that the Kenyan public universities have been considerably overstaffed. From this perspective, the University of Nairobi had approximately 740 more teaching staff than it needed during the 1990s. The tendency for the public universities to have faculty/student ratios that are too low to support is the negative side of offering a wide range of

Table I.8: Academic staff by university, rank and sex, 2000/01

University	Full professor		Associate professor		Senior lecturer	
	M	F	M	F	M	F
Nairobi	88	4	141	26	234	55
	(58)	(36.4)	(57.1)	(60.5)	(47.6)	(55.6)
Moi	17	1	39	2	63	6
	(11)	(9.1)	(15.8)	(4.7)	(12.8)	(6.1)
Kenyatta	28	2	20	3	97	26
	(18)	(18.2)	(8.1)	(7.0)	(19.7)	(26.3)
Egerton	5	2	22	7	34	4
	(3.3)	(18.2)	(8.9)	(16.3)	(6.9)	(4)
Maseno	13	1	10	1	28	5
	(9)	(9.1)	(4)	(2.3)	(5.7)	(5.1)
JKUAT	1	1	15	4	36	3
	(0.7)	(9.1)	(6.1)	(9.3)	(7.3)	(3)
Total	152	11	247	43	492	99
	(100)	(100)	(100)	(100)	(100)	(100)

Source: Generated from personnel records in public universities
Note: Figures in parentheses represent percentages.

programmes and courses, some of which have very low enrolments. In a better co-ordinated system, some of the programmes would be offered at only one university, thus leading to the evolution of centres of excellence. A case in point is offering programmes in medicine, pharmacy and dentistry that for various reasons admit a few students each instead of developing a centre of excellence approach.

The high number of non-academic staff in the universities can be explained by the influence of political patronage that has the effect of compelling university authorities to employ more workers than they may actually need.

Following the execution of the first phase of the retrenchment exercise in 2001 and the rapid expansion of university enrolment due to the privatization of education in the public universities, staffing ratios have been changed. Staff:student ratios now range from 1:12 at the University of Nairobi to 1:33 at Maseno, with an average of 1:20 for the other public universities. The non-academic staff to student ratios average 1:5, with the exception of Kenyatta

Lecturer		Assistant lecturer/tutorial fellow/graduate assistant		Totals	
M	**F**	**M**	**F**	**M**	**F**
488	151	120	38	1,071	274
(34.5)	(35.6)	(27.2)	(17.8)	(39)	(34.6)
329	67	79	41	527	117
(23.3)	(15.8)	(17.9)	(19.2)	(19.2)	(14.8)
175	100	113	75	433	206
(12.4)	(23.6)	(25.6)	(35)	(15.8)	(26.0)
194	50	71	40	326	103
(13.7)	(11.8)	(16.1)	(18.7)	(11.9)	(13.0)
107	32	4	13	162	52
(7.6)	(7.5)	(0.9)	(6.1)	(5.9)	(6.6)
121	24	54	7	227	39
(8.6)	(5.7)	(12.2)	(3.3)	(8.3)	(4.9)
1,414	424	441	214	2,746	791
(100)	(100)	(100)	(100)	(100)	(100)

and Maseno universities whose ratios are 1:7 and 1:12 respectively. Nairobi, Moi, Egerton and JKUAT, which are still overstaffed with administrative personnel, will have to continue their phased staff rationalization reform if they are to achieve the optimal size of non-academic staff.

The gender gap in staffing

Table I.8 shows the staffing position of academic staff in the public universities during the 2000/01 academic year. With a teaching force of 3,537, this represents an increase of 686 per cent from the early 1970s. The University of Nairobi (1,071 male and 274 female academic staff) has 38 per cent of this total staff, Moi (527 male and 117 female) accounts for 18 per cent; Kenyatta (433 male and 206 female), 18 per cent; Egerton (326 male and 103 female), 12 per cent, JKUAT (227 male and 39 female), 8 per cent, and Maseno (162 male and 52 female), 6 per cent. Women constitute a mere 22 per cent of the total academic staff. Such a low female/male ratio is directly related to the numbers of female graduates, as it is from this category that the universities' academic staff are recruited. The gender gap is widest at JKUAT, because most of its courses are science- and technology-based.

Only 1 per cent of the female faculty are at the professorial level, as against 4 per cent of men. The greatest concentration of both males and females is at the lecturer grade (52 per cent for men and 54 per cent for women). Major reforms are needed in order to correct the gender imbalance in staffing. However, as indicated earlier, this is an issue that calls for reform of the entire educational system and not the university system alone. The public universities could nevertheless play their part by initiating affirmative action with regard to further training for female junior members of staff.

Facilities

Despite the financial constraints occasioned by a reduction in government funding, the University of Nairobi has been able to oversee the completion of a number of important projects including two state-of-the-art lecture theatres at Chiromo with a seating capacity of 300 each, a lecture theatre at the Kenyatta National Hospital Campus with a seating capacity of 250, the Faculty of Engineering Complex and a lecture theatre at Parklands Campus. There are also a number of on-going projects nearing completion, including the construction of a large laboratory complex for medical and dental students at the College of Health Sciences and the extension of the Faculty of Architecture and Design building. Other projects approved by the university for the 2002/3 academic year are construction of the Faculty of Pharmacy and the Department of Nursing Sciences and the completion of the stalled 8:4:4 building at the College of Education and External Studies in Kikuyu.

Physical planning in the public universities is not commensurate with their rate of growth and expansion. When innovations crop up, university managers accommodate them within the existing infrastructure. This has often led to the over-stretching of existing facilities. Thus, Egerton University has had to convert twelve staff houses into offices for various uses. AVU-Egerton is currently housed in a building that used to contain two of the largest lecture halls in the university. These conversions have led to a further squeeze on the already inadequate infrastructure. Moi University also had to convert some staff houses into hostels while students' common rooms were turned into lecture rooms. Overstretching of infrastructure is visible in lecture halls and halls of residence. The situation in the halls of residence has been worsened by the phenomenon of 'squatting' – the practice whereby non-resident students reside unofficially on the campus under private arrangements with the official tenants (allocated students). Clearly, major reforms are needed in physical planning and space utilization. Most of the them could probably be accomplished by aggressive fund-raising based on a strategy of partnership between the universities and the private sector. For example, all the public universities possess plenty of land that could be their contribution to a partnership aimed at improving and increasing physical facilities. This kind of partnership would, however, require more trust than is currently in stock.

The management of human resources

The terms of service for staff in the public universities provide a framework for recruitment, training, development and appraisal for all cadres. At Kenyatta University and JKUAT, the Deputy Vice-Chancellor (Administration) is responsible for the overall management of staff, while the Deputy Vice-Chancellor (Administration and Finance) handles this at Egerton and Nairobi universities. But in these and other public universities, the daily supervision of staff is vested in heads of departments or sections, deans and other senior academic and administrative officers.

Among other concerns, the efficient management of staff involves providing remuneration packages that insulate them from the ravages of inflation. In this regard, the public universities compare badly with the private universities, which pay well, and with salaries in some other African countries and elsewhere. This has had consequences for the public university system, where the inability to offer good salaries has led to an exodus of lecturers to southern Africa and Rwanda, among other countries, that offer superior remuneration and other terms of employment. While most of the private universities in Kenya do not pay well, United States International University (USIU) has attracted a number of staff from the public universities because of its attractive remuneration package, which in 2002 was roughly twice as high as that offered in the public universities (see Figure II.1 in Part II). Nonetheless, the public universities are making efforts to raise salaries in order to attract, motivate and retain highly qualified staff. So far, however, these changes are small compared with the magnitude of the problem.

The tendency to peg administrative to academic salaries without demanding similar academic qualifications from administrators is a

61

bone of contention among academic staff in the public universities. They argue that the only criterion used in promoting administrative staff is length of service. Moreover, administrators are accorded favourable treatment in terms of office space, office facilities and secretarial services, all of which have tended to create resentment that affects productivity among the academic staff. Two members of the teaching staff from Kenyatta University observed that:

> ... if there is one thing which undermines esprit de corps in what we call corporate life in this university, it is the problem of lack of communication.... As a consequence of lack of communications and the apparent laissez-faire attitude of the administration over matters that affect staff and their general welfare, there appears to be little rapport between the administration and members of staff. The academic staff and the administration seem to be working at cross-purposes rather than as a cohesive team. (Darkoh and Wambari, 1994: 78)

This situation is exacerbated by the fact that the academic staff in the public universities do not have unions. Most of the universities have staff welfare associations instead, but Egerton does not even have one of these. Without staff unions, it is left to each university to try to improve the welfare of academic staff according to its own resources, administrative practices and statutes. One good practice has been the representation of academic staff in key university decision-making organs. An overdue reform is the reinstatement of academic staff unions that were banned in the mid-1980s.

Health & recreation activities

Apart from Kenyatta University, most public universities have little to show by way of staff recreational facilities. In 2001 Kenyatta University established a Health and Recreational Centre for its staff, students and members of the public, under the management of the Physical Education Department. The centre includes a 33-metre swimming pool, a fitness testing programme, indoor games and two gymnasia (for staff and students), both of which have treadmills and bicycles and other exercise machines. Three full-time exercise instructors and one swimming instructor staff the centre. The overall objective is to create a sports academy with the centre as its nucleus. In the context of dwindling resources, the centre is an innovation well worth emulating by other public universities. For the first time, a public university has taken physical fitness seriously, especially among its staff, a milestone in a context where hypertension and other forms of stress are becoming more common.

Management of student needs/affairs

All the public universities have established offices or units dealing with the management of student affairs and welfare. At Nairobi and JKUAT, the Dean of Students Office handles student welfare issues, while at Kenyatta University the management of student affairs is under the Directorate of Student Affairs. Maseno has set up a Students' Welfare Office. Student welfare issues are also handled by the respective student organizations, including the Kenyatta University Student Association, the Nairobi University Student Association, the Student Union of Egerton University, the Jomo Kenyatta University Student Organization and the Moi University Student Organization. Parallel organizations have also been formed to cater for students enrolled in self-sponsored programmes, such as the Jomo Kenyatta University Alternative Degree Programme Student Association.

Although some universities have experienced relative tranquillity owing to a spirit of dialogue between management and the student organization, the Kenyan public universities are better known for student unrest and riots resulting from grievances over issues ranging from food to national politics. It would appear, however, that public university administrators are beginning to utilize the art of dialogue in the management of student affairs, including the management of student-government relations. With regard to the latter, the universities have also begun to appreciate the need to protect students from the state by keeping the dreaded anti-riot squads off campus. Good university leadership has been a key factor in the institutionalization of dialogue as an instrument of conflict management. In all the public universities, Vice-Chancellors are keen to reduce the distance between themselves and the students without jeopardizing their authority. At Egerton University, for example, there has been a noticeable positive rapport and general improvement in student-administration relationships under the current Vice-Chancellor who interacts frequently with the students. The previously dormant academic guidance system has been reactivated to help students academically, in addition to improving relations between students and the administration. Each member of staff at Egerton serves as an academic adviser for up to two students whose academic and social welfare is monitored. However, academic advisers sometimes find that the system is ineffective since few students turn up to seek advice. At Nairobi University, the management board has established a working committee with the brief to investigate matters related to students' requests.

63

In some universities, efforts have been made to enhance students' leadership skills by sponsoring them for study tours both within and outside the country. In the 2000/01 academic year, Kenyatta University student leaders travelled to the University of Dar es Salaam in Tanzania, Makerere University in Uganda and the University of Eastern Africa, Baraton (a private university in Kenya) to study the mode of operation of student organizations in these institutions. These tours enabled them to interact with their peers elsewhere and to gain valuable exposure. On their return, the students reported favourably on Makerere University, in particular. The Guild [student parliament] oversees student academic and social problems at Kenyatta University and handles them appropriately at the grassroots level. This greatly minimizes incidents of student rioting and unrest. The Guild officers meet the university administration frequently for briefing and presentation of sensitive issues that they are unable to handle (Kenyatta University *Tribune*, October 2001).

Strategies for managing HIV/AIDS

There are no accurate data on the actual numbers of staff infected with the HIV virus, but it is well known that HIV is taking a heavy toll on both staff and students. In recognition of this, the public universities have set up AIDS control units (ACUs) to develop programmes for the management of HIV/AIDS as well as to help raise community awareness. The general objective of these units is to reduce the prevalence of HIV/AIDS among the university community, to reach out to infected and affected groups both within and outside the universities, to offer counselling services for those living with AIDS and their families, and generally to demystify the disease. Activities currently being undertaken include student-based peer counselling, HIV/AIDS awareness days and the distribution of condoms.

Kenyatta University has an AIDS Outreach Programme that works on awareness creation. In addition, KU has now taken the lead in teaching about HIV/AIDS at certificate, diploma and postgraduate levels. Similarly, the university provides compulsory HIV courses for all undergraduates. The Egerton University Health Centre Project is an on-going project focusing on the intensive training of students about HIV/AIDS and related issues. JKUAT has also established an HIV/AIDS board whose role is to sensitize and provide information to the university community on HIV/AIDS. In addition, JKUAT hospital is a designated Voluntary Counselling and Testing Centre (VCT).

The University of Nairobi's AIDS Control Unit was launched in late 2002 after more than six months of consultations and study visits to other ACUs, including the Kenyatta University unit. The university's ACU cautions staff and students on HIV/AIDS, while also advising them to test their personal status at VCTs. The unit puts forward a range of policies and strategies in dealing with HIV/AIDS including non-discrimination against HIV-positive staff and students.

65

4 Reforms Related to University Financing

Cost-sharing & the unit-cost system

From independence in 1963 until the 1970s, public higher education in Kenya was free of cost to students. Cost-sharing in Kenya's public universities dates back to the mid-1970s when the government introduced a student loan scheme. In spite of that, many students and parents continued to regard university education as free; hence the low recovery levels of these loans. In June 1991, the government introduced the current cost-sharing scheme that requires students to pay in full or in part through a direct charge depending on their perceived need for tuition, food and accommodation. The introduction of direct charges acknowledged that, in the context of growing enrolments and diminished funding, the government could no longer finance university education without compromising education standards. The introduction of a direct charge was also influenced by the general policy of introducing cost-sharing measures as part of the Structural Adjustment Programmes (SAPs) prescribed by the World Bank and the International Monetary Fund. The understanding was that no deserving student should be denied university education simply on the basis of financial inability. Consequently, the government set up loans and scholarships schemes under the Higher Education Loans Board (HELB). Some 90 per cent of the current crop of regular undergraduate students benefit from loans and/or scholarships.

The annual cost for an average undergraduate is estimated at Kshs.120,000 (US$1,667) and is based on unit cost.[3] This is defined as the amount of money a university spends on one student per year per degree programme. Of this unit cost, Kshs.86,000 (US$1,194) is earmarked for tuition and Kshs.34,000 (US$472) for catering, accommodation and other costs. The government's capitation per university is computed by multiplying the total number of students by Kshs.70,000 (US$972), which is the government's annual grant per student. The balance is supposed to be met by the student, except in cases of need where a loan of up to Kshs.52,000 (US$722) and a bursary of Kshs.8,000 (US$111) may be considered. As general policy, only 20 per cent of the student population are expected to receive bursaries, regardless of precise needs during the year. These bursaries are evenly distributed among the public universities. Since

[3] US$1=Kshs. 72 in February 2006.

the demand outstrips the amount available, the competition for them tends to be very high. In cases where deserving students fail to obtain a bursary, the public universities have introduced various means of student assistance, including work-study programmes.

The present unit-cost system (computed in 1995, using figures from the 1991/2 audited accounts of the public universities) is grossly inadequate as a basis for funding the public universities. Moreover, the method does not take into account the differential costs of the various degree programmes and tends to reward universities such as Kenyatta and Maseno that offer more of the cheaper arts-oriented programmes over those offering the more expensive science- and technology-based programmes, since the same unit cost is used for all programmes. Even then the predominantly arts-based universities such as Kenyatta and Maseno are still under-funded, as the cheapest degree training per student costs Kshs.182,000 (US$2,528) and the most expensive one Kshs.470,000 (US$6,528) per academic year, amounts that are way above the government capitation per student. The depth of the financial crisis afflicting Kenya's public universities is reflected in the chronic deficits shown in Table I.9. The brief reprieve of the 1994/5 academic year notwithstanding, the deficits keep rising, due to the fact that essential services have to be kept afloat despite increased costs. At Kenyatta University, the deficits have increased from approximately 2 per cent in the mid-1990s to the current level of about 14 per cent. The University of Nairobi, which has a gross monthly payroll and operational expenditure of Kshs.195 million (US$2.7 million), with a monthly capitation of only Kshs.119 million (US$1.65 million), records a deficit of 39 per cent annually. Moi University's debt portfolio had approached Kshs.155 million (US$2.2 million) by 2000.

Table I.9: Cumulative recurrent deficits for all public universities

Year	Deficits in Kshs.	Deficits in US$
1991	22,705,554	315,355
1992	310,858,544	4,317,480
1993	216,326,145	3,004,530
1994	147,715,640	2,051,606
1995	135,313,271	1,877,963
1996	503,280,783	6,990,011
Total	1,336,099,937	18,556,948

Source: Data from Ministry of Education, Science and Technology, Planning Division, 2002.

Despite this stressful financial situation, the public universities seem unable to collect fees from their students. Thus the current fee arrears at the University of Nairobi, for example, stand at around Kshs.240 million (US$3.3 million). The pay-as-you-eat (PAYE) cost-sharing system in the catering services has aggravated the financial situation of the public universities, in that students find it expensive and therefore opt to cook in their hostels, which in turn inflates the cost of running the hostels due to high electricity bills (discussed in further detail below).

Income-generating activities & privately sponsored students

In an effort to make up the financial shortfalls and enhance their missions, the public universities have mounted innovative income-generating activities (IGAs). These are organized around self-sponsored academic programmes, business and productive ventures (non-academic commercial units), consultancy services, study-abroad programmes and hiring out university facilities to external users. Non-academic IGAs include running guesthouses, farms, bakeries, cyber-cafés, bookshops, restaurants and mortuaries. New study programmes and courses have also been initiated in response to public demand, on the basis of charging full-cost fees plus overheads. The introduction of these courses has not only increased access to university education programmes during evenings and weekends but has also contributed to generating valuable income for these institutions.

In 1994, the University of Nairobi appointed a committee to look into income-generating activities in the university and make appropriate recommendations. In its report, the committee came to the conclusion that, through the use of experts and business-like management styles, the institution could generate substantial revenue in a sustainable manner. Consequently, it recommended the formation of the University of Nairobi Enterprise Services (UNES), whose responsibility was to promote, manage and co-ordinate income-generating activities and consultancies.

Maseno University initiated similar measures in 1995 when its Academic Board and Council established the Investment and Economic Enterprises Unit to co-ordinate and manage all non-teaching income-generating units,[4] including the university farm, bookshop,

---

[4] The Investment and Economic Enterprises Unit was disbanded in 2001, with all IGAs coming to be managed by a limited company, as discussed in Chapter 5 below.

catering services, guesthouse, tree nursery and staff housing. Kenyatta University has likewise launched a number of income-generating activities: the bookshop in 1992, the Child Care Unit in 1993, the Bureau of Training and Consultancy in 1993 and a Postgraduate Diploma in Education programme in 1995, among others. Moi University responded by forming the Moi University Holdings Company Limited to run non-teaching income-generating activities such as mortuary services, transport, a bookshop, farms and staff housing. JKUAT adopted a different approach from the other public universities. Under the auspices of the Continuing Education Programme, it has been accrediting middle-level institutions where JKUAT programmes are offered. Egerton University has also ventured more recently into income-generating activities.

These various activities, especially the self-sponsored programmes, have been successful in generating significant income for the public universities. During the 1998/9 and part of 1999/2000 fiscal years, for example, the University of Nairobi earned a total of Kshs.224 million (US$3.1 million) and Kshs.240 million (US$3.3 million) respectively from parallel degree programmes. Indeed, it is expected that in five years' time these programmes will bring in an estimated gross revenue of close to Kshs.1 billion (US$13.9 million) a year (University of Nairobi, 1999). Currently, the university raises about 20 per cent of its budget from the parallel-degree programmes and pays close to 60 per cent of its utilities bill from its own internal resources. At Moi University the revenue from student fees in the Privately Sponsored Students Programmes (PSSP) was approximately Kshs.103 million (US$1.4 million) in the 2000/01 financial year.

While parallel programmes and self-sponsored students have succeeded in bringing the universities some additional income, the income does not yet seem to offset the costs involved. At the same time, staff motivation is low, and the universities themselves have failed to realize the income potential of consulting services provided by their staff. At Maseno University the permanent personnel emoluments in the income-generating units were Kshs.5.9 million (US$82,000) compared with a total net profit of Kshs.3.6 million (US$50,000) in the 1998/9 fiscal year. In the 1997/8 financial year total emoluments amounted to Kshs.5.2 million (US$72,000), whereas only Kshs.3.2 million (US$44,000) had been realized as the total net profit from all income-generating units (Gravenir and Mbuthia, 2000).

At Kenyatta University, the total income from IGAs was Kshs.22 million (US$305,000) in 1996/7, while total expenditure amounted

69

to Kshs.33 million (US$46,000). In 1997/8, the annual revenue from IGAs was Kshs.30 million (US$406,000) while the total expenditure amounted to Kshs.51 million (US$708,000). This bleak picture was reversed during the 1998/9 year when the income-generating units realized Kshs.112 million (US$1.6 million) compared with expenses of Kshs.79 million (US$1.1 million). In general, therefore, the cost of personnel emoluments has reduced the profit potential of the IGAs. While staff retrenchments carried out at Kenyatta University in 2001 might have reduced the total expense on personnel emoluments related to the IGAs, no data were readily available to show the impact of this exercise. The motivation of staff involved in IGAs is generally low as a result of poor remuneration, lack of proper training opportunities and lack of mechanisms for staff recognition and reward.

Although the provision of consultancy services by university staff members for the government or for private enterprise ought to generate significant funding for the universities, this has not been the case in Kenya. At Kenyatta University, for example, the Bureau for Training and Consultancy Services, which was expected to harness this resource for the university, has failed to make a breakthrough into the consulting world. It has opted instead to concentrate on offering training programmes. Consequently, academic staff who offer research and consultancy services at the university do so exclusively for their own benefit and often at a cost to the university through loss of time and free use of university facilities. The situation in the other public universities is similar. To reverse this situation, the public universities need to convince both the consumers of the value of such services and the academic staff who provide them of the potential advantages of having these services centralized within the university.

Cost-reduction measures & constraints

Cost-reduction measures in public universities have included the following: staff retrenchment, stringent financial management procedures and controls and staff cost-sharing schemes. During the 2000/01 academic year, public universities scaled down their expenses by retrenching 3,203 employees in the lower cadres. This brought down the number of non-academic staff from 13,420 to 10,217. As noted above, since government capitation to the public universities is based on the number of students and not employees, overstaffed universities spend most of their funds on salaries. In view of this, the public universities are striving to develop a model of determining optimal staff numbers. From the 2000/01 retrenchment exercise, Nairobi and Moi universities saved about Kshs.18 million (US$240,000) and Kshs.1.8 million (US$24,000) per month, respectively.

Other measures have been taken with the aim of ensuring that the public universities strive to live within their budgetary allocations. To this end, strict controls are being instituted in all areas of expenditure, in particular the use of the telephone, electricity, water and university vehicles. All account holders (deans and heads of departments, units or projects) have been advised to keep books on general accounts such as income and expenditure. Assistance on how to maintain these accounts is being provided by finance departments, since it requires some training in basic accounting to maintain proper records.

At the University of Nairobi, for example, all purchases over Kshs. 100,000 (US$1,333) must have the approval of the Deputy Vice-Chancellor (Administration and Finance), whereas college principals can sanction purchases of between Kshs.50,000 and 100,000 (about US$700–1,400). Non-statutory expenditures over Kshs.500,000 (US$7,000) require the knowledge and approval of the Vice-Chancellor. To ensure that these financial practices are complied with and expenditures are within the approved university budgets, internal auditors have been called upon to carry out appraisals of the financial procedures being practised at all levels of the public universities. This may arise from whistle-blowing or routine audits. In order to ensure their independence, the internal auditors report to the Vice-Chancellors; their management reports are made available to the heads of units.

Some public universities appear to use their limited resources more prudently than others. For example, Moi University, which has two Teaching Practice (TP) sessions – a short four-week session for second-year students and a longer twelve-week session for third-year students – has a budget of Kshs.4 million (US$55,500) for the two exercises, while Kenyatta University spends Kshs.15 million (US$208,000) on one twelve-week session. Moi University manages to do this by having the two TP sessions run concurrently and by restricting the exercise to schools west of the Rift Valley region, thus reducing transportation expenses. At Maseno University, the university has introduced a cost-sharing scheme in medical services for staff in the form of a medical levy.

The public universities are also being urged to borrow from the restructuring strategies that were applied in businesses faced with

71

shrinking revenues and rising costs between the 1980s and 1990s. During this period, corporations re-examined their missions and reduced their less essential activities. In this context, the public universities are considering hiring out services that are marginal to their core missions, such as management of estates, security, transport and catering.

The most logical response by universities to falling government allocation of resources has included the 'double entry' solution of reducing expenditures and generating more income. These efforts are sometimes derailed by the misappropriation of funds. The Auditor General's reports have on occasion raised concerns about this problem and the associated loopholes in financial management. At Moi University the loopholes have included the many bank accounts in operation (some 65 in 2000) and cases where records are not properly kept. During the 1995/6 financial year, it was reported that Maseno University lost over Kshs.50 million (about US$700,000), most of it through theft and false allowance payments (Ondiek, 1997). Reports of the Auditor General have also pointed at the Kenyatta University administration for flouting tendering procedures. In 1994, for example, the university management awarded a tender for the supply of office furniture to a supplier at a cost of about Kshs. 400,000 (US$5,600) on account of its being the lowest bidder out of four quotations received. However, it was observed that the furniture was actually supplied by another firm, which had not initially tendered, at a cost of Kshs.1.5 million (US$21,000). During the 1998/9 fiscal year, the university spent a total of Kshs.2.4 million (US$33,000) purchasing furniture and equipment from various suppliers for the residences occupied by the Vice-Chancellor and Deputy Vice-Chancellor (Finance). These purchasing decisions were not, however, based on competitive bidding. The university purchased other stock items for Kshs.2.8 million (US$39,000) without following proper procurement procedures. Questions have also been raised about the construction of the biochemistry laboratory between 1990 and 1993 (Republic of Kenya, 1994, 1996, 1999).

Financial enhancement & management measures

Financial discipline is the key to the public universities' efforts to improve utilization of their available resources in order to expand the level and diversity of their sources of income. In this regard, purchases of provisions, stationery, insurance and contract awards where the cost involved is above Kshs.200,000 (US$2,800) are processed through tender committees. Other specialized items such as computers, printers, copiers and vehicles are procured via a minimum of three quotations and technically approved specifications. Where three quotations are not available, approval is sought for single sourcing. As detailed above, the Auditor General has on several occasions decried the manner in which some universities flout these procedures. In the meantime, as the government attempts to increase its funding to the public universities from the original Kshs.70,000 (US$1,000) to over Kshs.105,000 (US$1,450) per student per year, the student component of direct fees has not changed. The public universities are therefore proposing that the students' contribution should also be increased.

Other proposals being contemplated by the public universities to enhance their revenue base include charging students for catering and accommodation on a full cost-recovery basis for all materials, utilities and maintenance costs at halls of residence and kitchens, and the adoption of a 'no fees, no registration policy' so that students will not have access to any university services or facilities until they have paid their fees. In the same vein, it has been suggested that students be charged interest at prevailing market rates on any outstanding fees. Measures have also been taken to enhance the productivity of university real estate holdings. Currently there is an on-going review of the utilization of universities' residential real estate. In addition, a number of related policy initiatives are being implemented, including new staff housing policies, for example, charging market-based rents for their property while at the same time progressively eliminating the subsidization of housing facilities.

Although most public universities follow the priority incremental budgeting system that requires a description of what incremental activities or changes would occur as well as the ranking of all activities in order of their importance, the University of Nairobi is considering the merits of adopting a zero-based budgeting procedure. In the zero-based budgeting system, budgets are prepared from zero as though they are being prepared for the first time, thus allowing close scrutiny of every proposed expenditure. It is expected that this budgeting model will facilitate the realization of efficient budgets. It has also been suggested that all cost centres should be granted greater autonomy in managing their budgets by being allocated funds on a block basis.

The current asset portfolio of the public universities is estimated to be in excess of Kshs.60 billion (US$833 million). Unfortunately some properties lack clear or registered titles. Although the universities have implied, and indeed enjoy, *de facto* ownership status, they lack legal ownership, a situation that compromises the control of securities and the related unlocking of the investment potential or commercialization of such assets. Most universities are currently investigating these possibilities.

The public universities are trying to reach out to their alumni. In the broadest sense, alumni (sometimes referred to as 'the con-vocation') include all persons who are graduates of their respective universities. However, the public universities are attempting to formalize alumnus status through the payment of a fee. Active membership is also maintained through payment of regular convoca-tion dues. Alumni associations are meant to help their respective universities attain their educational goals. They also encourage their members to continue their university friendships after graduation through annual reunion activities. The alumni of the private univer-sities in Kenya take the lead, with many fund-raising activities for their institutions. At the University of Eastern Africa, Baraton, the alumni sponsored a project christened 'Step out of the mud' that puts concrete slabs on sidewalks on campus to reduce the mud carried into buildings on campus. Following this private university experience, public universities have embarked on aggressive and pro-active processes of image-building, fund-raising and developing supporters through their alumni, a practice which is a standard method of raising resources for most leading universities all over the world.

Impediments to the new financial practices

Nonetheless, the most serious impediment to the implementation of innovative financial management practices remains the requirement that universities operate within strict government financial regula-tions, typically characterized by tedious bureaucratic procedures. These procedures require that, for any payment, documents must go through 12 stages of approval starting from the request for an advance to the dispatch of the cheques or payment in cash for amounts less than Kshs.3,000 (US$42). In order to purchase goods or procure services, there are 13 stages of approval. When the cost involved is between Kshs.5,000 and 200,000 (US$70–2,800), quota-tions are required. Any amount exceeding Kshs.200,000 necessitates a call for tenders and approval of the Tender Committee. The processing of tender applications alone can take up to six months.

Then there is the issue of raising local purchase orders, which must be dispatched to the supplier or service provider before the goods are supplied or the services rendered. After this, a voucher is prepared and taken through various stages of approval before a cheque is written, signed and dispatched – a process that may take days, weeks or even months, depending on the availability of funds. These procedures are quite different in the private universities where one designated finance officer can process payment once it is approved and still manage the finances with accountability. The former Vice-Chancellor of Moi University tried to speed up the process by allowing a number of approval signatories and introducing other measures to expedite payments as well as to guarantee accountability.

5 Motivation for & Management of Reforms

Motivation for reform

Numerous factors are involved in the reforms currently being implemented by the public universities in Kenya. They include the need to survive in the face of adversity, growth in primary and secondary schooling, competition from the private universities, prompting by foreign universities and the private sector, pressure from the government and from development partners and dynamic leadership in some public universities.

The need to survive in the face of adversity

The motivation for public university reforms needs to be understood in the context of the financial constraints faced by these institutions, especially from the mid-1980s on. During this period, government funding declined steadily as a result of a number of factors, the main one being the overall reduction in budgetary allocations to the service sectors, including education, as Kenya's economic fortunes began to experience a downturn due to the mismanagement of national resources and poor leadership. Related to this were the SAPs sponsored by the Bretton Woods institutions – the World Bank and the IMF – which, among other things, recommended a reduction in social sector spending and the need for the beneficiaries of higher education to contribute towards the cost of their education.

Secondly, increased worldwide focus on basic education (since the 1990 World Conference on Education for All held in Jomtien, Thailand) led to an increased proportion of the education budget being devoted to lower levels of education with less to higher education. In addition, the public universities were arguably losing favour with the government, as the latter began to view them as bastions of opposition at a time when there was little other dissent. Consequently, while the budget allocation to higher education was expected to grow at an annual rate of 4 per cent in order to support the expanding public university system, funding for the universities plummeted, with the exception of the 2000/01 fiscal year.

The overall effect is that the public universities have been operating under difficult budgetary constraints, characterized by rising payroll and operational costs, and escalating debts and deficits. The University of Nairobi's monthly payroll averages Kshs.145 million in addition to a monthly operational expenditure of Kshs.50

Table I.10: Capitation vs. expenditure at Kenyatta University, 1995–9

Financial year	% increase in capitation	% increase in expenditure	% increase in deficit
1995/96–1996/97	5.6	7.8	2.2
1996/97–1997/98	9.2	15.0	5.8
1997/98 – 1998/99	4.0	17.9	13.9

Source: Generated from the Finance Department, Kenyatta University, 2002.

million, while the institution's monthly income is only Kshs.119 million. The result of these constrained financial conditions is a cumulative debt portfolio running into millions of shillings. Financial records from Kenyatta University indicate a similar situation. The capitation versus expenditure from 1995 to 1999 at Kenyatta University (Table I.10) shows increasing deficit levels.

The under-funding of the public universities was intensified by their mismanagement of the limited resources available and by their failure to initiate any meaningful cost-sharing measures. Instead, students continued to insist on more privileges, while both the government and the respective university administrations lacked the will to implement much needed cost-sharing measures. The problem was exacerbated by rapidly increasing student numbers, partly due to populist expansion-related decisions of the kind that led to a presidential directive to the public universities to increase their intakes to accommodate more students in 1988, resulting in the now famous 'double intake'.

The twin pressures of under-funding and expanded intakes resulted in extreme over-stretching of public university human and physical resources (Sifuna, 1998). The universities have therefore been forced to cut out some of their teaching and research programmes and reduce some essential services including transportation, communications and other benefits previously enjoyed by students and staff. These developments partly explain many of the disturbances emanating from students and academic staff during the last decade or so. Academics in these institutions have had a myriad of genuine reasons for discontent, including worsening salaries and other terms and conditions of service.

Other causes of concern include disabling teaching environments, and diminished research votes and other benefits such as support for participation in conferences. These difficulties have played a major

77

role in encouraging the flight of academic staff to other countries and other local universities in search of better opportunities. In the meantime, the universities have had to stay open somehow, even as they have continued to increase in numbers and as new providers of education have begun to make their presence felt. This has meant that, even when the economic imperatives seemed to dictate otherwise, social and political concerns demanded that the institutions somehow find a way of remaining open.

However, the permanent closure of the institutions has never been, and is not ever likely to become, a public policy option. This is what is called 'the imperative of survival'. It is a zero-option situation that is not peculiar to Kenya, since no African country has even temporarily, let alone permanently, closed a university on economic grounds. What is peculiar to Kenya and a handful of other African countries is the need to survive in a highly competitive environment with private universities and low-key competition for scarce public resources between the public universities. On the basis of public policy statements by the relevant authorities, there are strong indications that the government will never fully finance the public universities. Instead, they have been advised to devise ways and means of raising additional funds to support their activities.

Pressure from students in the pipeline

An increasing population base of learners in the primary and secondary sub-sectors has driven the rapid expansion of university education in Kenya. There has been a dramatic increase in the primary school population since 1963, from 0.9 million in 1963 to 1.4 million in 1970, 3.9 million in 1980, 5.4 million in 1996 and 5.8 million in 2001. For the last ten years, the country has registered approximately 0.5 million candidates for the Kenya Certificate of Primary Education (KCPE) every year. Of this number, some 221,250 (46 per cent) enter secondary schools. The number of primary schools has also risen tremendously since independence: from 6,058 in 1963 to 6,123 in 1970, 10,268 in 1980, 14,864 in 1990, 16,552 in 1996 and 17,000 in 2001.

Table I.11 suggests that the greatest expansion in Kenya's education system has been in secondary education. The number of secondary schools in the country was 3,029 in 2000, compared with only 151 in 1963. Secondary enrolment has also grown rapidly, from 31,120 in 1963, to 652,283 in 2000, largely driven by public expectations of economic returns from investing in education. In addition, the government has also emphasized secondary education

Table I.11: Growth of secondary education in Kenya, 1963–2000

Year	No. of schools	Increase (%) over 1963	No. of pupils	Increase (%) over 1963
1963	151	–	31,120	–
1966	400	165	63,193	103
1970	783	419	126,855	308
1972	849	462	161,910	420
1976	1,268	740	274,838	783
1980	1,682	1,014	410,626	1,219
1986	2,395	1,486	500,000	1,507
1990	2,678	1,674	580,441	1,765
1996	3,004	1,889	658,253	2,015
2000	3,029	1,906	652,283	1,996

Source: Data from MoEST, Planning Division, 2002.

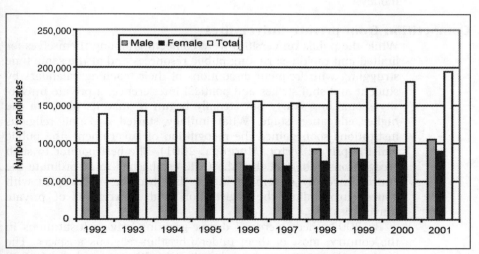

Figure I.5: Kenya Certificate of Secondary Examination candidates by sex, 1992–2001

Source: MoEST Planning Division, 2002.

as the country's immediate source of middle-level human resources and the feeder of tertiary education institutions. This expansion has been accelerated by pressure from an explosive population growth, increasing at just under 4 per cent per year during the 1980s and 1990s.

79

Entry to the public universities is based on performance in the Kenya Certificate of Secondary Examination (KCSE). The minimum requirement for university admission is a mean grade of C+ in KCSE. MoEST statistics show that between 1992 and 2001 nearly 1.6 million students sat for the KCSE (see Figure I.5).

Although 40,000 to 60,000 students qualify for admission to the public universities, only about 10,000 are admitted; about 3,000 students join private universities and another 5,000 go to national polytechnics. In addition, between 7,000 and 10,000 students a year attend universities overseas. Between 1990 and 2001, it is esti- mated that some 60,000 students travelled outside the country on self-sponsorship to universities in the United States, India, Britain, Australia and elsewhere. Kenyans spend a colossal amount of money – some Kshs.16 billion per year (University of Nairobi, 1999) – on university education abroad. The self-sponsored programmes in the public universities have been initiated partly to retain some of this money.

Competition from private universities

While the public universities were competing among themselves for limited and rapidly shrinking public resources and at the same time struggling with frequent disruptions of their teaching calendars by student and staff strikes and political interference, a private univer- sity sector has slowly but steadily begun to take its place on the higher education stage. What initially started as small religious institutions soon gained the recognition of government, the public and the private sector (Murunga, 2001). The best pointer to such recognition is the fact that the CHE, established to co-ordinate the entire university system in Kenya, has become preoccupied with issues surrounding the registration and supervision of private universities.

By 2002, there were 17 degree-granting private institutions in the country, most of them under Christian-religious auspices. The total enrolment in private universities in 2002 was about 10,000 students, approximately 17 per cent of the university student population in Kenya. By the mid-1990s, the educational prominence of the private universities was becoming quite apparent. Much of the credit for this attention must go to USIU, which came to epitomize the success of private university education with its elaborate advertising and recruitment strategies and its well organized and publicized graduation ceremonies, all of which were a real challenge to the public university sector.

However, students and parents were attracted to USIU and other private colleges for other reasons. First, students at these universities stood a good chance of completing their degree programmes faster than their often more academically qualified counterparts enrolled in the public universities. Second, the private universities offered working people a much-needed second chance to pursue their dreams of advancement through evening and weekend teaching programmes. Third, perhaps due in part to their relatively higher socio-economic backgrounds, private university graduates seem to enjoy greater success in finding employment – an added incentive for those who could afford it to join these universities.

In addition, the private universities have gained a measure of respect for their more professional governance structures. This is demonstrated by their more efficient use of staff and institutional infrastructure and more co-ordinated and predictable scheduling of teaching programmes, and by the de-linking of academic affairs from welfare services. This respect has translated into high market opinion of graduates from private universities (see Table I.6, above). Finally, the public universities are gradually losing some of their best teachers to private universities, some of which offer more stability of operation and opportunities for generating supplementary income in night and weekend teaching. During the past decade, Nairobi and Kenyatta universities lost about 20 full-time lecturers to USIU. This is in addition to USIU's part-time lecturers, the majority of whom are drawn from the two public institutions. The exodus of lecturers from the public universities to other destinations and the failure of those sent abroad for further training to return to their home institutions aggravate this loss. The negative effects of this brain-drain from public to private universities have yet to be fully appreciated. The private universities have a better gender balance, better ICT facilities and strong alumni associations, which suggests that they value their graduates more than the public universities do.

Prompting by foreign universities

Since higher education has become an international business, foreign universities are aggressively advertising their programmes in Kenya, challenging the appeal of local public and private universities. The advertisements are aimed at attracting Kenyan students to academic institutions abroad or persuading them to enrol in locally based programmes of foreign universities. This competition by foreign universities for Kenyan students is likely to escalate in light of the University Amendments Bill, 2000, one of the key features of which is the provision allowing foreign universities to set up campuses locally without having to go through hitherto rigorous inspection procedures. Under this Bill, recognized foreign universities have only to obtain certificates of recognition from the CHE before beginning their programmes. Although this may save thousands of Kenyans vast amounts of money that would otherwise have been spent on education in foreign countries, the move is sure to lead to a significant loss of potential students and teaching staff from the public universities.

The Australian Studies Institute (AUSI), established in Nairobi in 2002, is one of the beneficiaries of this new legislation. The institution has none of the playing fields or large lecture theatres and faculty offices generally associated with traditional university settings. AUSI's one-floor 'campus' prepares students for degree courses in Australian universities, some of its affiliated universities being Deakin in Melbourne, Macquerie in Sydney and University of South Australia. Learning is personalized and technology-driven. In addition to AUSI, about 15 Australian universities have sent Australian educational consultants to Kenyan schools. In partnership with Hillcrest Schools in Kenya, they have inaugurated an Australian universities schools' day fair, a strategy which is likely to enhance the number of Kenyan students in Australian universities.

There are also Kenyan middle-level tertiary institutions mounting degree programmes for foreign universities. The Kenya School of Professional Studies offers the Bachelor of Law (LLB) degree of the University of London and a Bachelor of Technology degree in library and information studies with Technikon, South Africa. The Kenya College of Accountancy is the official University of South Africa (UNISA) centre in Kenya. A survey of the advertisements that appeared in the *Daily Nation* and *Sunday Nation* throughout 2001 revealed a wide range of foreign university advertisements with information on the nature of the programmes offered, the background of the universities and institutions and the academic standing of their Kenyan partners. Out of a total of 639 advertisements, the main advertisers came from Britain (150), Australia (130), the United States (112), South Africa (88), Canada (74), India (40), Switzerland (23), Japan (10), Seychelles (4), Mauritius (2), Cyprus (2), West Indies (2) and Malaysia (2) (Ogot, 2002). Between 35 and 40 British universities hold education fairs annually under the auspices of the British Council to popularize these universities in Kenya.

An initiative by British Premier Tony Blair to make higher education more accessible to international students (dubbed Education UK Brand) was launched in June 1999 and provides for a number of waivers aimed at reducing learning costs and expanding access for many students. Among other things, the UK Brand provides for relaxed work restrictions and visa requirements for international students. Under the new policies, foreign students are allowed to work part-time for up to 20 hours a week to supplement their income. The acquisition of student visas for the UK has also been made much easier so long as one has an admission letter and the required fees. Initially, the process of obtaining a visa was a tall order, requiring from six months to a year and a stack of documents of proof to go with it. Little wonder, then, that the Kenyan student population in Britain rose by about 12.1 per cent in one year alone. Besides the British Council, other agencies such as the British Education Training and Technology Association and Lawrie Green Education promote British universities and interview students. By 2002 about 6,000 Kenyan students were studying in Britain, the majority taking undergraduate courses.

These aggressive attempts by foreign universities to gain advantage in the marketplace over local public as well as private universities has served as a wake-up call to the Kenyan institutions of higher learning to market themselves more aggressively to ensure their survival at a time of liberalization in higher education. The first exhibition in May 2002 by 14 Kenyan universities should be seen in this light. According to the Commission on Higher Education, the exhibition provided an opportunity for the public to learn more about what goes on in Kenya's institutions of higher learning. The exhibition was critical to those public universities which now operate self-sponsored degree programmes and have to enter the market to recruit students.

Pressure from government

Universities continue to admit many students on government orders, despite declining funding from the exchequer. The presidential directives to the public universities to double their intakes in the late 1980s are notable examples. Along with these directives came the pronouncement that no eligible student should be denied university education because of inability to pay fees. The dilemma arising from this action was that the majority of the students could not pay fees, yet the institutions were not able to send them home for fear of repercussions from the government. Coupled with the inadequate funding in relation to their student populations and methods of operation and encouraged by the government to look for alternative sources of funding, the public universities are moving to create innovative means of generating income to finance their programmes.

83

At the University of Nairobi's 27th graduation ceremony in November 1999, President Moi reiterated the need for universities to became self-reliant:

Indeed, I have on a number of occasions advised public universities to work out mechanisms of raising additional income through income-generating activities. In this respect, I am pleased to note that you have addressed this issue seriously and have formed a university company to enable you to enhance and co-ordinate income-generation activities (*Daily Nation*, 30 November 1999).

The government started exerting pressure on the universities through the Kamunge Report (Republic of Kenya, 1988), which recommended that the public universities should increase their revenue bases as well as raising money from the public and private sectors to strengthen their programmes. The requirement that students pay for their accommodation and food as a cost-sharing measure, together with the initiative to recruit holders of master's degrees to substantive teaching posts, arose from the recommendations of this report.

Influence of development partners

The public universities have also been influenced by donors to rethink their methods of operation in regard to education provision in a context of changing trends and new challenges. From 1990, the World Bank required as a basic condition for funding that the public universities formulate development plans to articulate their direction. Since the preparation of the initial development plans based on World Bank guidelines, the design of such plans as a way of taking stock of the past and charting the future has now become standard practice. Similarly, the World Bank's displeasure at failure to forward audited accounts in time has been instrumental in the evolution of improved accounting practices. Donors also prompted the line-budget system and accountability in financial management. These were positive initiatives for the universities.

At the 6th General Conference of the Association of African Universities held in Arusha, Tanzania, rectors, Vice-Chancellors and presidents of African universities were called upon to reform or risk perishing (AAU, 1999). It was noted that reform was a must for universities, if they were to remain relevant in the twenty-first century. In addition, such donors and international development partners as the German Academic Exchange Service (DAAD), the US Agency for International Development (USAID), the Japanese International Co-operation Agency, Pathfinder International, the Joint Financing Program for Co-operation in Higher Education (MHO, Netherlands), the International Centre for Insect Physiology and Ecology and the Ford and Rockefeller Foundations have all played a significant role in supporting the public universities in capital development, human resource development, research and in some specific school- or faculty-based projects. MHO has assisted Moi University in the establishment of information and communication technology systems in critical areas of administration, including student admissions. This has made it imperative for Moi University to change the way it registers students. The exercise now takes a shorter time, as the admissions office is able to handle Higher Education Loans Board queries from students quickly and competently.

Similarly, the Universities Investment Project, a World Bank-funded project, has enabled the University of Nairobi to create a modern information and computing infrastructure. Another donor-led initiative is the Kenyatta University Peer Counsellors, a collaborative project between KU and Pathfinder International. The project, which began in 1987, addresses problems of pregnancies and drug abuse among students on campus. Over the years it has been expanded to include education on HIV/AIDS issues. Development partners have also influenced on-going efforts in public tertiary institutions to rationalize their functions and reduce their staff, a project that was initially promoted by the World Bank. The first phase of this exercise, the retrenchment of non-academic staff in the lower cadres of the public universities, was executed in 2001.

Prompting by the private sector

The demand for market-oriented courses has compelled the public universities to update their curricula regularly in order to ensure that the skills they teach are relevant to the labour market. To achieve this aim, experts from the private sector are incorporated at either the design stage or at programme review seminars. The partnership between JKUAT and Micro Mini Systems, Inc. is an example of emerging collaboration between the private sector and the public universities. Micro Mini Systems, Inc., an American company, and Diamond Systems (a local company) have designed ICT courses at JKUAT at certificate, diploma and degree levels that are offered at the university as well as in several middle-level tertiary institutions nationwide accredited by JKUAT.

At Moi University, the Faculty of Technology and the Department of Tourism regularly use personnel from the private sector in their curricula review workshops. The ICT infrastructure at Maseno University was partially sponsored by the Business and Information

85

Technology Centre, a private firm which not only helped in the completion of the building that houses the ICT operations, but also installed 65 computers for use by staff and students. The Otto Essein Young Professionals Programme at Kenyatta University, its hurdles in implementation notwithstanding, seeks to improve students' hands-on experience by attaching them to various companies in an effort to expose them to the world of work. Most of the parallel programmes offer degrees designed to respond to market demands. As indicated earlier, the most popular of these degrees are those clearly leading to employment or self-employment.

Importance of leadership

Any reform package requires a determined leader whose vision and support make possible the success of reform strategies. The pace and tempo of the reform initiatives taking place in the public universities in Kenya vary widely among these institutions, depending on the style of leadership among their respective chief executives. For example, many of the changes taking place at Egerton University were designed in the past decade, but the sluggish pace at which they were being implemented was disappointing, partly because of the conservatism of previous Vice-Chancellors. The current Vice-Chancellor, appointed in late 2000, managed to reverse that trend within a period of about two years. Being more supportive of reform initiatives and a team player, he raised staff morale and created an environment conducive to change. Although there is still a lot to be accomplished, a sense of optimism was rekindled in the institution.

The importance of dynamic leadership is also noticeable at Kenyatta University. Many of the reforms accomplished at the university could be attributed to the Vice-Chancellor's commitment, energy and imagination during the past decade. The Vice-Chancellor has made several bold structural decisions, including the introduction of a new admissions policy, based on the highly successful trimester system which allows students to register on a semester basis and so complete their degree programmes in a minimum period of three years as opposed to the usual four. Previously, admission had been strictly tied to the Joint Admissions Board (JAB) guidelines that peg enrolment to programme capacity and available bed space. Kenyatta University now admits students each trimester – rather than once a year – and students complete their studies in a shorter period of time, thus creating more space. When fully operational, this flexibility will considerably reduce the long periods school leavers must now wait before they enter university.

The role of intermediary bodies in mediating reforms

The Commission for Higher Education

Many Commonwealth countries in Africa have now established bodies to mediate between governments and universities regarding funding and other pertinent issues. The logic of such intermediary bodies is based on the proposition that public universities require large resources for highly specialized needs. In order to protect the universities' interests and adjudicate between competing claims, statutory bodies outside both the civil service and the universities are set up to provide a bridge between the two. University people largely staff these bodies so that the universities can make their case in the confidence that it will be understood and judged fairly. Thus, an intermediary body becomes the advocate of the universities' needs vis-à-vis the government; it consults universities and advises government on university policies and helps interpret policies once decided by the universities. In addition, such a body divides the budgetary cake between universities using official policy priorities and planning criteria, which are known to all concerned. The universities then receive their grants of public funds from the intermediary body, not the government, in order to avoid the suspicion of political bias (Coombe, 1991:18). In Kenya the CHE was established in 1985 under the provisions of the Universities Act to play this role.

The Commission for Higher Education has 20 members, the majority (85 per cent) of them appointed by the President of the Republic of Kenya, who also appoints the Chancellors of the public universities. Representatives from the private universities and post-secondary institutions are among the Commission's members. Only two Vice-Chancellors from the six public universities are members. The CHE's functions give it massive statutory powers to regulate and monitor the growth and development of public universities in Kenya. The Universities Act empowers the CHE to establish a Universities Grants Committee and to delegate some of its functions to that committee. In practice, this has not worked well. All the public universities present their individual budgets and proposals directly to the Treasury through the Committee of Vice-Chancellors of the respective universities and, in some cases, to the President. Commenting on this issue, Sifuna (1997:226) notes that:

... interestingly, Vice-Chancellors who are normally represented on CHE and praise its work on the accreditation of private universities effectively bypass it when it comes to their own plans and budgets. They defend their

87

institutional autonomy, which each university enjoys by virtue of its own statute and clearly resent the notion of ceding part of it to CHE.

In fact, some Vice-Chancellors believe that they can best handle the rationalization of departments and related planning issues themselves, without the support of the CHE. For budgetary control, the public universities favour a statutory University Grants Committee separate from the CHE and have drafted legislation to this effect. The consequence of Vice-Chancellors bypassing the CHE has been a disproportionate allocation of grants to particular universities (Sifuna, 1997: 226). The relegation of the CHE to the background with regard to financial planning for the public universities has led the Kenyan government to use unit costs as a basis for financing the institutions.

Furthermore, the requirement that the CHE make regulations in respect of admission to the public universities and provide a central admissions service through the JAB has not been fulfilled. The JAB is made up of the six Vice-Chancellors from the public universities, Deputy Vice-Chancellors, academic registrars and deans of faculties. It selects students for the public universities and distributes them to various faculties without any input from the CHE. Since the Central Universities Admissions Committee that was to be managed by the CHE under the Universities Act never became operational, it has been removed from the statute book. Consequently the JAB has been given legal recognition under the CHE umbrella. Apart from this, the CHE has no other relationship with the JAB, and is never consulted before or during the process of student selection.

In addition, although one of the functions of the Commission is to advise the government on planning higher education in accordance with human resource projections in the public and private sectors and in conformity with national skills and employment patterns, the establishment of Kenyan public universities has been carried out without consultation with the CHE. Kenyatta University (1985), Egerton University (1987), Jomo Kenyatta University of Agriculture and Technology (1994) and Maseno University (1999) were all established on the basis of presidential decrees. Thus, the CHE has been marginalized because much of the formulation of higher education policy in Kenya has always revolved around the country's President.

Finally, one of the responsibilities of the Commission is to inspect each public university at least once every four years for purposes of quality assurance. With the crisis in the public universities that is manifested through overcrowding, the brain drain, deteriorating physical facilities, poor library resources and insufficient scientific equipment, the CHE has been expected to carry out an inspection into teaching, research, general administration and organization at each of the universities to help them redefine their objectives in the context of current realities. It has failed to live up to its mandate in this sphere. This poor performance by the Commission largely reflects the weaknesses in the Universities Act that led to its inception.

The need for assistance from the World Bank in financing the expansion of the public universities has, in some ways, resuscitated some of the CHE's functions, particularly in regard to planning. Dissatisfied with the haphazard growth of higher education, the World Bank insisted on rational planning and management in the mid-1990s as one of the conditions for the provision of funding for the public universities. The CHE was offered the opportunity to co-ordinate this planning. In this connection, it required each public university to prepare a consolidated development plan reflecting its mission as well as the procedures followed in its financial management. According to two senior officers surveyed at the CHE offices, five out of the six public universities complied with this requirement to develop their plans (personal interview, 2002, Nairobi).

Except for the accreditation of private universities, the Commission has fulfilled few of its statutory functions due both to loopholes in the 1985 Universities Act and to contradictions between this act and the individual acts that established the public universities. As already stated, the Commission does not have a mandate to oversee the public universities. This has created an inconsistency in the law and an opportunity for the public universities to ignore the CHE. The President appoints the Vice-Chancellors of the public universities, while CHE's chief executive is appointed by the Minister of Education, Science and Technology. This creates confusion in terms of seniority and lines of communication. Although the CHE is supposed to guide Vice-Chancellors, they tend to see themselves as being superior to its chief executive and thus often bypass the Commission. It also needs restating that the role of planning and the provision of financial needs for the public universities was given to the Commission without modalities on how this should be accomplished. The CHE's Universities Grants Committee – intended to co-ordinate the funding of the public universities – was established without provisions regarding its composition and powers and with no arrangement for obtaining external funds. Until these hurdles are eliminated, the CHE will remain powerless.

89

The Higher Education Loans Board

The provision of loans to help finance higher education dates back to 1952, when the colonial government started giving out loans under what was then called the Higher Education Loans Fund to Kenyans pursuing university education outside East Africa. After independence in 1963, university education was offered free of charge, the full cost being borne by the government. Beginning in the mid-1970s, undergraduate students received a government loan to finance their education, covering the costs of tuition, accommodation, subsistence and books. The recovery procedures for these loans were inadequate; the original concept of developing a revolving fund from which more students would benefit was thus thwarted. In 1995, the IMF and the World Bank advised the government to set up a body with responsibility to manage the government-sponsored student loan scheme. This led to the establishment of the Higher Education Loans Board (HELB) in 1995 to facilitate the disbursement of loans, scholarships and bursaries to needy Kenyan university students, to recover all outstanding loans supplied to former university students by the Government of Kenya since 1952, to establish a revolving fund from which funds could be drawn to lend out to needy Kenyans pursuing higher education, to invest surplus funds in any investments authorized by law and to seek funds from other organizations (the private sector, philanthropic organizations, foundations and so on). The board's main sources of funding at the moment are the exchequer and funds recovered from former students.

The board is also mandated to seek funding from private organizations and individuals. For example, the Visa Oshwal Jain community in Kenya provides scholarships that benefit more than 100 students for the full duration of their studies in the public universities. The board provides loan application forms to needy Kenyans pursuing higher education in Kenyan universities recognized by the CHE. The students must also be selected by the JAB if they are attending the public universities. The board uses a means test to identify needy students through the information supplied in the student's application form. HELB loans to applicants range from Kshs.35,000 (US$490) to Kshs.50,000 (US$700) and bursaries range from Kshs.4,000 (US$56) to Kshs.8,000 (US$110). Out of the university fees, the board pays tuition fees of Kshs.8,000 direct to the universities for every student who is awarded a loan, with the balance paid direct to the student for his/her personal welfare.

In effect, and in line with the government policy of cost-sharing, the board supplements parental contributions towards a student's financial requirements. Upon completion of their studies, students must repay the loans, whereas bursary awards do not require repayment. Some 40 per cent of the funds the board lends to students comes from money repaid by previous students, although disbursement management and practical problems related to recovery are, at times, problematic. Reports from the loans recovery department indicate that the board has done reasonably well in the domain of loan recovery since 1994.

The board started off by giving loans to needy Kenyan students studying in the public universities, and two years later extended this facility to students in private universities as well. In addition, it began giving loans for the first time to a few postgraduate students in the public universities in 2000, extended to postgraduate students in the private universities in 2001. The provision of loans to students in the private universities is a logical outcome of HELB's mandate to assist needy students in all tertiary institutions in the country.

Despite noticeable improvement in HELB's service delivery, some students benefiting from the loans complain that what they receive is not enough for them to pursue their studies without having to resort to menial and sometimes unacceptable jobs (*Daily Nation*, 5 June 2000). This is largely due to the relative inadequacy of the board's funding capacity. The HELB relies heavily on the exchequer, which provides some 60 per cent of the total loans it gives out to students annually, with the balance coming from monthly loan recoveries (HELB, 2001).

The means-testing instrument used to identify needy students is unfortunately insufficient to measure real need. A Vice-Chancellor at one of the public universities attributes the escalating number of student appeals to the inability of the initial application form to draw a clear distinction between needy and non-needy students (HELB, 2001). According to media reports, 'HELB has over the years been cheated into giving loans to undeserving students.... 25% of the student applicants have been found to have been dishonest with the board' (*Daily Nation*, 5 March 2000). Although the HELB has improved its means-testing mechanisms (personal interview, Nairobi 2002), the task is a daunting one in developing countries such as Kenya where large numbers of families operate in a semi-subsistence mode that makes verifying income data extremely difficult (Assie-Lumumba, 1994). It has further been noted that some groups of students, especially female students and those from pastoral communities, have disproportionate access to loan funds. Such

91

imbalances have exposed the HELB to criticism from politicians and parents.

In addition, the board experiences major difficulties in recovering loans from unemployed beneficiaries, especially those who have graduated since 1993, the majority of whom are either still looking for jobs or are hired as casual workers, thus making it difficult for the board to demand payment. The Act of Parliament that established the HELB empowers it to recover loans only from those who are in formal employment. On the other hand, when the idea of a loans board was first introduced, it encountered some degree of hostility from both students and parents who wanted grants rather than loans. As noted above, most students still regard the loans as free grants from the government, an attitude that slows down repayment. In addition, *the* HELB has had difficulty tracing some of the people who were advanced loans since the scheme was introduced in 1974. Despite the databases built by the HELB, a number of past beneficiaries could not be located.

The Joint Admissions Board

The Joint Admissions Board was established in the 1980s for the purpose of regulating entry to Kenya's public universities. It comprises the six Vice-Chancellors from the public universities, their deputies, registrars and deans of faculties and schools. It was established on a goodwill basis by the Vice-Chancellors; as such, it is not recognized under any legislation. It is, however, recognized by the Commission for Higher Education and the Higher Education Loans Board. The JAB is charged with selecting students for admission to the Kenyan public universities and distributing them to various faculties. Its chairmanship rotates on an annual basis among the Vice-Chancellors of the six public universities.

Every year members of the board hold a number of meetings to determine the cut-off points for admission which vary from year to year. Based on capacities within individual universities and faculties/schools and in the light of students' preferences, selected students are allocated to various courses. Since some courses are more competitive or have smaller capacities, individual faculties/schools and/or departments may have specific admission criteria and different cut-off points. Thus, the main criteria for admission to the public universities and specific courses are the available space, performance in the Kenya Certificate of Secondary Education (KCSE) Examinations and the level of demand for courses. Recent disclosures by the JAB show that the number of students applying for public university places has been declining. Even so, on average only 30 per cent of applicants are able to secure a place.

Since its establishment in the 1980s, the JAB has managed to streamline the admissions process in all the public universities. The 1990/91 admissions process, for instance, had to handle both 'O' and 'A' level applicants, a total of 170,000 applicants. One of the main challenges was to establish selection criteria which were perceived to be fair by both students and parents (Sifuna, 1997). Following a series of consultations with Ministry of Education officials, it was agreed that 8,500 and 11,500 'O' and 'A' level students, respectively, should be admitted (Mwiria and Nyukuri, 1992). Equitable distribution of places has also been made possible by including additional criteria such as gender and regional disparities, as is manifested in differentiated cut-off points in respect of such disadvantaged groups. In the 1996 intake, for instance, the cut-off points were 63 and 62 points for male and female students respectively. The JAB has been criticized for lacking the muscle to win the confidence of all the Vice-Chancellors, partly because it lacks a legal base, thus enabling those who have any complaint about its operations to call openly for its scrapping, and so making it highly vulnerable.

The JAB has also been accused of sluggishness in selecting students for admission to the universities. Thus, when the Kenya Certificate of Secondary Education is completed, these results are announced almost a year before the JAB publishes its admission cut-off points. Parents whose children meet the previous year's cut-off points are often shattered to learn that the cut-off points have been raised. Some critics have agreed that it is 'outrageous' that it takes two years after secondary school for students to begin at the university (*Kenya Times*, 4 March 1995). Kenyatta University has therefore worked out and implemented its own admission programme on a semester basis, a move some regard as a positive one, since it will reduce the length of time KCSE candidates have to wait before entering the university. Others view the change as an attempt to admit students outside the JAB, sparking a behind-the-scenes struggle amongst public university administrators. However, details emerging from the JAB itself, the HELB and the CHE indicate that Kenyatta University acted within its rights in admitting students earlier than other universities (*Daily Nation*, 17 January 2002).

In order to strike a balance between the universities and the courses available, the board ends up admitting students to universities and degree programmes they never requested. To address the problem of qualified students being denied university admission as a

93

result of restrictions on the number to be admitted, some universities have gone ahead with admitting more students to parallel degree programmes. Some administrators have contended that it is dishonest for the universities to admit regular students through the criteria set by the board, and then admit others separately for parallel programmes. Viewed in this way, it may appear that the JAB has reduced the whole admissions process to a gamble. Aware of these weaknesses, the Vice-Chancellors of the public universities issued a directive to the JAB to admit only those students who meet the board's criteria. They also argued that the same criteria for admission to regular programmes should be applied to privately sponsored students, and that the CHE must ensure that the public universities adhere to the established procedures in order to avoid compromising academic standards (*Daily Nation*, 8 December 2001).

Finally, the board has occasionally been a scapegoat in the ongoing struggle to define the role of donors in development. It has thus been perceived as lacking autonomy vis-à-vis donor agencies, and unable to insulate itself from their direct manipulation. The *Daily Nation* (Aduda, 1997) expressed this view in an article stating that the public universities were 'still under a donor-imposed condition to limit admission to less than 10,000 students each academic year'.

The management of reform initiatives

Most reforms pertaining to university programmes emanate from academic staff via departments, faculties and schools. Sometimes, however, university councils or senates or management boards may issue directives to departments to look into certain academic matters and make appropriate recommendations. This was the case at Egerton University, when course loads were revised to ensure that students had between 15 and 21 credit hours per semester. Each department was required to revise its syllabus in view of this requirement. Except for such cases, whenever new programmes have been contemplated, the initiative is routed through the department where the programme will be domiciled to the faculty or school board to which the department belongs, which considers the proposals and their rationale. If it endorses the departmental request, it is then forwarded to the university senate for consideration. This participatory planning process has seen the successful launching of new academic programmes in the public universities. Sometimes those suggested by the management are forwarded directly to the university council and implemented, especially when the changes have to do with cost-cutting. The withdrawal of the transport service at Moi University and the subsequent increase in the commuting allowance were handled in such a manner.

University councils, senates and management boards control reforms at different levels, especially those concerned with income generation, staff appointments, job descriptions and the allocation of funds through policy guidelines. Here we are mostly discussing the administration of income-generating activities, since university entities such as senates, councils, deans, committees and department chairs administer the other types of reforms.

The monitoring and administration of the reform process has in most cases been decentralized. The University of Nairobi has established the University of Nairobi Enterprises and Services Ltd (UNES) as the business-oriented institutional framework for the co-ordination of income-generating activities. Egerton University runs its income-generating units and self-sponsored programmes through directors, while the Income-Generating Activities Board (IGAB) co-ordinates those of Kenyatta University, with peripheral support from the Income-Generating Activities Department. Kenyatta Virtual University Ltd has recently been formed as a private company with the mandate of managing the university's short courses and diploma programmes. At Moi University, such non-academic income-generating activities as mortuary services, transport, the bookshop, farms, staff housing and catering are administered through Moi University Holdings Company Ltd, whereas the Privately Sponsored Students Programme (PSSP), headed by a director, manages all the self-sponsored academic programmes. From 1995 till early 2001, Maseno University co-ordinated all its non-academic income-gene-rating endeavours through its Investment and Economic Enterprises unit. In February 2001, this body was disbanded and all income-generating units – academic and non-academic alike – were to be managed by a newly formed limited company. JKUAT has accredited several middle-level tertiary institutions to offer its programmes in commerce, business and information technology through its Con-tinuing Education Programme. Despite this decentralization of the management of reform initiatives, most management units do not have direct access to the funds they generate, since their financial transactions all go through designated university signatories.

There has been some concern about the rapid increase in centres running JKUAT courses beyond the point where they can be adequately supervised. Most of the personnel managing the JKUAT

95

income-generating units are not professionally qualified and are poorly paid. To ensure that the changes being implemented at the public universities succeed, it is critical to strengthen the administration of the reform process by engaging qualified staff who are paid competitive salaries, just as the University of Nairobi has done with its UNES employees. Continuous upgrading of the managers' skills will also be necessary. Those universities with parallel degree programmes are finding it difficult to manage the income from the programmes in such a way that lecturers do not overwork themselves in pursuit of the direct payment to be earned. Some feel the best way to manage the parallel-degree students would be to integrate them with the regular students and offer the lecturers an extra flat fee for the additional students. This should reduce the incentive to overwork, while regular students would no longer feel neglected in favour of the parallel students.

Financing the reforms & gaining support

The reforms carried out at the public universities have generally depended on the institutions' own resources, with only limited financial support from the government and development partners. This is why offering self-sponsored academic programmes is the most viable of all the innovations. Beyond these programmes, universities are experimenting with numerous non-teaching alternative sources to generate additional income. These non-teaching activities are financed from both internal and external sources, although the universities always provide the start-up capital or 'seed money'. At Kenyatta University, departments or individuals planning to launch an income-generating unit must prepare project proposals, which are submitted to a projects appraisal committee for assessment of their viability. Those proposals considered feasible then qualify for seed money, with the funds being released at intervals and on condition that the project receives a satisfactory monitoring report at each stage.

Sometimes the reforms are financed through external donations, grants and joint business ventures. The joint ventures of JKUAT and Maseno University with the private sector have already been discussed above. The University of Nairobi has been able to translate some of its programmes and research findings into basic community development components through donor support. Its Nutribusiness Project, discussed earlier, evolved from its linkage with American universities, the American bilateral aid organization and an American non-governmental organization. The UoN has enjoyed support from many international organizations, including the Sasakawa Foundation of Japan, the German Development Authority, the Swedish International Development Authority, the International Development Research Centre of Canada, the United Nations Development Programme, the United Nations Educational, Scientific and Cultural Organization, the World Bank, the Rockefeller and Ford Foundations and the Flemish Inter-University Council (VLIR) in Brussels. For instance, in 1999 it signed an agreement with VLIR for the provision of university-wide computer networking and internet linkages, training methods in reproductive health and HIV/AIDS and support for marine science and coastal management, an agreement that brought in some Kshs.48 million (US$670,000) in assistance (Gichaga, 1999).

Most of the reforms taking place at Kenya's public universities have won both local and international support. Increased local and national political support reflects a number of factors. First, the self-sponsored academic programmes have widened access to university education. The emergence of specialized courses previously available only in foreign universities has provided a convenient and cheaper local alternative. Universities are also meeting strong demand from the private sector by organizing courses that update professional skills. This initiative has been applauded as an effective way for the public universities to serve the country, while generating supplementary income at the same time.

The public universities have been pro-active in encouraging an open-door management policy. Aggressive marketing of academic programmes has been pursued through the local media, and when questions have been raised, the institutions have been quick to respond. Thus, when regular students of the University of Nairobi protested about the self-sponsored degree students on the grounds that the latter had lower entry grades than their counterparts in the regular programmes, public anger and disapproval against the protesters was unmistakable. The cultural week of festivities that Kenyatta University has organized for the past decade has been a great public relations exercise. Notwithstanding some grumbling that KU had turned its priorities upside down, particularly when its library was in such a sorry state, the public still had an opportunity to watch KU students demonstrate their artistry, creativity and performing talents. Recently, both Moi University and the Catholic University of Eastern Africa have emulated such public programmes.

Public advertising by the universities is a relatively new development. All now widely advertise their programmes in print media supplements on the annual graduation day; some have taken to advertising on television and jointly organizing an annual 'public universities day' during which they present themselves to the public. Needless to say, one way the universities have won political support has been through avoidance of political controversies and engagements at almost any cost. From the perspective of the reforms, this has called for a low-key approach to the reform process.

There are several high points in the international community's recognition of the reform initiatives taking place in Kenya's public universities. The AVU project at Kenyatta University is seen as one of the most successful virtual university projects in Africa. Until recently, the university hosted the AVU regional office (it has since been moved to a different site in Nairobi). Following the introduction of an online registration system for students, Kenyatta's innovations have been widely acknowledged. In this connection, the *Daily Nation* noted that 'educational institutions in Kenya are fast catching up with new technology – with Kenyatta University becoming the second university in the country to introduce online registration for students; [the first is] the United States International University, which is private' (*Daily Nation*, 4 September 2001).

6 Impact of the Reform Process

Increased access

The most visible effect of the reforms in the past decade has been the widening of access to university education for Kenyans. Before the implementation of the reforms documented here, the public universities admitted between 8,000 and 10,000 students a year. Approximately another 17,000 secondary school graduates missed university admission every year, after about 1,200 were absorbed in private universities and 3,000 travelled abroad to join foreign universities. Since the launching of self-sponsored degree programmes in the public universities, thousands of Kenyans who would have had to go abroad for study are now enrolled locally. The self-sponsored degree programmes also offer those already in employment an opportunity to further their education through evening and weekend classes. Teachers wishing to upgrade their teaching skills may attend classes during the April, August and December holidays when their students are away.

The popularity of these programmes is demonstrated by their high enrolments. Since the 1995 inception of the Kenyatta University self-sponsored postgraduate diploma in education, over 2,000 students have benefited from it, while its Institute for Continuing Education and Special and Early Childhood Education Departments host nearly 4,000 teachers who are pursuing undergraduate degrees in education. The University of Nairobi had a parallel-degree enrolment of 6,410 students from 1998 to 2002; Moi University had 3,799; JKUAT, 605; Maseno, 230 and Egerton, 328 students. Furthermore, the opportunity to learn in the public universities has not been limited to those seeking university diplomas and degrees but has also been extended to students at certificate levels and members of the public from all walks of life.

Beyond the introduction of self-sponsored degree programmes, the recent adoption of new delivery mechanisms – including the AVU, bridging courses, the semester system and distance-learning – has made public university education accessible to a larger number of Kenyans. A critical issue that remains, however, is the question of regional imbalance.

Equity

Despite the massive expansion of student enrolment, the public universities continue to exhibit socio-economic and gender inequalities.

Most beneficiaries of the increased access to higher education in Kenya still come from the economically advantaged areas and are predominantly male. The reforms have therefore not yet had much impact in this respect. Thus, with the declining level of state subsidies and bursaries for students admitted to the public universities, the emerging trend of privatized education is likely to maintain, if not exacerbate, social inequities by excluding students from certain groups from tertiary education. As mentioned above, the higher one ascends the educational ladder, the lower the female participation rate. As a result, female students make up only about 30 per cent of total enrolments in the public universities.

In addition to being under-represented in the overall enrolment, female students are deplorably under-represented in scientific subjects. The low level of female participation in the sciences is more pronounced in engineering and technology-based courses where their enrolment stands at slightly over 10 per cent. This relative lack of female students has its origins in the under-representation of girls in science at the lower levels of education. In most cases, the public universities admit applicants on the sole basis of performance in the Kenya Certificate of Secondary Education (KCSE) examinations. Although the Joint Admissions Board has recently instituted affirmative action by lowering girls' admission index by one point, this has not changed the situation much, since remedial measures do not lie entirely with the university but with society and the entire education system. However, the university can certainly institute more appropriate affirmative action for science-based programmes.

Quality

With the advent of self-sponsored academic programmes in the public universities, one critical issue of concern for the public is that of quality. Critics have questioned the standards of newer programmes, especially those mounted in centres outside the universities. For example, JKUAT's courses are offered in other centres, including commercial colleges. Since the major objective of these commercial colleges is to make a profit, there is a strong likelihood that quality will be compromised. In addition, the entry criteria to these self-sponsored programmes are less competitive than those for the regular programmes, which has also raised doubts with regard to the quality of some of the graduates. The decision by Egerton, Maseno and Kenyatta to mount medical courses in their self-sponsored programmes, for which they have limited capacity to teach effectively, also exacerbates public fears about the quality of these institutions' graduates.

A look at other proxy measures of quality points to a discouraging trend. The high population of students sitting supplementary examinations or retakes, the poor quality of examination answers and the poor remuneration for lecturers all imply low-quality education. Discussions with lecturers quite often indicate, for example, that there is a drop not only in the level of participation in class but also in the quality of verbal and written communication. This is one reason for the mounting of common foundation courses such as in communication skills. Such courses, however, have not made a big difference, because students do not take them seriously compared with what they consider their core courses. In any case, students in these overcrowded classes have limited meaningful inter-action with the lecturers. External examinations are one way of main-taining some quality. Unfortunately, some of the external examiners have not lived up to expectations. As their reports indicate, some of them pay more attention to the marking and distribution of marks than to the quality of the students' answers. Another pointer to declining quality is the fact that cases of cheating in examinations are becoming more common.

A less common but occasional quality issue is that of undeserving students gaining admission into the public university system. As an example, in the 1999/2000 academic year, a student from North Eastern Province irregularly secured admission into the Early Child-hood Education degree programme at Kenyatta University through the influence of a Permanent Secretary in the Ministry of Education. When such admission malpractices occurred at Makerere University, they were exposed, and the concerned students were expelled. In March 1999 Makerere University expelled the Minister of State for Primary Education and a Member of Parliament from its Master of Business Administration programme because of the irregularities dis-covered in their admission papers (Wakabi, 1999). On the other hand, when the press exposed the Kenyatta University incident, university administrators and Ministry of Education officials main-tained a studious silence. That the Makerere University registrar could expel a minister of education, whereas the Kenyatta University administration could not expel an ordinary student could be explained by Makerere's greater autonomy The lack of university autonomy in Kenya is a more serious problem than the few cases of irregular admissions that might go uncorrected.

Relevance

During the past decade, the public universities have been striving to rethink their programmes by designing and diversifying their courses with a view to enhancing their relevance. Under the auspices of the International AIDS Vaccine Initiative, the Department of Medical Microbiology of the University of Nairobi, the University of Manitoba and Oxford University have been working together on HIV research and are generating a wealth of information on the virology and immunology of HIV infections. The Centre for Complementary Medicine and Biotechnology (CCMB) started by Kenyatta University to conduct scientific research on herbal medicine jointly with herbal medicine practitioners is part of the on-going national effort by the Kenya government and KEMRI to integrate the use of herbal medicine into conventional medical practice. By enlisting at the CCMB the help of herbalists who do not hold university degrees, Kenyatta University has been able to benefit from their wealth of experience at the same time as helping the institution shed some of its elitist image. Along the same lines, the public universities can bring a relevant practical touch to their teaching by utilizing the many highly qualified academics working in industry, commerce, international and national private and voluntary organizations to teach and undertake research with university personnel and to run seminars and short-term courses in their areas of expertise.

In addition to these initiatives, the public universities are making attempts to widen and strengthen their outreach and community service programmes as indicated above. As we have seen, most of the self-sponsored degree programmes offered are those in high demand because of their relevance.

Kenya's quest for industrialization

In Sessional Paper No. 2 of 1996, Kenya articulated its intention to industrialize by 2020. Universities are expected to play a critical role in helping to achieve this goal. They are not only charged with the responsibility of developing human resources to facilitate the process of industrialization but are also expected to provide the research base for these efforts. The challenges in industrialization mean that the public universities will need to identify the skills needed in the world of work so that they align the curricula appropriately and provide students with sound academic training backed by practical skills. Between 1990 and 1995, the public universities admitted a total of 151,740 students (see Table I.5 above), of whom only 9,113 (7,974 male and 1,139 female) enrolled in programmes in engineering and architecture. Thus, of all the students in the public universities, only 6 per cent (5.2 per cent male and 0.8 female) enrolled in engineering and technical sciences, a figure too low to promote the country's industrial development effectively.

If Kenya is to meet its objective of industrializing by 2020, in addition to imparting the necessary academic and practical skills to university students, it is imperative to train more engineers and technologists. The underproduction of engineering and technical-based human resources stems partly from the inadequate teaching of science and technical subjects at secondary school level. Approximately 3 per cent of KCSE candidates study vocational and technical subjects at this level (personal interview, Kenya National Examinations Council, July 2002). With regard to curricula re-orientation, the Otto Essein Young Professionals Programme (a partnership between UNDP, the Federation of Kenyan Employers and the Ministry of Planning and National Development, launched at the University of Nairobi in 1997 and at Kenyatta University in 2002) is designed to help realign the curriculum. The initiative aims to promote a sustainable link between academic training and the world of work through organized industrial attachments for students enrolled in commerce degree programmes.

Planning & management of university programmes

The most important impact of the reforms in planning and management lies in the acceptability of change by the university community. Although still at the nascent level, there are noticeable efforts to decentralize management of the reform process. The key manifestation of this decentralization is the existence of companies, boards, bureaux and committees that play a crucial role in the planning and management of the reforms, as described above. Nevertheless, powers of decision-making are still largely vested with central administrations in some key areas. In some areas, certain management decisions are still being made on an ad hoc basis. This is because change in organizational culture is still viewed as incremental and has to be nurtured until the larger system permits more radical change.

103

Utilization of financial, human & physical resources

The profits realized through income-generating activities have been used to top up staff salaries, recruit part-time teaching staff, maintain existing facilities, purchase relevant teaching materials, improve the university's transport system and support programmes for curriculum development. Service providers – mainly academic staff members and support personnel – are compensated for services rendered to the self-sponsored academic programmes and the non-teaching income-generating activities in the public universities. Increased compensation to lecturers is helping resolve some of the problems over which the unregistered University Academic Staff Union (UASU) called a strike in 1993/4. Although attempts were made to address staff welfare and salary packages, many academic staff felt that the recommended salary increases did not match the high rate of inflation. Consequently, many lecturers chose to supplement their income by teaching in private universities and middle-level tertiary institutions. With the advent of self-sponsored academic programmes, lecturers have been compensated for their extra services at rates that are comparable to, if not better than, what they were earning elsewhere. For example, the University of Nairobi has decided that the best method of compensating academic staff is through income-sharing, so that the more the university receives, the more staff are paid.

In addition to staff remuneration, income-generating programmes contribute funds to various sections of the universities, including library maintenance and capital development funds. Although modest, the recent addition of vital textbooks and journals to the libraries at Nairobi and Moi Universities was made possible through such allocations. At Kenyatta, one of the visible effects of these income-generating initiatives has been the renovation of the Nyayo Complex Hostel, which had been in a pathetic condition for several years. Other improvements that have been undertaken at KU include the provision of additional office space and the installation of perimeter fencing in the main sections of the university. The University of Nairobi has used the additional revenue to pay for medical services, electricity, telephone, water and insurance and for general infrastructure improvement. Moreover, the university was able to acquire six new buses. In 2002 the self-sponsored academic programmes were meeting close to 60 per cent of the university's entire utilities bill.

The introduction of privately sponsored student programmes has to some extent enhanced the efficiency of universities in utilizing

104

existing human and physical resources. Lecturers do more teaching, and existing facilities such as libraries and lecture theatres are used more intensively. However, there is another sense in which these resources have been overstretched. This is manifested in the escalating complaints by lecturers about the increased workload that, in turn, has negatively affected their performance in other professional areas. At another level, in some departments or stations, the available non-academic staff are inadequate to serve the increasing number of students. Such problems are clear at key facilities such as libraries, where the inadequacy of staff, coupled with low staff morale, has left these facilities in a state of disorganization.

Challenging the relevance of the Joint Admissions Board

On-going reforms in the public university sector raise questions about the relevance of this institution. In particular, the slowness with which the JAB conducts the admission exercise is increasingly viewed as an impediment to reform. As mentioned earlier, it takes the JAB almost a year after the KCSE results to announce its cut-off points for entry into various degree programmes and about two years before the eligible students join the universities. The introduction of the trimester system at Kenyatta University (including a summer term) enables hard-working students to earn their degrees in three years instead of four. The university has potentially reduced the length of time KCSE graduates have to wait to join the university from two years to one.

Yet the majority of students selected for admission to Kenyatta University – those who apply for loans from the HELB – cannot take advantage of the reform. The HELB only processes loan applications after the JAB has finished its selection exercise. Only the few students who can sponsor themselves are benefiting from this innovation. Furthermore, the introduction of privately sponsored programmes whose admission criteria are determined by each public university without reference to the JAB points to the increasing irrelevance of this organization.

Cost-sharing measures & student welfare

Cost-sharing has had a negative impact on student participation in academic programmes. Student admission records in the public universities reveal increasing failures in reporting back to the

105

institutions. Between 1995 and 1999, Moi University reported that 7.5 per cent of the students admitted failed to report, while most of those who did report encountered financial problems. At least 1,000 students out of the total enrolment of 4,923 in 1995/6 faced expulsion for their inability to pay fees, a situation that prompted questions in Parliament. The pay-as-you-eat (PAYE) system has been very expensive for students and has turned out to be counter-productive in all the public universities. With students finding PAYE too expensive, the majority are opting to eat outside the university or to prepare their own meals in the hostels, even though university rules forbid cooking in these facilities. Before the practice became so common, students who were found cooking in hostels were disciplined for breaking university rules and for denying the university revenue from the catering services offered in the dining halls. The universities also incur huge electricity bills from the student residences. The financial implication of students' cooking in hostels is best illustrated by Kenyatta University, whose electricity bills increased from about Kshs.6 million to over Kshs.30 million per financial year during the 1990s. In the 2000/01 fiscal year, the university spent over Kshs.36 million on electricity alone. In addition to escalating electricity costs, cooking in residence halls poses a grave danger to students due to the electricity overload, as the hostels in most of the public universities were not designed to accommodate mass cooking and because students often dismantle overload control switches (Standa, 2000:49). A lecturer in the physics department at one of the universities cautioned that 'overloading due to cooking in rooms could easily ... result in fires' (personal interview, March 2002, Nairobi).

When students are not cooking in the halls of residence they prefer to eat outside the university in nearby locations, some of which leave a great deal to be desired from a public health standpoint. For example, Kilomita Moja, a slum situated 1 km from Kenyatta University, is a popular eating point with roadside kiosks registering booming business when the university is in session. Given the university's history of strikes, the authorities are reluctant to ban cooking in the halls of residence and they are, of course, powerless to stop students from 'dining out'. The public universities should perhaps weigh the costs of providing cheaper meals against the high electricity bills and the potential tragedy of fires and their aftermath. In the long run, the universities might contemplate providing hostels with kitchens for students.

106

Public perception of the public universities

Perhaps one of the most noticeable effects of the reforms discussed here is the change in the public perception of the universities. Before the reforms, the universities had an ivory tower image, with most of the public viewing these institutions with suspicion. This is a perception that the government had arguably fostered as a way of isolating the universities from the public. This perception has now changed, especially with the introduction of parallel degree programmes that have made it possible for the public universities to enjoy a more positive image with the wider public.

7 Concluding Observations & Questions Raised

Kenya's public universities continue to make a prominent contribution to national development through the training and preparation of human resources in various professions for the private and public sectors. The main lesson they have learned from the reform process of the past decade is the critical importance of using and managing available resources efficiently. This way the institutions will effectively grapple with many of the financial constraints that have faced virtually all tertiary institutions in the country.

The experience of the public universities with the reform process reflects both achievements and costs. Obviously, the ability to enhance their mission and build on their vision depends on how well they manage the achievements and minimize the costs of implementing reform. The main achievements of the reform programmes include opening up university education to more Kenyans, improving institutional revenue bases and being able to offer demand-driven and relevant academic programmes. The challenges that have resulted from the process have shed some light on the strategies that need to be undertaken to ensure that the benefits of reform are not lost.

Growing student enrolments, without a commensurate rise in the level of government funding, has been a major motivation for the reforms. At the same time, external pressures from the government, the private sector and donors have continued to challenge the public universities to justify their existence by reforming their programmes and approaches. But reform has also been motivated by the influence of donor organizations and the competition provided by the private university sector. In a few cases, reform-minded institutional leadership has fuelled the reform process and outcomes.

Overall, the reform initiatives have been fairly well managed. The process has involved significant consultation with university constituents, including staff and student committees, in planning the reforms, restructuring some administrative bodies to improve service delivery and the improved use of available human and physical resources and of the academic year itself. Thus facilities are shared across faculties, staff are used more intensively, and the academic year is organized in such a way that instruction takes place nearly every month of the year.

On the positive side, the reforms have been credited with expanding access to university education (especially improving the

108

access of female students, though not in science); the acceptance by staff and students of the inevitability of change; improved staff motivation through financial rewards made possible by the admission of self-sponsored students and the provision of scholarships for staff spouses and children enrolled as private students; the expansion of physical facilities using self-generated funds; challenging the Joint Admissions Board's centralized student recruitment in favour of admission by each university individually; the enhanced perception of the public universities among civil society, government, the private sector and the donor community; and increased accountability to the recipients and consumers of university education.

The negative aspects of the reform initiatives include some dilution of the quality of education; an intensification of inequality as ability to pay becomes the main criterion for access to university education; decline in the level of support services available to students, especially with the introduction of cost-sharing; and the high level of dependence on student fees and donors to fund the reform initiatives, along with new income-generating projects and a range of physical and human resources that have been stretched too thin. A further disadvantage has been the limited interaction with the relevant government ministries and the private sector in designing and implementing the reforms.

Many of the reforms would seem to have limited potential for long-term sustainability because universities are less business-like in their operations than they need to be. This shortcoming would require the recruitment of competent managers and improved training for existing ones, the implementation of a financial system that is more in keeping with current business practice, and the development of both internal and external evaluation mechanisms for gauging performance and the quality of output. While the public university sector's response to falling resource allocation from the government has included the double-entry solution of both reducing expenditure and generating more income, these efforts are unfortunately being derailed by the misappropriation of funds. The Auditor General's reports have raised concern about possible loopholes that need to be sealed.

Winning and maintaining the support and collaboration of relevant stakeholder groups remain a major challenge. This challenge could be met if the quality of university education, as well as services such as research and consultancy, is perceived to be high, priced competitively and responsive to Kenya's development needs. Thus universities will have to attract qualified staff and create

109

conditions and incentives that enhance their retention and motivation. Another challenge is addressing the infrastructural aspects of an inadequate learning environment in terms of lecture theatres, residential hostels and libraries. While the image of the public universities in the eyes of the wider public and potential students and staff is slowly improving as a result of the reform process, improved student and staff governance systems should go some way toward further improving it.

Improving the reform process & winning support

It appears that the public universities are responding well to their mandate to produce high-level human resources for the country. Yet the question of whether their output is really meeting national human resource needs is worth addressing. To begin with, there is no clear picture of what those requirements are. No recent survey of human resource needs has been undertaken to guide the universities in planning their programmes and admissions. In the absence of such a survey, the emphasis given to certain programmes will vary with the perceptions of the universities' management and the perceived demand. Under such circumstances, it will be very difficult for output to match real needs in any systematic way. To improve this situation, better communication is needed between university administrators and both the Ministry of Labour and Human Resources Development and the Ministry of Education, Science and Technology. This would help the public universities to focus their programmes on areas of greatest national need. Similarly, closer contacts need to be forged between university teaching departments and potential employers from both the public and private sectors.

At the institutional level, there is need to bring all the key stakeholders aboard through a bottom-up approach that allows for potential differences to be addressed well in advance in order to ensure ownership of the change process as well as consensual agreement to the targeted changes by all those affected. These consultations have to be viewed as on-going processes, because changed circumstances call for changed priorities and changing ways to address them. Thus the targets and vision arrived at during the initial discussions should benefit from regular revision. In addition, there is a need to set up and strengthen structures of change management such as strategic planning offices backed up by functioning management information systems. Institutions will further need to mobilize the resources needed to ensure the implementation of change from both internal and external sources and through the identification of relevant local, regional and international partners.

Realization of these goals implies three things that may prove stumbling blocks to the reforming institutions. One is that universities will have to restructure their procedures and bureaucracies in order to respond quickly and effectively to needs as they are identified. Their sluggish adaptation to accepted priorities reduced their credibility and caused a notable degree of demoralization among their own staff. Second, if university programmes are to be tailored to fit users' needs more closely, academic standards may have to be redefined. In this connection, the institutions' promotion procedures – which place heavy emphasis on traditional forms of scholarly publication and give less credit to strengths in teaching or in forging links between academic training and the world of work – may have to be revisited. Third, universities need to make a greater effort to influence the direction of the intermediary bodies that have emerged out of consensual agreements with the relevant stakeholders, because these bodies support university programmes by overseeing accreditation, quality control and university relations with government.

Confidence-building among public university stakeholders is a critical element in promoting the sustainability of the reform process that, as noted, is dependent on improvements in all aspects of public university education. To improve the quality of their programmes, universities will have to attract qualified staff and create conditions and incentives that enhance their retention and motivate them to work hard. The provision of an environment conducive to learning in terms of lecture theatres, residential hostels and well-stocked and well-kept libraries and science laboratories and other facilities should enhance the quality of university services. The public universities will have to offer competitive rates for their programmes, given the competition for fee-paying students among them and with the private universities. More important is the need to ensure that new programmes respond to market needs. The relevance of public universities' programmes can be achieved in part by the use of private-sector experts as part-time lecturers and their involvement in curriculum design and intensification of students' industrial attachment schemes. In undertaking this, the universities need to tap the potential of their alumni. Although the spirit of philanthropy has yet to be properly established in Kenya, the universities have large numbers of alumni, including both their graduates and their current and former staff, some of whom hold senior positions in government and the private sector.

Public and private universities in Kenya influence and complement each other in several ways. The scheduling of most teaching in self-sponsored academic programmes on weekday evenings and at weekends and holidays was an idea borrowed from the private university sector. Private universities, on the other hand, have benefited from public universities utilizing their academic staff on a part-time basis to supplement their own shortfall. Both the private and the public universities (through self-sponsored programmes) are expanding access to university education at no extra cost to the public and are responding flexibly to market demands for specialist skills. Although in the past there were limited contacts between them, recent initiatives such as KENET have provided a bridge between these two types of institutions.

Intermediary bodies need strengthening in numerous ways. The Higher Education Loans Board requires more funds for the establishment of a revolving fund from which it can lend money to more needy students. To enhance its services, the Commission for Higher Education needs to develop an accreditation and evaluation mechanism that is less restrictive on private universities. Also necessary is the revision of the Universities' Act of 1985, which has no legal provisions for regulating offshore campuses. Although the Joint Admissions Board has done some streamlining of the admissions process in the public universities, it will have to adopt even more efficient procedures in order to keep pace with changes taking place in institutions such as Kenyatta University.

Lessons learned & questions raised

Redefining university education in Kenya

The results of this study point to new ways of viewing the mission and vision of the university in Kenya.

The ivory tower image of universities is fading. Universities no longer restrict admissions to an elitist cadre of students, but have begun opening their doors to average people, strengthening distance-education programmes, opening up campuses in remote parts of the country, pairing with middle-level colleges to expand opportunities, mounting outreach programmes and enlisting outside experts to teach and research. While few can argue with a mission statement that seeks to place the university within 'the people', it is still worth asking whether this process should be shaped by certain parameters and, if so, who should define them?

Public universities are striving to be more relevant. Opening doors and emphasizing relevance comes at a cost. In some cases universities have developed courses they are poorly equipped to teach, have recruited more students than the available human and physical capacity can handle and have introduced changes that negatively affect both student and staff welfare and academic quality. It seems doubtful that the current trade-offs are inevitable. These problems deserve more thought by both the university community and the larger society, including the government.

The more market-based approach has consequences for university autonomy. As they develop products demanded by the consumer and embark on income-generating projects, universities are becoming more businesslike, less concerned with the pursuit of knowledge for its own sake, more flexible in delivering services and more appreciative of the need for strategic planning. As a result, the government may have to yield some of its traditional authority over universities. Academics may also have to cede some of their traditional autonomy to the market, since they can no longer sincerely and effectively defend the doctrine of 'academic freedom' as the basis for determining what to teach and research. And student freedom to disagree with the university authorities is now tempered by the presence of 'private', fee-paying students. Moreover, universities will have to allow the wider society more say in determining what goes on within their walls and will have to be more accountable to all their constituents.

The locally relevant university or the global university? While the universities strive to become locally relevant, they are also building up links with the international higher education network, which in turn is assuming an increasingly global character. The tension between local and global forces is plainly evident in all the public universities. Perhaps this tension does not need to be resolved but just calls for greater awareness of the contending forces. A more pro-active approach would require that the universities consciously devise mechanisms to balance the effects of the two forces. The current practices seem to reflect a general 'laissez-faire' policy.

Should public universities transform society? Some of the reforms of the past decade are quite innovative; some are even transforming the universities' sense of their own mission. This research indicates that some of the reforms could indeed have a transforma-

113

tive potential outside the universities. Should this become a permanent feature of the university mission?

Challenges for the implementation of reform

The formulation and implementation of reform have highlighted a number of specific challenges, which should form the basis of identifying new ways of supporting these initiatives.

Co-ordination and standardization of university curricula. In order to ensure that universities do not mount courses that are already offered in institutions better placed to teach them and that they are in a strong position to mount particular new programmes, the Commission for Higher Education and relevant professional bodies need to be more involved in determining new curricula offerings.

University funding and student support. Increased access, the introduction of new programmes and commercialization of university education all call for a re-evaluation of the ways in which university programmes and students are funded. Rather than funding universities solely on the basis of the number of students enrolled, a new funding strategy should take into account the actual cost of educating students in specific programmes in order to ensure the survival of disciplines that are more expensive to teach (architecture, engineering and medicine, for example) and of universities that have a more technological orientation. Second, universities need to design fair criteria for distributing the resources emanating from parallel degree programmes and income-generating projects. Third, the Higher Education Loans Board needs to tighten its criteria for funding needy students so that its decisions are more transparent.

Strengthening institutional governance. As universities are forced to become more accountable to their respective constituents, it will be important to strengthen student and staff associations to ensure their continued participation in the change process. In addition, universities need to devise more effective means of involving the business community, government and civil society in the process of designing and implementing reform. Co-ordinated participatory involvement is likely to result in greater acceptance of, and commitment to, the reform process.

Promoting long-term sustainability. If the reforms are to continue to strengthen university programmes, the public universities

114

need to recruit competent administrators and reward them competitively, to upgrade the management skills of the reform managers on an on-going basis, to design customer-friendly yet transparent financial accounting systems and to strengthen internal and external evaluation systems.

National consensus-building. Interest in and commitment to the reform process are more likely to be realized under conditions where there is broad agreement among the constituencies likely to be directly or indirectly affected by the reforms and their outcomes. The CHE may be well placed to co-ordinate this effort.

Future funding possibilities

Future donor support is likely to have the greatest impact if it is directed to (i) areas that should be given higher priority than they currently are by both universities and donors and which therefore require a catalyst of some kind, (ii) areas that need greater resources than the universities could hope to generate, and (iii) areas that lie outside the realm of individual public universities.

(i) Areas that need higher priority include:
* identifying mechanisms for improving student welfare;
* strengthening consultative identification and implementation of reform;
* strengthening quality control and internal/external evaluation systems;
* enhancing equity by recruiting more students and staff from traditionally disadvantaged groups/regions and providing facilities for physically challenged students; and
* improving internal governance systems.

(ii) Areas that already rank as high priority but where the scale of available resources limits action include:
* research votes;
* procurement of modern teaching and learning equipment, textbooks and journals;
* electronic linkage to other institutions and resources outside Kenya;
* training and upgrading the skills of reform managers and academics; and
* supporting staff participation in local and international academic and non-academic gatherings.

115

(iii) Areas outside the realm of individual universities where donor support may be most valuable include:

- reinforcing the capacity of the Commission for Higher Education to play a more effective co-ordinating role by supporting staff training, computerizing of databanks, funding seminars aimed at building consensus around its supervisory function and introducing it to funding networks so that it can obtain funds for itself and for some inter-university programmes;
- enhancing the capacity of the Higher Education Loans Board to improve its ability to identify needy students, to raise funding from sources outside government and to increase its capacity for loan recovery;
- strengthening linkages between the public universities themselves and between public and private institutions by promoting collaboration in training and research; and
- strengthening regional and international linkages by funding collaborative teaching and research programmes and student and staff exchanges.

Final thought: Are the reforms innovative or transformative?

The reforms that we have seen in the public universities during the past decade or so are both innovative and transformative. In order to survive the rapid expansion of enrolments since the mid-1980s in the wake of declining government financial support, the public universities have had to face up to an urgent need for change. These changes have been premised on the need for greater relevance, efficiency and effectiveness in the way the institutions fulfil their vision, mission and objectives. The search for more innovative ways of generating supplementary sources of income, the enhancement of the relevance of their academic programmes, and the introduction of staff appraisal to review their performance are changes that are both innovative and transformative. They represent a departure from the old way of doing things, and they have altered the outlook of the universities significantly.

The approach pioneered by Jomo Kenyatta University of Agriculture and Technology of introducing part-time courses by accrediting middle-level tertiary institutions in several parts of the country is transforming the public university system as well as the new constituents JKUAT is now able to reach. It has enabled the institution to take its programmes to people living in remote parts of the country such as Lamu at the Coast and Kisii in Nyanza Province, who would not otherwise have been able to gain admission even to the self-sponsored programmes. Kenyatta and Nairobi Universities are emulating the JKUAT initiative through their distance-education programmes. In order to enhance the effective management of its distance-education programme, Kenyatta University has become the first public tertiary institution to operate an FM radio station.

The early admission in January 2002 of the first batch of year 2000 KCSE candidates who applied to Kenyatta University through the JAB could be viewed as a radical and transformative innovation. Early admission, which allows students to register on a semester basis and to complete their degree programmes in three as opposed to four years, is likely to transform the system by clearing the backlog of potential students as well as transforming Kenyatta University itself.

The establishment of the African Virtual University sites at Egerton and Kenyatta could also be seen as transformative. The AVU uses the power of modern information technology to increase access to educational resources. By means of this project, two universities are tapping the potential of new technologies to overcome existing barriers, including declining budgets, outdated equipment and limited space and facilities, that prevent increased access to higher education for a significant number of students from all walks of life, including housewives and peasant farmers. Properly implemented, the AVU will transform the educational delivery system as well as the lives of many graduates. It also has the potential to transform the institutions by making them more technologically inclined.

The collaboration between the University of Nairobi, the University of Manitoba and Oxford University in developing a vaccine to assist in the war against HIV/AIDS will be a significant transformative change if these efforts bear the much-awaited fruits. By enlisting the help of traditional healers from various parts of the country, the Centre for Complementary Medicine and Biotechnology at Kenyatta University has shed the old elitist tendency in staff recruitment. Some of those recruited as researchers may not have gone beyond primary school. The healing community has been truly transformed in becoming university teachers. Furthermore, no one can deny the effect they will have on university campuses, accustomed as the latter are to stiff academic gowns.

Perhaps the most potentially transformative reform is the introduction of fee-paying students to university campuses. These students are on average much older and more business-minded than the average undergraduate. They have less time to waste and

117

demand accountability and value for their money, taking no part in street demonstrations as do their younger colleagues in the regular programmes. The overall effect is that they are helping to democratize the universities in a perhaps much more transformative way than their youthful and more demonstrative colleagues.

Appendix

Research methodology

The research process included the following steps:

- requesting the assistance of the six Vice-Chancellors in the exercise;
- consultation and appointment of one or two researchers from each of the six universities;
- a follow-up meeting between university officials and the chief investigators to further explain the study, followed by a letter from the latter requesting permission to conduct the study and introducing the researchers to the university administration;
- a workshop between the chief investigators and the research teams to study the research proposal and design a research strategy;
- institutional planning workshops to map out research strategies for each university;
- data collection and preparation of 'initial impressions' or 'pre-drafts' for each university, followed by a second researchers' workshop to fine tune methods of data collection, especially statistical data;
- further data collection and preparation of draft reports, followed by a researchers' workshop to discuss drafts;
- revision of drafts followed by validation workshops/reviews in each university;
- finalization and editing of each university report;
- preparation of a synthesis report;
- a validation workshop for the synthesis report.

Data were collected between November 2001 and November 2002 from university personnel (junior administrators, Vice-Chancellors and/or their deputies, finance officers, registrars, deans, heads of departments, directors of institutes, heads of income-generating projects and academic staff); university council members; administrators of higher education intermediary bodies; Ministry of Education officials responsible for higher education; and student representatives. In addition, data were gathered from institutional primary and secondary sources including newspaper reports, commencement statements and graduation lists of the previous decade, published materials from a variety of large and small education documentation centres and basic institutional data over a ten-year period (including data on enrolments, staffing and financing). The research teams also

119

undertook systematic observation of the physical infrastructure of the universities, including visits to halls of residence, lecture halls and staff offices.

The researchers collected basic statistical data on enrolment, staffing, finance, income-generating activities, new programmes, degree classifications and so on, all of which were analysed to yield, for example, the gender dimensions. In all the universities, this type of data was collected around 21 common 'dummy 'tables in order to facilitate data aggregation for the synthesis report. In addition to statistical data, qualitative information was collected from observations and from key informants.

Two main problems were encountered in the process of the data collection; the incompleteness and questionable accuracy of the available institutional data and the difficulties of scheduling interviews with university officials. However, these problems were ameliorated by the fact that university staff were by and large very co-operative.

The research team consisted of two senior researchers – the authors of this synthesis report and editors of the six institutional reports – and nine researchers based in the six public universities. Of the nine researchers, four were women. In addition, five of them were young education researchers working for their Ph.D. degrees. The results of the research project include this synthesis report and six other reports, one on each public university.

II Private Provision of Higher Education in Kenya

Trends & Issues in Four Universities

DANIEL WESONGA, CHARLES NGOME, DOUGLAS OUMA-ODERO & VIOLET WAWIRE

Acknowledgements

Profound gratitude goes to the Ford Foundation for the grant that made this project possible. Special mention goes to Dr Tade Aina, the Ford Foundation Representative in Eastern Africa, and Anne-Marea Griffin and Mary Ngolovoi, also of the Nairobi Office of the Ford Foundation, for their untiring assistance.

We would also like to thank Godwin Murunga, project co-ordinator, for initiating the research idea, writing the proposal and identifying the research team. Individual researchers who handled the various themes include Dr Charles Ngome (governance and management), Violet Wawire (equity and access), Douglas Ouma-Odero (curriculum and ICT) and Daniel Wesonga (financing). Research assistants Jane Mbagi, Kaari Miriti, Eva Ayoo, Pamela Marinda and Godfrey Omondi also made valuable contributions.

Our thanks also go to the following people: data analysts Calvin Kayi and David Mumo; peer editors Dr Ibrahim Oanda of Kenyatta University and Wycliffe Otieno of E-PARSE; Advisory Board members Dr Sheila Wamahiu, Professor Daniel Sifuna, David Aduda and Dr Regina Karega, all from Women Educational Researchers of Kenya (WERK); project advisory team members Dr Karin Hyde, Dr Grace Bunyi and Dr Sheila Wamahiu for quality assurance and Esther Wangui, project officer, for day-to-day management of the project.

We appreciate the time and co-operation of all the individual respondents involved in the study, with special thanks to Dr Freida Brown (Vice-Chancellor, USIU), Professor Leah Marangu (Vice-Chancellor, ANU), Professor Rev. Caesar Lukudu and Professor Mavira (CUEA), Professor Talitwala and Professor Katia (Daystar), and Professor Mutunga and Dr Walemba (EUAB).

We are also grateful to David Court and Lisbeth Levey for their comments on the initial draft and Wangenge Ouma for his editorial assistance. Many other people assisted in many ways and to all of them we offer our sincere appreciation.

Daniel Wesonga, Charles Ngome,
Douglas Ouma-Odero and Violet Wawire

1 Origins of Private Higher Education in Kenya

Christian missionaries were at the forefront of the development of Western education in Kenya. The many primary and secondary schools as well as teacher training colleges they established in different parts of the country testify to their untiring efforts (Abagi and Nzomo, 2001). The establishment of university education in Kenya is largely associated with the birth of the Royal Technical College in 1956 and its metamorphosis into the fully-fledged University of Nairobi in 1970. However, a few private institutions of higher learning existed in Kenya before independence, namely, St Paul's Theological College and Scott Theological College. These institutions became pioneer private universities in Kenya following the relaxation in the 1990s of the government's hitherto firm grip on the provision of higher education. The establishment in Nairobi of a Kenyan campus of the United States International University (USIU) in 1970 signalled the arrival of the first private university in the country with a secular orientation. Since then, many other private universities have been established.

The establishment & location of private universities

Figure I.1 in Part I showed the location of the 17 private universities that are chartered, registered or operating in Kenya with a letter of interim authority from the Commission for Higher Education. Another four private universities are actually 'offshore' campuses of foreign universities, which are recognized by the CHE although not accredited.[1] Of the private universities (including the four offshore campuses), 17 are situated in Nairobi (the capital) and its peri-urban zones, while only four are located outside the capital. Those found outside Nairobi are established in agriculturally high-potential districts – Kabarak University in Nakuru, Kenya Methodist University in Meru, Kenya Highlands Bible College in Kericho and the University of Eastern Africa, Baraton in Nandi. This trend follows

[1] These are the Australian Studies Institute (AUSI), the University of South Africa (UNISA) centre in Kenya at the Kenya College of Accountancy, the University of London and Technikon of South Africa at the Kenya School of Professional Studies and the University of the Free State at the Kenya College of Communication and Technology (KCCT), all located in Nairobi.

closely the Christian missions' pattern of establishing educational institutions during the colonial era. The establishment of private universities in rural areas is less attractive than in urban areas; they are more expensive to set up and also to manage. The initial costs, including the provision of staff housing, access roads and medical facilities, are quite high. In addition, urban-based universities attract high enrolments of part-time students who work while attending classes in the evenings and at weekends.

In addition, by late 2002 some 14 other institutions had submitted proposals for establishment as private universities. These are Augustana University, Kenya Utalii College, University of Tropical Medicine and Technology, Hindu University, Gretsa University, Mbeji University of Science and Technology, Great Lakes University of Kisumu (being established by the Tropical Institute of Community Health and Development in Africa), Presbyterian University, Mombasa Islamic University, Concord University, Discipleship University, Kenya Medical College, Institute of Development Policy and Practice and St Andrews College of Theology and Development.

This widespread demand for higher education in Kenya has been triggered by the massive expansion of primary and secondary education over the last three decades, an expansion which was itself propelled by demographic pressures: population growth rates remained just under 4 per cent per year for most of the 1980s and 1990s. The increasing sophistication of the economy, which demands a skilled work force, has also fuelled the demand for higher education. The determination by some religious organizations to open tertiary institutions primarily for their followers has been instrumental in the emergence of church-sponsored universities in the country.

This high demand for university education compelled the government to increase the number of public universities from one in 1970 to six by 2001, but the demand for university education continues to outstrip the capacity of these institutions. The public universities admit some 10,000 students on government sponsorship, while, as noted in Part I, some 7,000–10,000 students annually go abroad to study, at great cost to the country in foreign exchange (Ngome, 2003). As the Daystar University web site (http://www.daystar. ac.ke/) proclaims, 'At Daystar, five African students can be educated for the cost of sending one student overseas'. It is within this context that the Kenyan government has encouraged the establishment of private universities.

124

Rationale for the study

Although private universities are still relatively scarce in African countries, they form a critical component of higher education in Kenya. Nearly 20 per cent of Kenyan university undergraduates are enrolled in private universities. Despite this high visibility, the missions, objectives and operations of private universities have not been clearly understood. With the exception of United States International University, many of the private universities have a strong religious orientation, leading most Kenyans to assume that these institutions exist primarily to increase the number of degree-level students bound for church-oriented work.

Despite their increasing visibility, the private universities have not generally been viewed as priority alternatives to the overcrowded public ones. Most Kenyans still believe that the public universities can provide a high quality of education and offer reasonable chances of employment. Most families cannot meet the high cost of private education and see their fees as a further cause of inequality harking back to the experience of the colonial period (Brown, 2001). More recently there has been a perception that the quality of the public universities is eroding, marked by unscheduled closures and over-enrolment in the face of dwindling government financial support. This is happening at a time when private universities are providing school leavers with a chance to benefit from university education at no extra public cost and making it possible for those already in the labour market to upgrade their skills.

This study was designed to shed light on the phenomenon of private universities in Kenya in terms of their curriculum and academic programmes, governance and management structures, financial base, community outreach, accessibility, equity and funding. The study also sought to investigate the role of the Commission for Higher Education (CHE) and its regulations with regard to the private universities, with a view to pointing out aspects that may require amendment to create a more equitable and supportive regulatory framework for private universities.

The four case studies

The four private universities selected for study – the United States International University (USIU), the Catholic University of Eastern Africa (CUEA), the University of Eastern Africa, Baraton (UEAB) and Daystar University – were chosen because they are the largest and best-established private universities in Kenya and are broadly

125

representative of the whole spectrum. Of the approximately 10,000 students enrolled in private universities in Kenya in 2000 about 70 per cent were students at these four universities. The institutions span the typologies of private universities in Kenya – with USIU representing the secular and liberal university, while Daystar, Catholic and UEAB are all under religious auspices but professing different Christian ideologies and criteria for admission. Each of the selected universities also has a unique niche in its course offerings: science-oriented programmes (agriculture, nursing, medical and automotive technology) at UEAB, business studies at USIU, education at CUEA and communications at Daystar. Lastly, they run the gamut in tuition fees from the lowest (CUEA) to the highest (USIU).

The Daystar University website describes it as non-denominational and as 'the largest Christian liberal arts college in Africa' with an enrolment of over 1900 students in 2004. Daystar's Athi River Campus is located on the edge of the Athi plains on the slopes of the Lukenya Hills, approximately 38 km from the city of Nairobi. The campus occupies a 300-acre parcel of land. A smaller campus two miles from the centre of Nairobi occupies a 1.5 acre site. Daystar has an evangelical mission and espouses a 'biblically oriented approach to training men and women for more effective service in church and society without the culturally disruptive and prohibitive cost of overseas training'.

The Catholic University of Eastern Africa (CUEA) was first founded as a theological institute, which opened in 1984 for the training of priests. The university is owned by the Bishops of the Association of Member Episcopal Conferences of Eastern Africa and received its charter in 1992. The campus covers 93 acres (website: www.cuea. edu).

The United States International University (USIU) was founded in 1969, and its website claims a status as 'the first and only secular university in East Africa'. The university's stated goal is to be the premier institution of academic excellence with a global perspective in East Africa (www.usiu.ac.ke). The university held its first graduation in 1979 with 23 students and numbered some 2,354 students in 1999/2000. The present USIU campus, to which it moved in 1991, occupies 120 acres of land in the Kasarani area of Nairobi.

The University of East Africa, Baraton (UEAB), affiliated with the Seventh-Day Adventist church, aspires to provide a 'wholistic [sic] Christian education [including] ... mental, physical and spiritual development' (www.tagnet.org/ueab). The campus is located on 339 acres in Nandi District, near Eldoret in the Rift Valley. Classes began in 1980 in temporary farm structures. As of 2004 UEAB enrolment was 1,200 students, from 20 different countries.

2 Accreditation, Governance & Management

Most private universities in Kenya were established between 1970 and 2002, with the majority having their origins in seminary-type institutions of higher education focused on theology and related subjects reflecting their concern for missionary and pastoral outreach. Their current academic programmes – both those with charters (apart from Scott Theological College) and those with letters of interim authority – concentrate on education, business, accounting, computer studies and theology. This curricular orientation has been criticized for being too narrow an intellectual base for both students and academic staff (Deloitte and Touche, 1994: 135), since a university, by definition, is a multi-disciplinary institution that should go beyond the social sciences and vocational education in its offerings. However, the private universities have found the cost of entry into such disciplines as medicine, engineering and science to be prohibitively high.

Another striking feature about these institutions lies in the range of nationalities among members of the student body. While public university students are almost exclusively Kenyan, the private universities tend to serve a broader constituency. This, too, reflects the theological and evangelical orientation serving the Eastern Africa region of many of these institutions. Several of the private universities maintain high percentages of foreign students (Pan African Christian College, 67 per cent; Nairobi International School of Theology, 25 per cent) (Deloitte and Touche, 1994: 135).

Accreditation status

The Commission for Higher Education serves as the link between universities and the government and has the overall responsibility of licensing higher educational institutions. The CHE categorizes the private universities into four main groups: accredited private universities, registered private universities, private universities operating on the basis of a letter of interim authority and foreign universities classified as offshore campuses. Of the 17 private universities, only 6 are accredited: University of Eastern Africa, Baraton (UEAB, 1992), Catholic University of Eastern Africa (CUEA, 1992), Daystar University (1994), Scott Theological College (1997), United States International University (USIU, 1999) and Africa Nazarene University (ANU, 2002). The 6 registered private universities are: East African

School of Theology, Kenya Highlands Bible College, Nairobi International Bible College, Nairobi Evangelical Graduate School of Theology, St Paul's Theological College and Pan African Christian College. Those granted letters of interim authority are: the Aga Khan University, Strathmore College, Kabarak University, Kenya Methodist University and Kiriri Women's University of Science and Technology. In addition, there are 14 applications awaiting consideration by the CHE.

Accreditation means recognition and confirmation in writing by charter, certificate or other documentation issued by the CHE. Before accreditation is granted, the CHE carries out an inspection of the human, physical, technical and financial resources available to carry out the institution's stated objectives. Requirements for accreditation include the establishment of institutional standards with respect to physical facilities, staffing levels and teaching loads, peer review, visitations and inspection, internal self-assessment and viability of financial resources on a long-term basis.

Governance structures

As Kenya's private universities develop, the issue of their instruments of governance acquires significance, because the attainment of institutional goals is dependent on the effectiveness of these structures. Saint (1992) suggested that a model of effective governance of higher education institutions should allow all the constituent groups to have dialogue at both formal and informal levels and should also guarantee the flow of information among the administration, staff and students. The governance and management structures of most private universities in Kenya consist of a board of trustees or directors, a university council, a Chancellor, a Vice-Chancellor or Rector, Deputy Vice-Chancellors and a senate. Below the senates are faculties or schools and departments. At each of these levels, there are variations in terms of power and authority. University councils oversee the operation of these institutions and ensure that their various departments are in harmony with policies outlined by stakeholder groups.

Management of human resources

The study examined the ratio of students to academic and non-academic staff in evaluating the resource utilization at the selected institutions.

128

Table II.1: Staff/student ratios, 2001/02 academic year

University	Teaching staff/ student ratio	Non-teaching staff/ student ratio
USIU	1:22	1:13
Daystar	1:23	1:10
CUEA	1:18	1:11
UEAB	1:20	1:10
Average	1:21	1:11

Source: Commission for Higher Education data, 2002.

Computations based on the 2001/2 academic year showed that both the average teacher/student ratio (1:21) and the average non-teaching staff/student ratio (1:11) were comparatively high at the private universities (Table II.1). These ratios highlight the efficient utilization of resources in the private universities, which have worked to keep their staff costs low. This contrasts sharply with the situation in public universities in Kenya, with a 1:12 faculty: student ratio and with staff costs by far the largest element in the budget, generally accounting for over 90 per cent of expenditures. On the other hand, the relatively low level of salaries at most private universities reflects a heavy reliance on part-time staff. At USIU, 65 of the 106 members of the academic staff are part-time employees and only 41 work full-time. A similar scenario exists at Daystar and CUEA, where about half the teaching staff are part-time. These institutions depend largely on part-time teaching staff moonlighting from the public universities. With the launching of self-sponsored degree programmes in the public universities, commonly known as 'parallel degree programmes', the private universities will be facing greater competition for the limited pool of academic staff. To eliminate this problem, they will have to invest more in training their own staff; otherwise the quality of education they provide may be compromised.

The effectiveness of a university depends on the quality of its staff, especially the academic staff. Based on educational credentials alone, the quality of academic staff in most of the church-sponsored private universities would seem to be quite low. For instance, at Daystar University, only 12 per cent of the teaching staff have doctorates, while 78 per cent have master's degrees. A similar situation obtains at CUEA and UEAB. Church-sponsored private universities often

129

consider the religious affiliation and motivation of potential employees more critical than their professional competence. Daystar University's Development Plan for the period 1999-2004 notes that:

The fast expansion of university education in Africa over the past decade combined with the shortage of qualified African academic staff is a major obstacle to the development of university level institutions in Africa. The shortage of qualified academic staff is further complicated for Daystar University because Daystar requires its staff to be committed Christians in addition to being academically qualified. Our efforts to hire a professor in business over the past two years have been fruitless. This is the biggest challenge to any Christian University in Africa today. (Daystar University, 1999:2)

In contrast, some 46 per cent of staff at the secular USIU have Ph.D. degrees, reflecting an emphasis on faculty qualifications and experience.

Human resources are the most important factor in determining the extent to which universities meet their missions and objectives. Their successful management encompasses staff recruitment, planning, retention, appraisal and development as well as negotiations over conditions of employment. In the universities studied, once recruitment has taken place, the management of staff (both academic and non-academic) usually devolves to deans and heads of departments or other sections within the universities. Interviews with deans and departmental heads indicated that they were quite familiar with policies governing recruitment, training, promotion and discipline. In spite of notable variations within these institutions, many try to motivate their staff by offering them a good working environment and a career path that includes opportunities and means of advancement in their jobs. Thus a great deal of emphasis is put on staff development as a means of improving organizational efficiency and effectiveness.

A number of staff members (both academic and non-academic) have benefited from the private universities' staff development programmes, which usually include education and training support for employees, their spouses and their children. At Daystar University, members of staff are entitled to a 10 per cent tuition waiver and transport to campus for approved training. Their children get a 20 per cent tuition waiver and reimbursement of transport costs. Council members of Daystar University and their children get a waiver of 50 per cent for tuition and full transport costs. At UEAB, staff members whose children attend a Seventh-day Adventist boarding school receive a scholarship grant amounting to 70 per cent of the tuition fees (60 per cent for day students). At USIU, the employee tuition

Box II.1 The Long Journey to my MBA
Stanley Mugwiria, financial accountant, USIU

The cut-off point for the Bachelor of Commerce degree had always been 13, and I was lucky to score 14. But because of the double intake on campus, the cut-off was suddenly raised to 16. I couldn't believe my eyes when I received my campus admission letter inviting me to study for a Bachelor of Education Degree in Business Studies and Economics instead.

I decided to study accounting while I pursued the degree, believing that I could still detour to Accounts. My first job as an accountant earned me Kshs.3,000, as I was still struggling to educate myself. I deliberately wanted a Master of Business Administration degree as consolation for the loss of the Bachelor of Commerce Degree. I first saw the USIU accounts post advertised in the newspapers.... This was it! I thought if I worked for a university, it could be easier for me to pursue an MBA. My highest hopes though were that the job would earn me a better salary to enable me to pay for tuition.

How can I explain my pleasant surprise when I landed at USIU! I pursued my MBA with relish. I must say it turned out to be even better than I had anticipated. Our class was full of practicing professionals, making discussions lively and practical. Of all the courses I have done, the MBA was the most enjoyable. It was June last year when finally my dream was realized. How can I explain my joy on graduation day? I felt good, great, better than I have ever felt before. I will forever be indebted to USIU for the benefit of free education, and I want to assure the university that we [staff] do plough it back into our work. Whether or not one is promoted, the increase in knowledge changes the way one approaches issues and looks for solutions. I have myself seen a metamorphosis in the way I handle students. Before, I felt under a lot of stress and often had to raise my voice. Today I am better equipped in logical problem solving; I am a better manager of my office.

(Source: *Sunday Nation*, 17 June 2001)

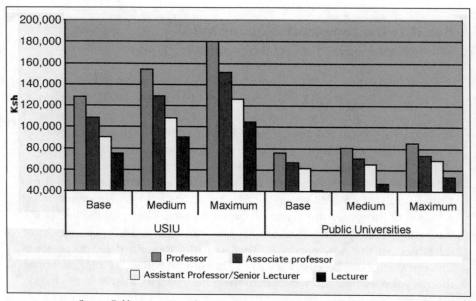

Source: Public universities administration divisions, USIU Human Resource Department, 2002.

Figure II.1: Faculty salary structure at USIU and other public universities, 2002 (Kshs.)

waiver covers full tuition costs. Discussions with USIU employees indicated that since its inception the university had helped many staff fulfil their career aspirations. USIU's financial accountant, Stanley Mugwiria, shared his experience with the education tuition waiver scheme (see Box II.1).

Adequate remuneration is paramount in attracting and retaining high-quality academic staff. At UEAB, remuneration is at basic levels sufficient to provide for living expenses, with maximum remuneration normally achieved in two stages, after five and ten years of service. Staff salaries and allowances at UEAB, CUEA and Daystar were all lower than those at the public universities. Among the four selected universities, USIU was the only exception to the pattern of low salaries. Its remuneration structure reflects competitive market rates in order to attract, motivate and retain qualified academic and senior administrative staff. While many Kenyan scholars have accepted employment in southern Africa (and more recently in Rwanda), where remuneration and other terms of employment are better (Brown, 2001), USIU has established itself as the highest bidder among local universities. Although many lecturers have left the public universities, the *Daily Nation* (22 July 2001) reports that USIU had lost only two lecturers to other institutions over a period of seven years. Out of 41 permanent teaching staff at USIU, about half had been recruited from the public universities. Over 80 per cent of the 85 part-time lecturers are also drawn from the public universities. While the good working environment is also a factor, this study found that USIU's pay package was the major attraction for lecturers from the public universities. Figure II.1 offers a comparison between the pay package structure in public universities and that of USIU.

USIU offered faculty members almost twice as much in remuneration as that offered at the public universities. Although the USIU lecturers surveyed indicated that they were still yearning for a pay rise, those who had previously taught at the public universities acknowledged that they were much better-off and that USIU's remuneration packages at least guaranteed them a comfortable life.

Inter-university networking & linkages

Most private universities have strong links with foreign universities, as many of them retain connections with their parent campuses in other countries. In addition, they are developing new linkages to broaden their networks and to meet some of the challenges facing them. USIU retains North American accreditation through several Alliant International University[2] campuses in California and in Mexico. It also exchanges students and faculty and collaborates in curriculum development with the other Alliant campuses (Brown, 2001).

Daystar University maintains links with several colleges and universities in the United States. It has established a staff and student exchange programme with the Christian College Consortium of 13 colleges in the US that is open to second-, third- and fourth-year students. At the same time, Daystar has hosted students from these colleges as well as visiting faculty members who stayed at Daystar for varying periods of time.

UEAB has linkages with the Tanzania Adventist College (TAC),

[2] In 2001 the North American campuses of USIU joined with Alliant University and the California School of Professional Psychology to form a new university – Alliant University International.

which offers a UEAB degree in theology and plans to run more UEAB courses. Negotiations for UEAB to accredit Akaki Adventist College in Ethiopia and Lakeview and Malamulo Colleges in Malawi are expected to bear fruit. In its 2001 *Self-Evaluation Report*, CUEA stated that it was developing linkages with other Catholic universities abroad in order to enhance quality education (CUEA, 2001). Although such linkages are healthy for universities the world over, the private universities in Kenya have been cautioned to develop relationships that respond to the institutions' and Kenya's socio-economic realities in order to ensure that their own priorities do not get sidelined (Deloitte and Touche, 1994).

Although these university linkages are still rather limited, they seem likely to improve. Through the East African Parliamentary Institute, USIU and the University of Nairobi, in collaboration with the State University of New York, are working jointly with parliamentary service commissions in Uganda, Tanzania and Kenya. The institute, funded by the Ford Foundation, is establishing a regional assistance centre for the Members of Parliament of the three East African countries to conduct research and facilitate regular gatherings of the three parliamentary service commissions in order to give parliamentarians resources that will encourage well-researched debates and new legislation.

Private university linkages with public universities were also being facilitated through the Kenya Education Network (KENET).[3]

Management of student affairs

Regarding the management of student affairs, this study focused on student activities, counselling and guidance, the governance of student associations, and channels of communication between students and university authorities. All four private universities have established systems for this purpose to deal with the management of student affairs and welfare. At UEAB, CUEA and Daystar, student affairs are handled through the office of the Dean of Students. At USIU this responsibility falls to the office of the Deputy Vice-Chancellor (Student Affairs). These offices provide opportunities for students to get involved in activities through various student organizations.

At the time of this study, the private universities surveyed had about 300 registered student organizations, clubs and associations.

---

[3] More information on KENET is provided in Part I, Chapter 2.

These included fraternities, sports clubs, special interest groups, and religious, social and welfare clubs. Student involvement in these groups facilitated the development of social, leadership and communication skills. All four private universities provided counselling and guidance services designed to foster personal growth and development and to help individual students with personal, social, career and study problems that might interfere with their education. Discussions with counsellors revealed that the most common problems addressed included academic pressures, relationship issues, family problems and concerns about sex and self-esteem. Most students interviewed appeared comfortable with their institutions' counselling and guidance services.

Student welfare issues in the private universities were also addressed by student unions – except at UEAB, where the union has been banned for activism. The student unions were the Catholic University Students Organization (CUSO), the Daystar University Students Association (DUSA) and the Students Affairs Council (SAC) at USIU. Membership in these student unions was open to all registered students upon payment of fees as prescribed by either student leaders or the university authorities. Student unions serve all students and represent the student body at university management meetings.

The university authorities at USIU, CUEA and Daystar have provided avenues for open communication with student leaders. At USIU, new officials of the Students Affairs Council attend a leadership retreat with university administrators to examine student leaders' role in the management and governance of the university. The university administration at USIU consults students before taking policy decisions on certain critical and sensitive issues. During the 1997/8 academic year, SAC officials met with university authorities to review tuition rates. The same year the SAC was also included in the search committees to choose a dean of students' affairs and the cafeteria services manager. During the 1999/2000 academic year, SAC negotiated with the administration to resolve a crisis involving the increase in fees for non–East African students.

The DUSA's success as a student government rests in its ability to engage in dialogue with the university administration. This, noted one student leader, 'has been achieved due to the fact that informal meetings have formed the core of their activities more than the formal contacts.... Doors in Daystar University are open for DUSA officials any time, any day without appointments' (personal interview, 2002). Since the student leaders had access to university adminis-

135

trators whenever the need arose, they were able to defuse potentially explosive situations.

Strategies for the management of HIV/AIDS

Sub-Saharan Africa accounts for only 10.4 per cent of the world's population, but it records 71.3 per cent of AIDS-related deaths and 11 million AIDS orphans (some 78.6 per cent of the AIDS orphans in the world). The epicentre of the disease in Africa is located in Eastern and Southern Africa. It is in this context that HIV/AIDS has been declared a national disaster in Kenya, with an estimated 900 AIDS-related deaths daily.

Private universities in Kenya have joined in the fight against this pandemic. Many university students are at high risk of contracting HIV through engaging in such risky practices as unprotected sex, frequent changes of partners and using sex for financial gain. Alcohol consumption is also common among students and often leads to risk-taking behaviour. In response to these challenges, the private universities have developed strategies to deal with HIV/AIDS both within the institutions and in the wider society. At UEAB, students and staff launched campaigns in the surrounding communities on the need to stop the spread of HIV, an initiative which attracted the support of the Adventist Development Relief Agency (ADRA). USIU focuses on prevention, control and awareness among its students, faculty and support staff. Although the institution had had only one AIDS-related death in six years (Brown, 2001), students have taken part in an on-campus survey to determine attitudes and behaviours related to AIDS. This survey will be used to assess the extent of the problem on campus and to develop a comprehensive HIV/AIDS awareness programme. USIU students have also launched AIDS awareness programmes through peer counselling. The institution's undergraduate course on Human Sexuality is also part of the effort to control the spread of HIV/AIDS on campus.

Daystar University has also dedicated time, resources and energy to alleviating the spread of HIV/AIDS. In collaboration with Norwegian Church Aid, the university launched awareness campaigns and raised funds for workshops and seminars aimed at making the Kyumbi Community in Machakos District aware of the impact of HIV/AIDS on their lives. During its 10th conference in Nairobi, in 2001, the Association of African Universities urged private universities to explore the possibilities of establishing AIDS control units to formulate programmes within the universities and their neighbourhoods.

Extension & community services

The private universities exhibit a good deal of commitment to local community development programmes, linking themselves to neighbouring communities by including programmes in their curricula that enable students to apply theoretical knowledge to practical life situations. At Daystar University, for example, a course on community development illustrates the importance the university places on community service, which the department considers 'holistic', involving spiritual, economic, social and political aspects of community life. In preparing the course Daystar University conducted a needs' assessment study of the Kapiti Plains that collected data from community members, leaders and government departments on the health situation and accessibility of water for domestic use in the area and made recommendations to improve community life (Chandran and Omwansa, 1999).

At UEAB, several community outreach efforts are in place. Services including free maternal/child health services, professional services at some local medical clinics and free health care for nearby primary schools have consolidated cordial relationships with the surrounding community. The university also serves as a learning centre for farmers and educators on new techniques in agriculture, as well as the dissemination of new ideas through visits, seminars and demonstrations organized by individual departments. The Department of Biology operates a snake park, which is popular with school children and adults in the community. The Department of Agriculture undertook an integrated agricultural project in Chamundu Location in conjunction with ADRA to educate farmers on modern approaches to environmental conservation and agriculture. In addition, the School of Education organizes periodic seminars for teachers and administrators to support and motivate them in their professional roles. The university has also contributed to charity, donating food and other material support for disaster survivors, as was the case after the 1998 bomb attack on the US Embassy in Nairobi.

The involvement of USIU in community service has included providing infrastructure within its neighbourhood, such as public access roads, sewer and water lines and electric transformers. The university has constructed and maintains a 2.5 km road connecting USIU to the Nairobi-Thika highway and has organized workshops on the delivery of public services, including one on 'Effective Police-Public Relations' for police officers from four divisions in Nairobi. It has also donated information technology equipment to the Kiambu

137

Institute of Science and Technology. Undergraduate students at USIU are required to work at least 100 hours without pay for non-profit organizations.

As part of its religious orientation, CUEA organizes and participates in community activities addressing marginalized and disadvantaged members of society. CUEA also started a project to improve the quality of education in local primary schools and non-formal education centres.

3 Issues of Access & Equity

The concepts of educational access and equity are intertwined and difficult to discuss separately. Access assumes the availability of educational opportunities for all those who are eligible by embracing the principle of inclusiveness for all potential learners. The concept of equity focuses on values of fairness and social justice in the way educational opportunities and resources are allocated, advocating the conscious elimination of all forms of discrimination based on sex, socio-economic status, geographical location or physical, mental and other handicaps (Koech, 2000). According to Schuller (1991), increased access entails making education available to a greater number of students. Wider access emanates from the creation of a more heterogeneous student population, including mature students and students from a range of socio-economic backgrounds, through admission criteria, course organization and credit transfers. He sums up the process thus: 'without the former [access] it is impossible to achieve the latter [equity] because access by competition to a scarce resource always favours the privileged' (Schuller, 1991: 33).

The private universities have come to play a critical role in taking in a large number of the increasing number of students who qualify to attend the public universities in Kenya but are unable to do so because of the limited number of vacancies available (Koech, 2000; World Bank, 1994). On average, only one-third of the Kenya Certificate of Secondary Education (KCSE) examination qualifiers get places in the public universities each year, due to the limited capacity of these institutions (*Daily Nation*, 24 May 2002). The private universities admit approximately 14 per cent of the total number of students who qualify on the basis of the KCSE (Brown, 2001). However, we should be quick to note that, based on their ability to pay, the clientele of both public and private universities are becoming economically segregated, with the private universities taking up students from the more affluent families. This tendency will be discussed further below.

Based on the general belief that the private universities only admit students based on their ability to pay (Murunga, 2001), the question then is whether they can play the social role of facilitating upward mobility, allowing talented students to access university education irrespective of their socio-economic origins. Similarly, the question emerges of whether private university education has been accessible to all students, irrespective of their sex, ethnic origin, age or physical disability. These are crucial questions that are inevitable in any discussion of equitable access.

Some argue that the private universities are not obligated to observe equity of access because of their private sponsorship. However, as reflected in their mission statements, the private universities recognize the need to provide equitable access. In addition, even though they receive government (and thus public) support through access to student loan programmes, most of them claim to be non-profit institutions established to serve the needs of society. Furthermore, they adhere to the same policies as the public universities as prescribed by the CHE. In fact, theoretically, the private universities are better placed to effect equity of access policies in view of the fact that they operate independently in most aspects, including budgetary allocations and admission of students – unlike the public universities, which are subject to government interference.

In their bid to fulfil the social role of providing higher education for all, the private universities must strive to increase and broaden participation in order to assist in meeting the nation's human resource needs in addition to advancing social equity. In this respect, therefore, we need to ask whether the private universities have transformed the traditional imbalance in university admissions and participation inherent in the public universities, especially in view of the heavy fees charged (Achola, 1997). The following section examines the private universities' recruitment policies and access to university education in terms of overall enrolments, followed by an analysis of equity indicators such as the regional distribution of students, their socio-economic backgrounds, age, physical disability and sex. Finally, support systems and strategies put in place to enhance equity of access to private university education are considered.

Access to university education

Recruitment & admission policies

Recruitment and admission policies have critical implications for equity of access to university education because they provide the procedures followed to realize the goals of the access policy. As an admission requirement, the four private universities utilize Kenya's national minimum cut-off grade of C+ in the Kenya Certificate of Secondary Education examinations for Kenyan students. For non-Kenyan students, minimum university requirements in their own countries are used. In addition, USIU and UEAB require international students to provide proof of proficiency in English. Although the minimum cut-off grade is C+, the quality of students in the private universities has continued to improve, with A and B students being attracted to these universities. USIU has had to set up a waiting list in response to the high demand for its courses, reflecting both the perception of the quality of its graduates and the success of its marketing strategies, which include advertisements through the print media, churches, exhibitions and alumni associations. The frequent interruptions of instruction that lengthen the training period at the public universities may also help to explain the growing preference for private universities. Furthermore, the private universities offer the only opportunity of pursuing university education for many qualified students who fail to gain admission to the public universities.

Apart from academic requirements, all the private universities in the sample except USIU made religious affiliation a criterion for admission. While CUEA and UEAB require students to respect the institutions' religious teachings and practices (Catholic and Seventh-day Adventist, respectively), Daystar looks for proof of students' commitment to Christianity. To this end, students provide reference letters from their pastors or church leaders, the content of which is verified by an oral interview. Religious considerations are crucial for students enrolling in the religious private universities because, as revealed by student interviews, survival at these universities is largely dependent on how successfully they can adhere to the religious practices and activities which constitute a major part of the university calendar.

Even though religion is a criterion for admission to the church-sponsored private universities, private university officials claimed that no student was turned away because of his/her faith. What clearly emerged from the study was the fact that students seek admission to universities where they think they will be 'comfortable' as regards religion. Furthermore, some students were sponsored by their churches, thus explaining their preference for particular universities. Religious affiliation was confirmed by statistics indicating that the majority of the students enrolled in religion-based universities had a religious background similar or related to that of these institutions. For example, while the Daystar students' sample was 100 per cent Protestant, data from the admission records showed that 69 per cent of students at CUEA were Catholics, and 54 per cent of the students at UEAB were Seventh-day Adventists. The fact that there were

141

students of other faiths attending most of the religion-based private universities meant that religion was not a compulsory requirement for admission. UEAB suggests that, while the university recognizes a serious responsibility to serve the Seventh-day Adventist community, admission is open to all students willing to abide by university policies (www.tagnet.org/ueab). However, the study found that some students misrepresented or exaggerated their religious commitment in order to gain admission to the religion-based institutions.

The study also found that the four private universities did not limit admissions on the basis of sex, age or nationality. Researchers examined the flexibility of admission procedures to determine whether they served non-traditional students such as older or mature students, part-time students and younger students who did not meet the standard requirements. Daystar and CUEA had pre-university programmes that provide a second chance of admission for students who initially do not meet the university entry requirements. USIU scrapped its pre-university programme in 1990, when demand for these courses grew tremendously. The programme's aim had been to feed students into the undergraduate classes. Working and mature students were catered for through evening and weekend classes as well as part-time provisions. With this flexible time structure, students could break off from and resume classes at their own convenience. UEAB does not have these provisions because its out-of-town location impedes accessibility for prospective working students.

All four private universities also attracted non-traditional students through their mature-entry programmes where work experience and other training are taken into consideration during admission. However, UEAB and Daystar limited access to this programme by considering ministry in their respective churches as a requirement. Similarly, all four private universities broadened access by allowing the transfer of credits from previous courses undertaken in other accredited universities and colleges. However, Daystar had additional innovations in admissions policy in terms of short-term and bridging courses in English for aspiring communications and language majors. Daystar also had an outpost programme, where the university conducted training sessions at locations accessible to students, thus catering for those who could not easily reach the university because of location or the university calendar.

Finally, the study also noted another innovative strategy not found in most public universities, in the form of an additional semester/ quarter, known as the 'summer' quarter, which enabled students to accelerate their studies, hence shortening their period of study.

Trends in enrolment

The rate of enrolment in higher education indicates the national effort being invested in education and the ground that remains to be covered, as well as imbalances that need to be corrected (Ronto-poulou, 1999). An analysis of the enrolment patterns in the private universities is important in view of the growing social demand for university education in Kenya and the inability of the public universities to absorb more than one-third of the qualified students.

Enrolments in the four private universities grew significantly over the years from 1997 to 2001. Table II.2 shows the enrolment trends in the four private universities studied.

Table II.2: Enrolment trends, 1997–2001: number of students enrolled

	1997	1998	1999	2000	2001
USIU	1,855	2,207	2,157	2,200	2,300
Daystar	1,212	1,616	1,851	1,596	1,727
CUEA	1,342	1,281	1,354	1,489	1,597
UEAB	862	851	1,065	1,067	1,200

Between 1997 and 2001, enrolment growth was highest at Daystar (43 per cent), followed closely by UEAB (39 per cent), while USIU and CUEA registered increases of 24 per cent and 19 per cent respectively. There is currently a waiting list at USIU, due to the fact that the number of qualified applicants exceeds its capacity. Explanations for this growth provided by top administrators and students in all four private universities were relatively similar: (i) the private universities are not affected by the same disturbances which bring about delays in the public universities; (ii) they provide an environment conducive to learning due to the availability of high-quality social amenities and learning resources; (iii) they provide a good social environment through strict discipline and high moral standards, especially in the case of church-sponsored universities; and (iv) they offer 'marketable' courses and in turn produce 'marketable graduates'.

The study went on to analyse enrolments in particular disciplines. Table II.3 gives the average student enrolment percentages in various faculties or schools in the selected private universities in the 1999/2000 academic year. Due to the small number of science

143

Table II.3: Average student enrolment per school/faculty/ discipline, 1999–2000

University/Faculty	Student Enrolment	%
USIU		
Business Administration	1,755	81
Arts & Sciences	404	19
CUEA		
Arts & Social Sciences	576	40
Theology	856	60
UEAB		
Business Studies	197	18
Science & Technology	543	51
Humanities	327	31
Daystar		
Arts	385	27
Social Sciences	1,046	72
Science & Technology	16	1
(mathematics only)		

students at USIU and for purposes of analysis, Science has been merged with Arts.

Business studies (including accounting, commerce, business administration and management, marketing and economics) seem to be quite popular wherever they are offered and attract the majority of students (50 per cent on average). At Daystar, for example, out of the 1,046 students in the Faculty of Arts and Social Sciences, 719 (69 per cent) were pursuing business studies. At USIU a stunning 81 per cent of students were taking business administration. A similar trend is observed at CUEA, where 18 per cent of the students in the School of Arts and Sciences study commerce, although it is only one of eight different departments. University administrators attribute this demand to the fact that business studies classes are market-oriented.

The low demand for business studies at UEAB is the exception, which might be explained in terms of its location and the competition offered by the equally marketable science and technology courses (comprising industrial technology and nursing). In the past, UEAB had enjoyed a monopoly in these science disciplines, being almost the only university to offer them. However, it now faces competition following the introduction of a nursing course at the University of Nairobi.

The findings of this study confirm the general impression that humanities, social sciences and especially business studies are the main domain of the private universities (Murunga, 2001). Given the proposed introduction of science and technology courses in all the universities' strategic plans, concerns about course diversity may be minimized in the future. In some cases, however, the private universities that did introduce science subjects have seen minimal results. At CUEA, for instance, science subjects only serve the Education Department.

We shall consider below whether the generally increased access indicated by the enrolment growth depicted above includes wider access for disadvantaged groups, in terms of students' regional origins, age, socio-economic backgrounds and physical disabilities.

Equity of access

Regional origin of students

In accordance with their mission statements which advocate non-discrimination as it pertains to nationality, the four private universities drew students from over 60 countries. Figures II.2 and II.3 give a breakdown of students' country of origin for CUEA and USIU whose student records were readily available.

Despite the international representation which might promote a diversity of cultural experiences for students, the great majority of them (91 per cent on average) were Kenyans. The study set out to

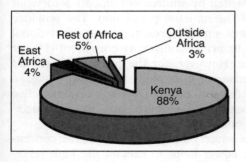

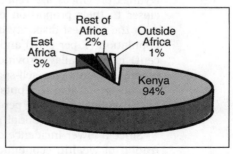

Figure II.2: Students' region of origin (CUEA)

Figure II.3: Students' region of origin (USIU)

145

Table II.4: Province of origin of private university students (%)

University	North Eastern	Eastern	Central	Western	Coast	Rift Valley	Nyanza	Nairobi
USIU	3	8	21	16	8	11	8	25
Daystar	0	19	32	3	2	19	10	15
CUEA	0	17	19	19	1	16	18	10
UEAB	0	9	3	12	5	29	30	12
Total average	0.75	13	19	13	4	19	17	16
% of national population	0.3	16	13	12	9	7	15	25

discover whether the private universities duplicate the experience of the public universities in drawing the largest share of students from the traditionally privileged provinces in Kenya's history of educational development (Court and Kinyanjui, 1980). Unfortunately, it was not possible to obtain details concerning students' home districts from the admission records. Consequently, information from student questionnaires was used to give a general picture of the students' regional backgrounds (Table II.4).

Table II.4 shows that the private universities, like the public universities, drew most of their students from historically advantaged districts such as Nairobi and Central Province, which experienced the early development of schools as a result of early missionary activity (Achola, 1997; Court and Kinyanjui, 1980). Central Province accounts for 13 per cent of Kenya's population and roughly 19 per cent of private university students, while Western and Nyanza provinces are represented by student enrolments somewhat closer to their proportion of the national population. The province with the greatest disparity between its representation in the national population (7 per cent) and its private university enrolment (19 per cent) is Rift Valley Province. However, for the private universities where students are self-sponsored, economic status also played a crucial role. Table II.5 puts regional economic power in perspective by providing regional percentages of poverty and the provinces' percentage of the national population.

Since a lower incidence of poverty should reflect a higher concentration of wealth, economic power helps to explain the high representation of private university students from Nairobi and Central and Rift Valley provinces and the low representation from North Eastern

146

Table II.5: Regional distribution of poverty

Region	% poverty incidence	% of national population
Nairobi	26.6	25
Central	31.2	13
Coast	48.3	9
Eastern	55.8	16
North Eastern	50.6	0.3
Nyanza	42.1	15
Rift Valley	41.2	7
Western	53.0	12

Source: GoK, 1998.

and Eastern Regions, the last despite its high population. However, location also emerged as an additional factor in explaining regional representation in the private universities. For example, the high representation of students from Rift Valley and Nyanza provinces at UEAB and from Central and Nairobi provinces in the other three universities could be explained by physical proximity to the universities.

Student socio-economic background

In view of the high fees charged by the private universities, the general impression is that most students come from higher socio-economic backgrounds. Student questionnaires regarding the highest educational levels of their parents as an indicator of socio-economic status (see GoK, 1998; Achola, 1997) reveal that a surprisingly large number of both parents have completed college or university education. Some 273 of the 565 fathers (48.3 per cent) were reported to have university degrees, while another 158 had college diplomas, bringing the total to 431 (or 76.3 per cent). Similar numbers were reported for the mothers of private university students surveyed: 40 per cent possessed a college diploma, while another 32 per cent had a university degree, suggesting a high socio-economic background and therefore presumably the ability to pay the high fees charged.

Concerns about gender, age & special needs

Although the education of girls has higher returns to society than that of boys, their participation in higher education continues to be less than expected (Achola, 1997; GoK, 1998). The lower enrolment of female students in Kenya's public universities has been documented by many studies (Achola, 1997; Eshiwani, 1983: 84). This

147

Table II.6: Undergraduate enrolments by sex, 1998–2000

	1998			1999			2000		
	M	**F**	**F%**	**M**	**F**	**F%**	**M**	**F**	**F%**
Daystar	726	935	56	-	-	-	666	930	58
CUEA	650	633	49	731	623	46	725	764	51
UEAB	458	393	47	548	517	49	540	527	49
USIU	923	1,052	53	925	1,035	53	1,056	1,144	52
Total	2,757	3,013	52	2,204	2,175	50	2,987	3,365	53

study, however, shows a markedly different trend for the private universities. The percentage enrolment of women in the four selected universities over the three-year period 1998–2000 is shown in Table II.6. The results show gender equity in enrolments, with an average female to male ratio of 53:47 for 2000.

The relatively higher participation of female students at private than at public universities can be attributed to four factors: (i) high levels of discipline and the good learning environments reassure parents of their daughters' safety in college; (ii) the private universities are not only cheaper than foreign universities but are close enough to home for parents to be able to monitor their daughters' academic and social progress; (iii) most courses in the private universities are in the humanities and social sciences which are popular with women; and (iv) many female secondary school leavers with good grades in humanities and languages fail to get admission to public universities. These explanations should be viewed within the context of the broader reasons for the choice of private universities, where affordability and the fewer interruptions in teaching during the academic year play a crucial role. Table II.7 below shows male and female students' enrolment by area of specialization at the four universities.

Despite higher female enrolment, the private universities mirror the situation in the public universities where female students are concentrated in supposedly feminine disciplines such as humanities and social sciences. The strong female participation in science and technology at UEAB is attributed to the large number of women who study nursing, considered a traditionally female specialty. Yet relatively similar numbers of women and men are studying business at all four private universities, suggesting that the older stereotypes may be changing.

Students made suggestions on how to increase the participation of female students in university education, including (i) the award of

148

Table II.7: Enrolment by sex and area of specialization, 1999

	Business studies			Humanities/ Social sciences			Science and technology		
	M	F	F%	M	F	F%	M	F	F%
USIU	887	886	50	129	275	68	–	–	–
CUEA	241	287	54	258	318	55	41	7	15[a]
Daystar	341	324	49	136	291	68	–	–	–
UEAB	112	96	46	152	165	52	285	256	47

Note: a) Science and technology programmes for CUEA include only mathematics.

scholarships, bursaries and loans to deserving female applicants; (ii) preferential admission for female candidates through affirmative action; (iii) tuition waivers for female students from poor socio-economic backgrounds; and (iv) persuading parents of the benefits of educating female children. For gender parity to be attained in the long run, however, these suggestions need to be implemented at the lowest levels of the education system, because gender disparities in education begin at the pre-primary level and cumulate as one goes higher up the education ladder (Kanake, 1997).

Flexible admission procedures and timetables facilitate mature students' pursuit of higher education. Although all four private universities had mature students, specific data were available only at USIU. Table II.8 gives a general picture of enrolments at USIU by age and sex.

Table II.8: USIU student enrolment trends by age and sex, 1996–9

	Under 25 years			26–34 years			35 years and above		
	M	F	F%	M	F	F%	M	F	F%
1999	786	897	53	149	150	50	96	95	50
1998	582	737	56	260	230	47	89	62	41
1997	608	638	51	311	249	45	58	54	48
1996	352	711	67	333	296	47	95	78	45

Source: USIU student admission records.

It shows that the great majority of students at USIU were under the age of 25, with most of them enrolled in undergraduate programmes. Adults over 26 constituted some 33 per cent of the total number, with 53 per cent women.

149

The study also considered physical disability as a variable in access and equity. All four universities had very few physically disabled students; three of them had fewer than ten, and Daystar had none. Even the few who enrolled tended to drop out. These findings confirm the fears that, even when physically challenged students are admitted, they are unlikely to remain because the universities do not cater adequately for their needs. Suggestions made by students to improve the general access of those with special needs were similar to those given for gender equity, except for the additional provision of special facilities and courses that address physical disability. However, it should be borne in mind that most physically challenged students in Kenya drop out of the school system early and may not be eligible for university enrolment.

Gender equity in university administration, teaching & research

Women in Kenya, as in many other African countries, have lagged behind men in their access to formal education (Koech, 2000). Consequently, fewer women are able to take up academic and administrative positions within the universities. In Kanake's study of the public universities, women accounted for a small percentage of university lecturers, especially in technical courses and in administration (Kanake, 1997). The results from the private universities showed a similar trend, as shown in Table II.9.

Table II.9: Staff participation in teaching and administration by sex, 2000

University	Deans			Heads of Departments			Senior Lecturers			Lecturers			Assistant Lecturers			Total % Female Staff		
	M	F	%F	M	F	%F	M	F	%F	M	F	%F	M	F	%F	M	F	%F
USIU	3	0	0	10	2	17	33	5	13	73	16	18	–	–	–	106	21	17
Daystar	3	0	0	9	3	25	23	16	41	36	18	33	18	7	28	77	41	35
CUEA	2	0	0	15	2	12	7	0	0	8	2	20	46	23	33	61	25	29
UEAB	4	0	0	14	3	18	14	4	22	37	4	10	18	8	31	69	19	22

Note: – represents cases where statistics were not available.

As can be seen in Table II.10, the majority of women academic staff at UEAB in 2001 were concentrated in family and consumer science (where they accounted for 100 per cent of staff) and in

Table II.10: UEAB academic staff distribution by subject and sex, 2001

Subject area Department	Distribution by sex		
	Male	Female	% Female
Languages & literature	4	6	60
Management	3	3	50
Technology	8	0	0
Biological sciences	3	3	50
Nursing	3	6	67
Educational guidance & counselling	3	0	0
Agriculture	6	0	0
Physical sciences & maths	5	2	29
Accounting	3	0	0
Geography & history	4	0	0
Theology & religious studies.	6	1	14
Information & computer science	1	0	0
Curriculum & teaching	2	2	50
Family & consumer science	0	5	100
Music	1	1	50
Total	52	29	36

nursing (67 per cent). Similarly, many women were concentrated in languages and literature (60 per cent). All these are regarded as feminine professions. Pertaining to the participation of women in teaching, Table II.10 confirms that the situation in the private universities was similar to that in the public universities (Kanake, 1997) where fewer women than men are members of academic staff. Of the four private universities studied, Daystar hires the most women for its teaching staff. According to administrators at Daystar, where personal salvation is a major criterion for recruitment, this situation has come about because there are generally more women than men who are 'born again' Christians to draw from in Kenya. Similar trends were observed at the administrative level, with fewer women holding positions of dean of faculty and head of department. UISU was the only university with a female Vice-Chancellor.

The relatively high female enrolments at the undergraduate level in the private universities were not reflected in the participation of female academic staff in senior administrative positions and higher academic grades that reflect attainment of higher degrees. This observation should be viewed, however, against the possibility that the poorer participation of women at lower educational levels hindered their effective participation at university.

151

Strategies to enhance equity of access

In addition to quantitative indicators of equity of access, this study examined qualitative measures of students' experiences within the institutions. This approach is based on the fact that success in meeting an institution's mission to broaden opportunities within higher education is achieved not simply by recruiting greater numbers of non-traditional students into the system but also by ensuring that the new students receive the support they need in order to thrive (Woodward, 2000). A look at institutional measures put in place to address equity of access is therefore imperative.

University policies & support systems

The policy statements of all four universities reveal the institutions' explicit commitment to providing equal opportunities for all. All four articulated policies of non-discrimination based on sex, nationality, ethnic origin, age or socio-economic status and religion (apart from Daystar in the matter of religion). However, a critical examination shows that, except for mature students (for whom flexible admission procedures apply) and the physically challenged (who are provided with special facilities), there were no specific measures in place for students in the other categories. Although the private universities attracted very few disabled students, for example, there are no specific strategies to recruit them. Similarly, it is not by design that the private universities attract more female students, because no specific efforts were made to recruit them.

Four particular support systems can help non-traditional and under-represented students to succeed in private universities once they are enrolled: guidance and counselling, orientation, financial aid and special facilities.

(i) Guidance and counselling departments play an important role in private universities in assisting students in academic, non-academic and social matters. The non-traditional students experience special problems in adjusting to new environments (especially for international students), issues regarding the payment of fees by students from poor families, and sexual harassment for female students. In addition to the presence of professional counsellors, the private universities also use peer counsellors to enhance the services of these departments. Found in USIU and CUEA, the novelty of this approach lies in the fact that students welcome the chance to interact with fellow students who identify with their problems.

(ii) Orientation programmes found in all four universities acquaint students with the manner in which the universities operate and their expectations of students. These are particularly useful for non-traditional students. The study noted that the quality of orientation in the private universities was better than that observed in most public universities, especially in terms of the content covered. While orientation in both categories of universities lasted one week, that at the private universities covered more aspects, including a thorough introduction to courses and units, acquaintance with academic premises and procedures and various social activities, including sports and clubs which most public universities do not cover. This process grounds non-traditional students in the university system, thus minimizing potential drop-outs.

(iii) Financial aid for students who cannot meet their educational expenses is an essential element in achieving equity of access, especially in the private universities where the fees are high. The private universities provide relatively substantial support for the promotion of equity of access through such financial aid programmes as work-study, scholarships and tuition waivers. However, these programmes meet only part of the students' needs. For example, while tuition fees on average amount to at least Kshs.40,000 per quarter, students can earn a maximum of Kshs.15,000 from the work-study programme, covering no more than 27 per cent of their tuition costs.

(iv) Institutional facilities of high quality encourage non-traditional students to participate in university activities and eventually to graduate. The four private universities had special facilities for the physically disabled in the form of ramps in the buildings and, at USIU, special toilets. However, these catered primarily for lame students; the needs of students with other disabilities were not necessarily addressed.

All four private universities provided separate accommodation facilities for female students, even though in some cases these were rather limited. CUEA, for example, provides accommodation only for a few female students and the clergy (priests and nuns). UEAB provided housing facilities for married students, thus catering for the needs of mature students with families. The study found that students were critical of transport facilities in all the universities except USIU, facilities that might be especially useful for mature students and part-time women students (see Table II.11).

The private universities studied tended to approach questions of equity indirectly through the curriculum and extra-curricular activities. For example, gender was addressed in courses on human sexuality, community development, sociology, psychology and other

153

Table II.11: Student levels of satisfaction with facilities and services

Facilities & services	% Satisfaction	% Dissatisfaction
Sports/recreational		
USIU	57	17
Daystar	26	50
CUEA	66	14
UEAB	49	40
Accommodation/residential		
USIU	50	20
Daystar	30	54
CUEA	12	72
UEAB	69	19
Food/catering		
USIU	43	51
Daystar	28	57
CUEA	25	59
UEAB	39	48
Transport/communication		
USIU	67	17
Daystar	18	77
CUEA	19	70
UEAB	29	61
Student financial aid		
USIU	46	24
Daystar	37	31
CUEA	38	53
UEAB	63	20

social sciences. Similarly, activities that promoted equity awareness included outreach programmes on HIV/AIDS, community service to hospitals, donation of food and clothing to the less fortunate and the Disability Awareness Day observed at USIU. Given the absence of direct approaches to equity, the private universities might consider setting up departments or institutes of gender studies or adding special education courses.

Officials at all four private universities said that they maintained an open-door policy in order to bring about better communication between students and the administration. While this is simpler in smaller institutions, there is no doubt that it is a sound communication strategy which plays an important role in creating a conducive atmosphere for students to discuss their problems. Less of the red-tape bureaucracy experienced in the public universities is noticeable in the private ones. Some students, however, expressed the opinion that good communications skills were scarce amongst staff members, and suggested that the latter should be trained in public relations.

Equity monitoring & evaluation

It is important for institutions to have a process in place for assessing periodically whether they are meeting their own goals of providing equal opportunity for all. USIU monitored two aspects of equity in the form of sex-disaggregated statistics in its prospectus and other documents and analysis of the number of students from poor socio-economic backgrounds in its financial analysis statements. The other three universities made no such attempt.

Private universities play a major role in increasing access to university education in Kenya through flexible admission procedures and programmes, including pre-university, mature entry, transfer of credit, bridging courses and outpost programmes. However, further access could be attained through a greater diversity of courses and the provision of increased admission for students from disadvantaged regions and poor socio-economic backgrounds, and the physically challenged.

155

4 Curriculum & Learning Systems

Political, social, economic and technological changes have had a profound impact on higher education in Kenya. This chapter discusses some of the challenges facing private universities with regard to curriculum and learning systems: improving the content of existing curricula, adopting appropriate teaching methods that go beyond lectures and audio-visual tools, building up a full-time faculty, improving library and learning resources, and developing structures and systems for managing change.

The private universities involved in this study offer programmes in liberal arts, social sciences and applied sciences. Each university has its own philosophy, mission and values that determine the curricula and courses offered. Apart from USIU, the curricula of the other three universities are informed by their Christian philosophies and values.

Academic programmes

The United States International University's core academic programmes are business studies and applied information technology. To develop students' ability to cope with global technological changes, the university mandates all students to take units in information technology. The extent to which USIU had achieved this goal was demonstrated by student respondents who registered a high degree of satisfaction with intellectual development (72.8 per cent), development of study skills and work habits (75.3 per cent) and relevance of courses to labour market requirements (71.6 per cent).

Courses offered at Daystar University are intended to be particularly responsive to the contemporary African situation. Such courses included Contemporary Conflicts in Africa, Communication Systems in Africa, Urbanization in Africa and Contextualizing African Christian Theology. These programmes were designed to offer comprehensive training based on biblical values defined as integrity, sacrifice, honesty, love, commitment and hard work. Like the students at USIU, respondents from Daystar registered satisfaction with intellectual development (71.7 per cent), development of study skills and work habits (72.9 per cent) and relevance of courses to labour market requirements (83.5 per cent).

The Catholic University of Eastern Africa's core programmes are education, business and religious studies. Before designing its curricular offering, CUEA carried out market surveys the results of which led to the introduction of bachelor of commerce, bachelor of science (computer science) and theology/religious studies programmes. New programmes in medicine and pharmacy are also planned in response to the surveys. The university has also initiated Masters and Ph.D. programmes to boost its research capacity. CUEA is the only one of the four universities to offer a doctoral programme. Student respondents' levels of satisfaction with intellectual development and development of study skills and work habits (66.3 per cent and 71.3 per cent, respectively) were much higher than their satisfaction with the relevance of their courses to labour market requirements (56.3 per cent).

The University of East Africa, Baraton offered courses in medical sciences (nursing and public health), automotive technology, agriculture, liberal arts and business studies, among others. All students are required to take courses in Christian beliefs and teachings. Student respondents at UEAB expressed high rates of satisfaction with intellectual development (79.3 per cent), development of study skills and work habits (75.6 per cent) and relevance of courses to the labour market (76.8 per cent). However, students criticized the lack of adequate staff to deliver some of the courses; programmes affected include nursing, Masters in public health (MPH) and electronics. Table II.12 shows the programmes currently offered by the four private universities and those they intend to introduce in future, along with a description of each university's competitive niche.

Table II.12: Courses offered at USIU, Daystar, UEAB and CUEA

Current Courses	Planned
USIU	
BA (International Relations; Journalism; Psychology)	Environmental Science, Physics,
BSc (Business Administration; Hotel & Restaurant Management; Information System & Technology; International Business Administration; Tourism Management)	Electronic/ Telecommunications Engineering
MA (Psychology; International Relations)	
MBA (Masters in Business Administration)	
MIBA (Masters in International Business Administration)	**Niche:**
MSc (Management & Organisational Development)	Business Studies

Table II.12: cont.

Current Courses	Planned
Daystar	
BA (Bible and Religious studies, Communication, Community Development, English and Psychology), BCom (Accounting, Business Administration and Management and Marketing) BEd (Accounting, Bible, Business Administration & Management, Economics, English, Marketing and Music), BSc (Economics, Applied Computer Science).	MBA MSc (Management, French, Management Information systems, Special Education) Postgraduate Diploma in Education, Law, Public Relations, Electronic & Chemical Engineering, Bio-Chemistry **Niche:** Communication Studies
CUEA	
BA (Geography, History, Religious Studies and Social Sciences) BCom (Accounting, Business Administration, Management, Banking & Finance and Marketing, Computer science) BEd (Social Education & Ethics, Geography, Christian Religious Education, History, Economics, Business Studies, English and Mathematics) MA (Education, Religious Studies, & Philosophy) PhD (Religious Studies)	Bachelor of Pharmacy Bachelor of Medicine BSc (Chemistry & Biological Sciences) **Niche:** Education & Religious Studies
UEAB	
BA (History, Geography, English, Kiswahili, Music) BBA (Bachelor of Business Administration) (Accounting, Business Information Technology, Marketing, Business Management, Networks & Communication Systems, Office Administration, Software Engineering), BEd (Guidance & Counselling, English, History, Geography, Kiswahili, Religion, Home Economics, Mathematics, Biology, Chemistry, Agriculture, & Physics), BSc (Agriculture & Agribusiness) BT (Agriculture) BSc (Biology & Zoology, Clinical Laboratory Science, Family & Consumer, Nursing, Chemistry, Mathematics) BST (Bachelor of Science & Technology) (Automotive Technology, Electronic Engineering, Technology with Education, & Construction Technology) MEd (Educational Administration, Curriculum & Instruction)	MA (Religion), Master of Divinity **Niche:** Agriculture, nursing & automotive technology

158

Even though these universities offered a range of courses, they have each carved out a niche for themselves in particular disciplines: communications (Daystar), business (USIU), education (CUEA) and medical sciences and technology (UEAB). USIU plans to introduce new programmes in communication and engineering, Daystar in business and law, CUEA in medicine and biological sciences and UEAB in theology and information technology. All four are in the process of introducing computer sciences and information technology as distinct courses rather than simply as supplements to their core subjects. The fact that they all have similar academic programmes offers them opportunities for collaboration in areas such as the exchange of external examiners, inter-university graduate work supervision and research and peer evaluation. Such collaboration could enhance the quality of their programmes, although specialization may offer different competitive benefits.

Students were asked their opinions on various aspects of the curriculum in their universities. Their responses were diverse but showed an overwhelming consensus on the need for improving computer facilities and internet access (see Table II.13).

The findings on intellectual growth, development of study and work habits and labour market requirements were in line with the guiding philosophy for education and training in Kenya as envisioned in Sessional Paper No. 6 of 1988 on Education and Training for the Next Decade and Beyond. The sessional paper emphasized that training should aim at producing individuals who are properly socialized and who possess the necessary knowledge, skills, attitudes and values to enable them to participate more productively in national development. A lecturer at CUEA said that the university inculcated in students the spirit of hard work and honesty and that a number of schools preferred its graduates because of these attributes. The registrar shared the same sentiments: 'Today what will help our students is if they are computer literate and if they are sincere. Nobody will take them if they are insincere. We are trying to inject morality and have students who are computer literate. New Zealand has taken more than ten of our students, Geneva and Cairo last week took two. There are things employers are looking for today, that is: academics and behaviour' (personal interview, 2000).

According to the former Vice-Chancellor of Daystar University, 'Education without character does not produce a leader in Africa. It is like educating a thief, which only makes one an educated thief.'

159

Table II.13: Student levels of satisfaction with the curriculum

Satisfied	Dissatisfied
USIU	
Adequacy and appropriateness of books and learning conditions in the library (76.5%)	Diversity of courses (69.2%)
Prestige of the university (76.5%)	Personal qualities of instructors/ lecturers (60.4%)
Development of study skills and work habits (75.3%)	
Computer facilities and internet access (59.3%)	
Daystar	
Relevance of course to labour market needs/ requirements (83.5%)	Computer facilities (36.5%)
Development of study skills and work habits (72.9%)	Adequacy and appropriateness of books and learning conditions in the library (44.7%).
Intellectual development (71.7%)	Method and criteria of student's evaluation (42.3%)
CUEA	
Content & structure of courses offered (73.8%)	Adequacy and appropriateness of books and learning conditions in the library (47.5%)
Quality of instruction (71.3%)	Methods of evaluating students (51.3%)
Development of study skills and work habits (71.3%)	Adequacy of computer facilities (50%)
UEAB	
Amount and quality of attention and feedback from instructor/ lecturer (85.3%)	Adequacy of computer facilities (42.7%)
Intellectual development (79.3%)	Adequacy and appropriateness of books and learning conditions in library (31.7%)
Quality of instruction (78.1%)	Prestige of my department (24.4%)

Curriculum delivery & teaching resources

Meaningful learning activities, organized in a systematic manner, represent the heart of the curriculum, as these shape the learners' experiences and education. The teaching and learning methods used in the four private universities included lectures, discussions, demonstrations, field trips, individual assignments/practicals, group work and seminars.

160

USIU has introduced e-learning (discussed below), for which students were required to take foundation courses in computer literacy. In addition, they made significant use of information and communication technologies for faculty-student communication on the Intranet, had a library stocked with up-to-date resources and subscribed to electronic databases with over 6,000 titles of full text materials, abstracts and indexes.

The challenge of delivering continuous lifelong learning at the learners' convenience requires these institutions to explore novel pedagogical methods including participatory training and learning approaches, e-learning and distance-learning. If higher education institutions embrace and sustain their redefined roles as 'facilitators of lifelong learning', they will reform their curricula accordingly.

Teaching and learning resources used in the universities investigated included computers, the internet, videos, visual aids (overhead and LCD projectors), books, online journals and CD-ROM databases. Significantly, students in all four institutions considered that these resources were insufficient (Table II.13). The institutions have developed strategic plans to address some of these constraints. For example, Daystar plans to network its two libraries (Athi River and Valley Road) and increase the libraries' collection to a minimum of 75,000 volumes. USIU's strategic plan (2000–04) sought to achieve the following: construct a new library to accommodate 1,000 readers, purchase 180,000 books by 2003, increase access to online databases and upgrade the existing media centre and make it fully operational to complement library and print materials. As for information and communication technology resources, USIU planned to increase and upgrade its computers and software. For its part, CUEA intended to establish a bookshop to help fill gaps in the library collection and to computerize its library services. UEAB planned to construct an audiovisual centre that would supplement books in the library. It also intended to set up a computer room in the library to enable it to expand its range of non-book materials.

Student dissatisfaction with learning resources, the personal qualities of instructors, and computer facilities and internet access at several of the universities indicates some deficiencies in the current curricula and their delivery.

Relevance & quality of new programmes

The introduction of new courses (applied computer science, management information systems and business administration) is in line

161

with the global trends in higher education, which place greater emphasis on the new (information) economy and technological advances. These new courses will give students a competitive advantage and sharpen the skills of those already working. The four universities surveyed were at various stages of introducing programmes in computer science and business studies. Their research divisions, in partnership with industry and alumni, conducted market surveys to determine interest in and the relevance of new courses, following which, proposals had to be approved by the departmental board, the faculty board, the senate, the council and finally the CHE. The urge to introduce new market-driven courses was so strong that one institution admitted students to a new computer science programme before the CHE had approved its curriculum. As it turned out, the CHE found the content insufficient, and major changes were recommended.

USIU offers courses in business, information technology, and cross-cultural skills and other internationally competitive courses to prepare students for the changing and increasingly technological world. In April 2000, the School of Business at USIU began applying for professional accreditation to two leading global associations for such institutions – the European Foundation for Management Development (EFMD) and the US-based Association to Advance Collegiate Schools of Business. In September 2001, in collaboration with the United States International College of Business in San Diego, it formally applied for accreditation by EFMD in order to ensure that its programmes met international standards.

UEAB introduced new programmes in business information technology, software engineering, networks and communication engineering, public health and clinical science. Apparently the university had not fully considered its lack of available faculty in some of these areas. For example, the lecturers handling the public health programme were all volunteers from Loma Linda University in the United States. This must have hindered satisfactory student/ teacher interaction, since the lecturers were able to come to Kenya only for specific periods. Secondly, the university had only two lecturers in information systems and computing, which meant that it had to rely on part-timers to teach these programmes effectively. Finally, when CUEA introduced an applied computer science programme, it faced similar staffing problems. The lack of a qualified faculty to implement the new programmes, especially in information technology and business studies, was a common problem among the universities surveyed, a problem that becomes more pronounced when they mount similar programmes in fields where qualified staff are scarce.

162

Student evaluation

Assessment criteria help to determine the competence of graduates of any given institution and provide a way of comparing the quality of graduates from similar institutions. While CUEA and UEAB used both internal and external assessment, USIU and Daystar used only internal assessment. By 2002, however, Daystar University had begun to engage external examiners, even though this was not yet official policy. Expert opinion from external moderators can help standardize and even improve the quality of examinations, and therefore help these institutions conform to external expectations of quality.

Administrators at the private universities that did not carry out external evaluation argued that its effectiveness varied according to the competence of the external examiners, even though it is their responsibility to identify external examiners well versed in the subjects being examined. Using internal assessment only may reinforce negative stereotypes about the quality of the education offered in the private universities, although such concerns might be allayed in response to greater 'intellectual cross-fertilization' through peer review of examinations as well as external regulation.

All four private universities used the Grade Point Average (GPA) system. The GPA is obtained by dividing the total number of points earned by the total number of units undertaken. Whereas some students were satisfied with the methods and criteria for student evaluation (USIU, 65.5 per cent and UEAB, 71.9 per cent), others were dissatisfied (Daystar, 42.3 per cent and CUEA, 51.3 per cent). Students at Daystar were dissatisfied with the grading system because they had to score above 90 per cent to get an 'A', which they felt was too high a standard.

Faculty/student ratios

Teacher/student ratios are one important determinant of the quality of instruction, as they foster (or militate against) continuous contact between faculty and students. It is essential in this context to distinguish between full-time and part-time staff. The faculty/student ratios for USIU, Daystar, CUEA and UEAB were 1:17, 1:18, 1:12 and 1:14, respectively. Although the general faculty/student ratio seemed reasonable, a disaggregated analysis reveals disparities across departments. For example, there were proportionately more lecturers in humanities than in applied science and business programmes, reflecting the difficulty of recruiting staff in the latter areas.

Recruitment policies also affect the ability of some universities to

163

Table II.14: Full-time/part-time academic staff ratios, 2001

| University | Academic staff numbers | | |
	Full-time (FT)	Part-time (PT)	FT : PT ratio[a]
USIU	40	100	1:2.5
Daystar	100	30	3:1
UEAB	51	31	5:3
CUEA	76	58	4:3

Note: a) ratios are broadly rounded.

attract qualified staff. For example, UEAB insists on full-time faculty being Seventh-day Adventists. The university administration admitted that meeting the twin criteria of academic competence and faith was difficult, resulting in a continued reliance on part-timers who were not required to be members of the faith. While having more instructors lowers faculty/student ratios and may improve the quality of instruction, part-time staff may devote less time to students. Table II.14 shows the distribution of full-time and part-time staff in the four private universities studied.

USIU began with entirely part-time staff but had built a sizeable full-time faculty by 2001. Although the other three universities insist on the importance of full-time faculty, they still have a high proportion of part-time staff. The difficulties in recruiting staff in the areas of business studies and information technology are likely to continue for some time.

Research

Research and teaching are the key components of higher education. However, the research component was found to be low in all four private universities. All undergraduate programmes were based on instruction rather than research, which was restricted to postgraduate studies and teaching staff. A faculty member observed during an interview that 'they train "products" for the market' and thus put more emphasis on teaching. The budgetary allocations for research in these universities also suggested that it was not a priority area. For the 1999/2000 financial year, for example, the funds allocated for research at USIU, Daystar, CUEA and UEAB amounted to 0.1 per cent (KShs.201,000), 1 per cent (Kshs. 4.3 million), 2 per cent (Kshs. 2.5 million) and 1 per cent (Kshs. 2 million) of recurrent expenditure, respectively.

Lecturers cited their heavy teaching workload and lack of financial resources as obstacles to conducting research. Lecturers at USIU had a teaching workload of 10 hours per week; those engaged in research received a reduction in workload of up to 5 hours (half the normal teaching load). Faculty at Daystar had a workload of 12 hours per week, and lecturers carrying out research were not given any reduction. The university was, however, working on a scheme to reduce the workload for those engaged in research. CUEA faculty had a teaching load of 9 hours per week; researchers were not given any reduction in workload and were encouraged to carry out research during their vacations. – an approach which makes time-bound research projects difficult to carry out. The university recognizes this critical problem and is making efforts to address it so that lecturers have time to conduct research.

It is clear that the four private universities put little emphasis on research even though their mission statements underscore the need for it. Research is one of the defining functions of universities world-wide, and enhancing research capabilities remains a challenge for the four private universities studied.

Library facilities

The library is one of the fundamental support facilities of a university. The institutions studied had varied ratios of books per student: USIU, 26:1; Daystar, 30:1; UEAB, 30:1 and CUEA, 40:1. These ratios fell below UNESCO's standard of 45 volumes per student, although three of them met the CHE's stipulation of 30 volumes per student.

The Commission on Higher Education stipulates that a university library's seating capacity should be equal to one-third of the total student population. The seating capacity of the USIU library was only 425, falling short of the CHE requirement mandating 800 seats. Daystar's capacity was 600, coming very close to the requirement (606). CUEA's library had a seating capacity of 440 students as compared with the required 534 students. UEAB's library had a capacity of 400 instead of a minimum of 500. Although the shortfall (except for USIU) was not big, the universities were already taking measures to accommodate the increased enrolments.

The four private universities had a comprehensive collection of both CD-ROM and online databases. Through the Programme for the Enhancement of Research Information (PERI) project, the Kenyan academic community and researchers are able to access over 8,000

165

electronic databases, free of charge, for a period of six years beginning in 2003. USIU, Daystar, CUEA and UEAB are all members of PERI, which is run by the International Network for the Availability of Scientific Publications (INASP) to support the dissemination of research information in developing countries.

Daystar University has no internet connection in its library and thus does not subscribe to online databases. However, it does have the CD-ROM version of the EBSCO databases. The university also subscribes to 150 academic and 30 non-academic journals and has annually updated subscriptions to CD-ROMs for the social sciences and business studies.

CUEA has internet access to electronic databases from Blackwell Publishers, African Journals Online (AJOL), the Online Computer Library Center (OCLC), Emerald and EBSCO. UEAB subscribes to electronic databases from Blackwell-Synergy, EBSCO and IDEAL databases, Cochrane Library, AJOL and the British Library Ordering Services. It also has CD-ROM databases.

All four university libraries offer related services, including reader services, interlibrary loan services, reservation/recall services and information and current awareness services. USIU and Daystar have multimedia centres that provide online and/or CD-ROM database searches, video viewing and audiocassette listening. The multimedia centre for USIU has 14 fully operational computer workstations in the library and on the campus-wide local area network (LAN). Daystar's media centre has 14 computer workstations used mainly for CD-ROM database searches.

USIU has a campus-wide LAN that enables users to access the online databases from anywhere on campus, giving them the convenience of searching the databases from their offices, laboratories and library. USIU's internet access is comparatively fast by Kenyan standards with a 64 kb/s leased line and VSAT (very small aperture terminal) technology. CUEA also has a 64 kb/s leased line, but database searches could only be undertaken in the library, where only five computers were reserved for online searches for both students and staff. UEAB initially relied on dial-up connections for internet access, which was slow and unreliable. However, when it acquired VSAT technology in 2003 the rate of information access improved greatly. Access to online databases at USIU, CUEA and UEAB has improved due to the use of leased lines and VSATs.

There were no systems in place at the university libraries to determine the usage of the CD-ROM databases and online databases. Sign-up sheets for students using the CD-ROMs in the four libraries are more of a security measure than a system to establish the usage and do not record the types of resources used.

University physical facilities

A university's physical facilities, including teaching and recreational facilities, determine student enrolment and the number of academic programmes it can offer. They also ultimately affect the quality of an individual student's experience. Daystar's physical facilities include an administrative block, 31 lecture rooms, two lecture theatres, six residential halls, a library, a chapel and an ultra-modern communication complex with communication studios, but most of the campus physical facilities are still under construction. Accommodation facilities at Daystar are inadequate, and most students have to commute between Nairobi and Athi River, limiting the degree to which they can utilize the Athi River facilities.

USIU has 20 classrooms, four seminar rooms, an administrative block, faculty conference rooms, a library, seminar rooms and a conference room at the student centre. All full-time faculty have dedicated offices, while part-time faculty use the faculty lounge and computer rooms as offices. The university also has two double-occupancy hostels with a capacity of 256 beds.

CUEA has an administration block, an auditorium, 19 lecture halls, three science laboratories, a microteaching laboratory, 14 seminar rooms, a geography laboratory, hostels and computer laboratories. UEAB has lecture rooms, seminar rooms, an administrative block, a library, a conference room, a computer centre, three workshops and three science laboratories (for biology, chemistry and physics).

Space utilization in all four universities is high, estimated at about 90 per cent throughout the year, with scheduled timetables for block study during semester breaks. The minimum learning facilities the CHE requires are classrooms/lecture rooms, staff offices and seminar rooms, central administration offices, a library, an auditorium/lecture theatre, staff common rooms, student common rooms with indoor recreational facilities, outdoor recreational facilities in the form of games or sports facilities and a dispensary. For residential universities, kitchen/dining facilities and hostels (or dormitories), including adequate laundry facilities, are also stipulated. CUEA, USIU, UEAB and Daystar meet all these minimum requirements, except for hostels. In all four universities, the hostels were inadequate and accommodated only a small percentage of students: USIU

167

(11.13 per cent), CUEA (19 per cent), Daystar (35 per cent) and UEAB (54 per cent).

Co-curricular activities

Co-curricular activities are important in facilitating the achievement of quality, all-round education. At USIU, sporting and recreational activities include basketball, rugby, Tae Kwan Do, swimming and aerobics. There are also clubs and associations including Red Cross, African Peace Initiative and Business Clubs. The university also has a gymnasium.

Daystar University also has sports and recreational facilities, clubs and associations. Co-curricular activities at CUEA include football, basketball, volleyball, table tennis, darts and 19 clubs and associations. There is also a student organization (CUSO) mandated to promote student welfare, the development and encouragement of their social and academic life and the establishment of co-operation with student organizations in other universities. Overall, students were generally satisfied with the co-curricular activities and facilities, although any substantial increase in enrolments is likely to strain the facilities.

5 Information & Communication Technologies (ICTs)

ICT resources and technologies enable institutions to receive/capture, process, store, transmit and display information in all its forms – audio, text and video. This chapter discusses the use of ICTs in the administration of the private universities and in the delivery of academic programmes. Mention has already been made in the previous chapter of ICTs with respect to the curriculum and learning systems. This chapter will focus on ICTs in themselves as strategic tools for the development of the private universities. In particular, it looks at ICT resources, utilization and management as well ICT strategic plans, policies and their implementation. Finally, the outcomes and challenges arising from the use of ICTs are discussed.

There is a positive correlation between economic development and telecommunications density. Compared with the rest of the world, Africa has the least developed infrastructure, with only 2 per cent of the world's telephones and an average teledensity of just over two telephones per 100 inhabitants (2.1 per cent in 1998). ICTs can be catalysts for development, providing the platform for knowledge generation and wide utilization.

The role of ICTs in higher education is succinctly stated in Article 12 of the World Declaration on Higher Education for the 21st Century: 'Higher education institutions should lead in drawing on the advantages and potential of new information and communication technologies, ensuring quality and maintaining high standards for education practices and outcomes in a spirit of openness, equity and international co-operation' (UNESCO, 1998). As Kenyan institutions of higher learning struggle to fulfil this role, the sector faces the following major challenges (Getao, 2001): limited infrastructure, telecommunications, networking and internet connectivity; prohibitive costs of laying down the necessary infrastructure, telecommunication equipment and tariffs; lack of proper content and standards and lack of ICT trainers.

ICT resources in the private universities

USIU, Daystar, CUEA and UEAB are at varying stages of development in the use of ICT facilities. The most notable constraint to full exploitation of these facilities is inadequate funding. This is largely because these institutions are tuition-dependent and reluctant to

169

transfer development costs to students in the form of increases in tuition fees.

USIU has e-mail, internet, electronic databases, CD-ROM data-bases, telephone (fixed line and mobile), fax machines and satellites (including DSTV for entertainment). Most of these were introduced between 1997 and 2000. USIU embraced ICTs to link the university to the rest of the world in order to facilitate worldwide (and local) communication and to market USIU.

Daystar also has e-mail, internet, telephone (fixed line and mobile), fax machines and CD-ROM databases, but lacks satellite com-munication. However, the university does have a communication studio with modern equipment for radio and television production. It has applied for a licence to operate an FM radio station within the campus. As at USIU, these changes were introduced, mostly in 2000, to improve communication between the two campuses of the univer-sity and with the outside world. UEAB and Catholic University also have telephones, e-mail, internet and CD-ROMs.

Most of the software used in these universities (both systems and application software) is from Microsoft. It includes Windows operating systems for stand-alone computers as well as for networks. Apart from Windows products, USIU also has a UNIX operating system (Linux) for the College Administration and Registration System (CARS), a data-base application that USIU uses for administration and management.

All the software used in the four universities is imported, because locally developed information systems were considered inadequate for the universities' requirements.

Strategic plans & policies

ICT strategic plans and policies are instruments to ensure effective management of information as a strategic resource by institutions of higher learning. Strategic management of ICTs includes formulating strategic goals, preconditions and starting points, drawing up policies and plans and finding ways to obtain material, human and financial resources (Looijen, 1998). The four private universities are all com-mitted to the development of strategic plans and policies to guide their use of ICTs. While USIU already has a fully developed ICT plan, the other three are still in the early development stages.

Among the highlights of USIU's five-year strategic plan for ICT development is the acquisition of increased bandwidth to facilitate distance-learning programmes and to help improve management information systems (USIU, 1998). To support the plan's implementation, the university made a budgetary allocation of Kshs.10 million, about 2 per cent of the total university budget, for the development of ICTs.

Daystar University's development plan has a component that sets out its vision towards embracing ICTs. The university has allocated an average of about 4 per cent of the total annual budget to support its ICT development, especially the networking of its two campuses.

The UEAB Development Plan recognises the inadequacy of its current ICT infrastructure, particularly the analogue line. The university intends to obtain a leased line to speed up data exchange and communications. In view of its rural location, the university also plans to install VSATs to facilitate information exchange through satellites. In addition, the number of computers are to be increased to 50, while an audiovisual laboratory is to be set up to complement existing learning resources. While CUEA is developing an institution-wide strategic plan with an ICT component, the CUEA information technology department has drafted in the meantime short-term plans to increase leased line bandwidth for more rapid data exchange and to prepare the university for e-learning.

A serious gap in all the four universities' strategic plans is the absence of the position of chief information officer who would lead the integration of planning and implementation of ICT programmes. None of them has a fully-fledged department in charge of ICTs, leaving only technical staff to manage the technology.

The use of ICTs has met with some resistance, especially in the areas of teaching and learning. Some faculty members are hesitant to put their lecture notes on the university Intranets for access by students. They prefer giving lectures where students take their own notes. Most of the networks, however, have the necessary security to check on unauthorized access. For example, USIU installed a firewall around its Intranet to keep out potential hackers and unauthorized users. A group of students cited the obsolescence of the notes—some lecturers were said to be using the notes they made during their student days – as the reason for not making them available on a public Intranet. Another factor might be some latent technophobia among faculty members, an issue that will need to be dealt with.

Utilization & management

The utilization of ICTs in the private universities is found mainly in two areas: academic – teaching, learning, research and library – and in administration and management. ICTs in both areas are managed by computer technicians, who ensure that the facilities are in sound condition.

The past two decades have witnessed an unprecedented transformation in both content and delivery of university education due to the use of technology in teaching and learning, especially in developed countries. But the use of ICTs in education does not necessarily guarantee effective learning. Technology only facilitates access to, storage and retrieval of information, which places the user at an advantage over a non-user. However, technology should not be seen as an end in itself but as a means to an end. ICTs were mainly used in the four private universities to facilitate learning and teaching. The universities also trained students in the use of ICTs in different disciplines.

As noted above, USIU has invested about Kshs.10 million in the development and maintenance of ICTs, including the introduction of e-learning. The university set up an integrated system for course delivery, students' information and financial information. Connecting faculty computers to the central network can improve academic productivity by providing online access to library resources, databases and teaching materials. Faculty at USIU have full internet access from their offices and can also access library databases and e-mail facilities.

Daystar University has not exploited the full use of ICTs because of infrastructural deficiencies (poor telecommunication facilities and lack of a network within and between its campuses). However, it has an ultra-modern broadcasting studio and, as already noted, has applied for a permit to start an FM radio station.

The use of ICTs in teaching and learning is still very low in these universities. Student access to computers is an indicator of their ability to tap into the information superhighway. CUEA has a computer/student ratio of 1:25; USIU, 1:19; UEAB, 1:30 and Daystar, 1:22. The average computer/student ratio in the four universities is 1:24. Although the CHE has not set standards for computing facilities, the above computer/student ratios indicate that students' access to computers is still very limited in these universities. This sense is reinforced by student interviews indicating dissatisfaction with the computer facilities (see Table II.15).

Even USIU, the pioneer in e-learning, will not be able to use this facility effectively without ensuring sufficient numbers of computers for student use. Internet access and on-campus connectivity will have little impact on future education if students cannot access the workstations needed to take advantage of these resources.

Table II.15: Student levels of satisfaction with computer facilities

University	Levels of satisfaction (%)	
	Satisfied	Dissatisfied
USIU	59	27
Daystar	37	45
CUEA	50	24
UEAB	43	43

As for the use of ICTs as tools in other disciplines, the challenge reflects on both the range and the availability of qualified faculty. The contents of these resources were mainly packaged in the West and are thus not contextualized for the Kenyan and African environment where the training takes place. The universities need a programme that empowers and/or motivates the faculty to package their own teaching resources for web communication. Also, there has been high turnover of ICT staff, and the universities find it hard to hire and retain such staff because of the higher salaries in the ICT industry than in the academic world. USIU tried to recruit ICT faculty from India but without much success.

ICT-mediated curriculum delivery

The internet and other ICTs present a strategic resource for universities to deliver teaching materials and to provide students with a good learning environment. By June 2001, USIU had pioneered the use of an e-learning environment to deliver pre-MBA graduate courses using the WebCT e-learning platform over the Intranet and internet (Kashorda, 2002).

Apart from the faculty learning how to develop courses in a new environment, students were also able to complete 50 per cent of the pre-MBA courses online. The project can be replicated in other programmes, especially in ICT and business programmes where there is inadequate academic staff. However, since much of the content is generated elsewhere, care should be taken to ensure that it reflects the needs of the diversity of learners in the university.

ICT-mediated research & administration

Universities can use ICTs to provide the information necessary for research. Moreover, the digitalization of research findings ensures wider dissemination and access. CUEA already has two of its journals

173

on the Electronic Supply of Academic Publications website. Computerization of libraries is another area where ICTs facilitate both research and teaching. So far, USIU is the only one of the four universities that has completely computerized its library and integrated it with other sections of the university. USIU's use of EURODITE library management software has significantly improved library acquisition, cataloguing and circulation. Through its interface with the campus Intranet, users can access the library from anywhere within the university.

USIU is also the only one of the four with campus-wide internet connectivity through its own Intranet. Only USIU has fully networked the various offices by setting up campus-wide area networks connected to both the internet and the library. The other universities have LANs mostly within computer laboratories and cyber cafés. Plans are under way, however, to establish campus-wide and inter-campus networking for Daystar's two campuses.

USIU has also embraced modern technology in its administrative functions and student information systems, financial and accounting information systems and office automation systems. Student registration, timetables, space allocations and utilization and budgets are also done online. The accounting and financial records at USIU are computerized using appropriate packages to monitor fee remission, enhance accountability and shorten auditing time and costs. With the USIU student information system, students are able to register for courses and obtain grade information online. Faculty and administrators are also able to pull out student records and compile reports, whether on enrolment or for accreditation purposes. The financial information system has been very useful for managing the financial resources of the university. Among its functions is maintaining a record of accounts for each registered student, an important tool for a private university that relies almost wholly on tuition fees. Departmental heads can also monitor their budgets online through this system.

Compared with USIU, the level of ICT use in the other three universities is still relatively low. CUEA, UEAB and Daystar universities suffer from poor telecommunications networks, which hinder maximum exploitation of ICT resources. They have not networked their libraries and therefore cannot offer the same comprehensive information resources as USIU. None of the three have developed comprehensive, institution-wide ICT strategic policies or plans to guide the planning for and development of these resources. They also require more training and user education to make better use of existing internet and CD-ROM resources.

174

ICT research & development

ICT research and development are critical for the identification of appropriate technologies that will bolster African development. While ICT research will be dictated by global technological changes, local ICT researchers should adapt international research results and technologies to the local context. ICT research in the private universities was still nascent at the time of this study, with the four selected using ICTs primarily to help in day-to-day management activities. The contents of their ICT programmes were biased towards computer applications rather than 'hard' computer science that would require substantial research. It is for this reason that the CHE had reservations about the contents of the computer science programme in one of the universities.

The Kenya Education Network (KENET), described above, aims at providing sustainable and faster internet connections for both private and public universities in Kenya. USIU and CUEA are already benefiting from the resources provided by the project, including access to over 7000 electronic journals. The project also provides funds for hardware, software and maintenance. When all these institutions are connected, the level of ICT research will improve, along with the sharing of research findings.

Benefits & constraints

Kenyan private institutions of higher learning would benefit tremendously if they fully embraced ICTs in their day-to-day functions. These benefits range from enhancing their efficiency to reducing costs and adding value to their programmes and services. The use of ICTs also saves time and enhances flexibility. At USIU, the electronic financial information system has drastically reduced audit time. Through this system, it is possible to implement an e–banking solution that completely eliminates the need to prepare and sign payroll cheques. After verification, the system communicates electronically with the bank, and payment is effected. The online registration of students has reduced registration time and eliminated complaints associated with the manual management of records. At Daystar, modern communication facilities, such as the communication studio, have helped to consolidate the academic programme in communications and contribute to its recognition as a centre of excellence in communication studies. Overall, these universities have made significant cost reductions in accessing journals by purchasing and subscribing to electronic databases.

In order to maximize the benefits of ICTs in the private universities there has to be sufficient preparation. The lack of appropriate infrastructure and staff has limited these universities from maximizing the potential of ICTs. For example, UEAB has a joint Master's in Public Health programme with Loma Linda University in the United States. However, due to the university's inability to exploit e-learning, the lecturers have to travel all the way from California to deliver the course.

Hardware acquisition and maintenance costs are among the major challenges facing these four private universities. The cost of acquisition of hardware for ICTs is relatively higher in Kenya than elsewhere, a problem that is compounded by the high import duty. Even though the duty on computers in Kenya has been reduced from 15 to 5 per cent, the cost of hardware is still 25–50 per cent higher than in North America. USIU spent US$110,000 on purchasing a server plus an additional US$60,000 for service. It also spends US$7,000 per month for maintenance of the internet (subscription and leased line). As most of these universities rely on student fees for their operations, an increase in fees to meet the cost of hardware would be prohibitive for most students.

Despite the challenges facing universities wishing to strengthen their information and communications technologies – the lack of ICT infrastructure, the lack of an enabling policy environment, staff technophobia, market forces and the inappropriate curriculum content of existing programmes – university leaders have recognized ICTs as central to the achievement of their objectives and are committing more resources to their acquisition and management.

6 Financing of Private Universities in Kenya

This chapter discusses the sources of finance for private university education in Kenya and the adequacy of such sources. It further analyses expenditure trends and the cost of private university education. Its findings are based on interviews with chief university financial officers and the analysis of secondary financial data obtained from the universities for the period 1994/95 to 2000/01.

Sources of university finance

Financial constraints bedevil both private and public universities and affect the entire African continent. In fact, the major financing challenge for Kenyan higher education is often 'how to do more with less', since available resources have been on the decline (Brown, 2001). In Kenya, furthermore, the legal distinction between a private and a public university lies in the source of funding. The Universities (Establishment of Universities) Standardization, Accreditation and Supervision Rules, 1989, stipulate that 'private university means a university with funds other than public funds. Public university means a university maintained or assisted out of public funds. In essence, law requires that private university funding be largely from non-public sources.' This definition is not only limiting but also challenges the concept of partnership in higher education.

The main sources of finance for private university education in Kenya include tuition and other fees; auxiliary enterprises; donations, grants and gifts; student loans, bursaries and scholarships and bank loans. Each of these sources is briefly discussed below:

Tuition & fees income

Tuition and other fees are the primary source of finance for private universities in Kenya. They rely on income from this source for their operations (recurrent) budget (see Table II.16).

Tuition income forms the base of private university funding, accounting for an average 100, 76, 72 and 40 per cent of the total annual income for USIU, Daystar, CUEA and UEAB respectively between the 1994/95 and 1999/2000 academic years. As can be seen from Table II.16, USIU was entirely tuition-dependent. Put together, the average contribution of tuition income to the total annual incomes of these four universities stood at 77 per cent.

177

Table II.16: Tuition income as a proportion of university revenue, 1995–2000 (Kshs. '000)

Item	1999/2000 Amount %	1998/99 Amount %	1997/98 Amount %	1996/97 Amount %	1995/96 Amount %
Annual Income					
USIU	477,233	434,500	369,260	274,800	228,118
Daystar	268,452	239,195	161,320	138,866	,566
CUEA	211,200	208,000	166,800	144,200	84.600
UEAB	222,000	183,000	184,000	164,000	169,000
Tuition income					
USIU (x = 100%)	477,233 100	434,560 100	369,260 100	274,800 100	228,118 100
Daystar (x =76%)	222,392 83	184,948 77	126,000 78	85,903 62	69,671 69
(CUEA) (x=72%)	157,500 75	136,300 65.5	131,100 78.6	104,200 72.3	58,700 69.4
UEAB (x =40%)	89,000 40	78,000 42.6	73,000 39.7	70,000 42.7	60,000 35.5

Source: Private Universities Survey, 2000.

x = average income from tuition.

Since private universities in Kenya rely heavily on tuition and fees income, the flexibility and stability enjoyed by these institutions becomes an issue of concern. Taylor and Massy (1996: 2) caution that:

> An institution's overall revenue structure reflects its diversity of funding sources. It is generally believed that an institution that derives its revenue from several independent sources enjoys greater flexibility and stability (in financial capital). By contrast, heavy reliance on one or a few sources – such as tuition or government appropriations – may result in greater volatility and unpredictability.

However, dependence on limited sources of funds may not necessarily be risky if the sources are dependable. For instance, USIU has a long waiting list (or 'queue') of applicants (owing basically to its attractive programmes, clientele niche, location and publicity), and therefore dependence on tuition income may not make it financially vulnerable. The same cannot be said of the other private universities. It was reported that universities such as UEAB, Daystar and CUEA, which used to have similar waiting lists, currently admit almost all qualified applicants. This was attributed partially to the

Table II.17: Tuition and fees as % of total recurrent expenditure, 1994/95–1999/2000

Year	Item, Amount & Percentage Surplus (or Deficit)		
	Recurrent Expenditure (Kshs. '000)	Tuition & Fees (Kshs. '000)	Percentage Surplus (Deficit)
1999/2000			
USIU	372,315	477,233	28.2
Daystar	294,404	222,392	(25)
CUEA	110,500	157,500	43
UEAB	204,000	89,000	(56)
1998/99			
USIU	381,302	434,560	14
Daystar	268,000	184,948	(31)
CUEA	96,600	136,300	41
UEAB	173,000	78,000	(55)
1997/98			
USIU	257,922	369,260	43.2
Daystar	210,000	126,000	(40)
CUEA	52,400	131,100	150
UEAB	180,000	73,000	(59)
1996/97			
USIU	205,694	274,800	33.6
Daystar	148,000	85,903	(42)
CUEA	40,500	104,200	157
UEAB	160,000	70,000	(56)
1995/96			
USIU	155,912	228,118	46.3
Daystar	130,000	69,671	(46)
CUEA	33,400	58,700	76
UEAB	164,000	60,000	(63)

Source: Compiled from data obtained from Private Universities Survey, 2000.

introduction of self-sponsored programmes in the public universities in Kenya. Increased reliance on tuition income may expose these private universities to financial volatility.

To remain financially stable, while at the same time depending on tuition as the primary source of income, the private universities must somehow ensure that student enrolments remain steady. Kenyan private universities are not alone in this predicament. Virtually all private higher education institutions are tuition-driven, with tuition and fees accounting, on average, for about 60 per cent of total annual income (Taylor and Massy, 1996). The adequacy of tuition and fees as a source of finance could also be scrutinized against their contribution to recurrent (operations) budgets in the institutions (see Table II.17).

Table II.17 reveals that USIU and CUEA could support their operations entirely from their tuition and fees income. UEAB and Daystar, on the other hand, could not sustain their recurrent expenditure with income from this source alone.

Auxiliary enterprises

Auxiliary enterprises are usually established to provide supplementary services for students, faculty and other staff. A fee is charged for such services, although the charge may not necessarily be equal to the cost of providing the service. Private universities in Kenya have generally made use of such facilities to generate revenue. Auxiliary enterprises established in individual universities vary in type and even level of development, but they all reflect innovation in the generation of finance for higher education. Income from auxiliary enterprises was rated as the second most important source of annual income at UEAB and Daystar (after tuition and other fees income).

UEAB may be the private university with the most developed auxiliary enterprises. The university generated 39, 35, 34, 38 and 33 per cent of total university income in 1995, 1996, 1997, 1998 and 1999 respectively from its auxiliary enterprises. In essence about 36 per cent of its annual income between 1994/95 and 1999/2000 came from auxiliary enterprises. The university benefits from the advantage of being located in an agriculturally productive area. The enterprises from which UEAB generates revenue include animal and crop husbandry (agriculture), a cafeteria, bookstore, clinic, laundry, carpentry workshop and snack shop. The university is self-sufficient in the production of milk, eggs, vegetables, maize and cheese and even offers a surplus for the market.

180

At Daystar University, auxiliary enterprises take the form of cafeteria and room/board services. These accounted for 31 and 17 per cent of the total university income in the 1994/5 and 1998/9 financial years respectively. At USIU, auxiliary enterprises accounted for 11 per cent of the total university operating revenues (less grants and scholarships) in 2000 and 2001. CUEA also generates funds from non-academic sources including a carpentry store, bookstore, canteen and leasing of facilities for conferences and seminars. Auxiliary enterprises were not well developed at CUEA, however, and some – like the canteen – operated at a loss.

Student loans, bursaries & scholarships

Students in chartered private universities benefit from student loans currently disbursed by the Higher Education Loans Board. The number of students benefiting and the amounts awarded vary from year to year and from one university to another. The HELB disburses Kshs.1 billion (US$13.9 million) every year, of which 2 per cent goes to students enrolled in chartered private universities. In 2002/03 some 332 of the 416 (80 per cent) who applied for HELB loans at UEAB were awarded Kshs.10.5 million, about 4 per cent of the university's total income that year, the number of loan awards having increased from 100 in 2000 to 225 in 2002 and 332 in 2003.

At CUEA, 303 students (86 per cent) of the 354 who applied for HELB loans in 2002/03 were successful, receiving a total of Kshs.9.5 million. Some 64 students at USIU received student loans in 2001. The university receives an estimated Kshs. 900,000 every year from the Loans Board. Interviews with student leaders and top university administrators in the private universities surveyed revealed that loans extended to students in these universities were generally insufficient to meet student needs. The HELB ceiling of Kshs. 52,000 was said to be inadequate, given the fee levels in the private universities. The Loans Board has fixed a similar ceiling on student loans for both the private university students and their counterparts in the subsidized public universities. Every student in a public university attending a regular programme receives a subsidy of up to Kshs. 70,000 per year.

Some of the students enrolled in the private universities in Kenya receive bursaries and scholarships from the Ministry of Education, which account for an average of Kshs.7 million per year (about 2 per cent and 4 per cent of university income at USIU and CUEA, respectively). UEAB students received government bursaries amounting to Kshs. 4 million (2 per cent of university income) in 2002.

181

In addition to loans, students can also qualify for bursaries of up to Kshs. 8,000 per year. In the 2004/05 academic year, private university loan recipients included, ranging from highest to lowest, 394 students at UEAB, 261 at CUEA and 233 at Daystar, to 36 at Africa Nazarene University, 29 at USIU and two at Scott Theological College.

Donations, grants, gifts & endowment

For private universities in Kenya, donations, grants, endowments and gifts constitute an important source of finance, especially for capital development. Donations constitute the largest portion of income for development expenditure at Daystar University. The university raises donations based on its development plans. By 2000 it had spent over Kshs.550 million, all obtained from donations and gifts, for the capital development of its new Athi River campus. Some 66 per cent of these donations came from overseas sources. Daystar solicits aggressively for donations and gifts and has even established two companies based in Canada (Daystar Canada) and the United States (Daystar US) specifically for this purpose. One of the fund-raising initiatives for Daystar US involved a capital fund-raising drive that was to raise US$6 billion over a six-year period. The majority of these donations and gifts came from churches (Lutheran, Baptist and Calvary).

Grants also formed a significant funding source for CUEA. The Association of Member Episcopal Conferences in Eastern Africa (AMECEA) bishops play a big role in making contacts for the grants and have also established the AMECEA Catholic University of Eastern Africa Endowment Fund. Many of the grantors for CUEA were from Germany, Switzerland and Italy, and most were Catholic organizations, funds or societies. It was estimated that 5 per cent of CUEA's total annual income came from grants.

UEAB also receives donations from both church and non-church organizations. As with Daystar, donations were the main source of funds for capital developments at UEAB. The Seventh-day Adventist Church fully funded the construction of a library, student centre and an auditorium. Other organizations' contributions included the health centre equipment (from Support Africa) and the construction of the technology building (from USAID). These donations were said, however, to have declined in both absolute and real terms over time.

Alumni contributions

Alumni are an emerging funding source with great potential for revenue diversification for the private universities in Kenya. The obvious limitation is that most of the private universities in Kenya are young, and their alumni themselves may not yet be well established financially. USIU has some 5,000 alumni, with branches in different parts of the country (the Mombasa branch, for example, has already set up a scholarship fund for students in the educationally disadvantaged Coast Province). An external alumni group (Uganda Alumni Association) had also been launched by 2001.

UEAB has already tapped this income source successfully. The Alumni Association of UEAB in conjunction with faculty, staff and friends has constructed over 1,000 metres of sidewalks connecting various buildings on the campus. This unique initiative dubbed the 'Step out of the mud project' raised US$100 for each three-meter sidewalk sponsored and US$50 for each 1.5 meter stretch of sidewalk. In return, the name of each contributor is inscribed on a footmark as a permanent mark of support. This project serves to demonstrate how initiative and innovation by the university can be an alternative source of finance and therefore a potential avenue for revenue diversification.

Bank loans & overdrafts

A few private universities in Kenya make use of credit facilities offered by banks to raise funds. The fact that the private universities are willing to access bank loans and overdrafts suggests the need to establish a higher education sector loan or grant for capital development. Resources for such a scheme could be pooled from the government, foundations, trusts and other donors and could be particularly useful for the private universities' introduction of expensive (science-oriented) programmes. Such a loan scheme could also support the public universities in the reconstruction of their dilapidated infrastructure. Under such a scheme, higher education institutions could borrow at below-market interest rates. The sector loan or grant could be national or even regional in scope.

Recurrent expenditure trends in the private universities

Recurrent expenditure drives the cost of private university education in Kenya. How an institution uses its funds to purchase various goods and services to support its current operations is reflected in its overall expenditure structure. The trends of an institution's recurrent expenditure structure can signal financial strength or financial vulnerability. The recurrent expenditure of the four private universities involved in the study was analysed over time.

183

Table II.18: Priority recurrent expenditure items, 1994/95–1999/2000

University/ Year		Items, Amount (Kshs.'000s) & Percentage							
	Recurrent Exp. ('000s)	Salaries Amount	%	Books/Journals Amount	%	Research Amount	%	Maintenance Amount	%
1999/2000									
USIU	372,315	135,171	36.3	17,698	4.8	201	0.1	-	0.0
Daystar	294,404	173,198	58.8	9,000	3.1	4,300	-	-	-
CUEA	110,500	61,800	55.9	10,500	9.5	-	-	-	-
UEAB	204,500	87,500	42.8	5,200	2.5	2,000	1.0	4,200	2.1
1998/99									
USIU	381,203	113,874	29.9	29,727	7.8	624	0.2	-	-
Daystar	268,000	146,000	54.5	8,000	3.0	4,200	1.6	-	-
CUEA	96,600	46,800	48.4	11,700	12.1	-	-	-	-
UEAB	173,000	70,300	40.6	5,200	3.0	2,000	1.2	3,500	2.0
1997/98									
USIU	257,922	100,724	39.1	1,084	0.4	-	-	-	-
Daystar	210,000	168,000	80.0	500	0.2	2,500	1.2	-	-
CUEA	52,400	24,700	47.1	8,600	16.4	-	-	-	-
UEAB	180,000	57,200	31.8	5,100	2.8	1,500	0.8	2,700	1.5
1996/97									
USIU	205,694	82,600	40.2	11,678	5.7	-	-	-	-
Daystar	148,000	60,000	40.5	0	0.0	500	0.3	-	-
CUEA	40,500	20,200	49.9	10,300	25.4	-	-	-	-
UEAB	160,000	23,500	14.7	4,700	2.9	1,000	0.6	1,800	1.1
1995/96									
USIU	155,912	50,409	32.3	3,875	2.5	-	-	-	-
Daystar	130,000	41,000	31.5	6,000	4.6	0	0.0	-	-
CUEA	33,400	15,900	47.6	1,100	3.3	-	-	-	-
UEAB	164,000	50,000	30.5	2,400	1.5	500	0.3	500	0.3
Totals									
USIU	1,373,046	482,778	35.2		0.0	825	0.1	0	0.0
Daystar	1,050,404	588,198	56.0	23,500	2.2	11,500	1.1	0	0.0
CUEA	333,400	169,400	50.8	42,200	12.7	0	0.0	0	0.0
UEAB	881,500	288,500	32.7	22,600	2.6	7,000	0.8	12,700	1.4

Source: Computed from data obtained from DVCs (Finance) at USIU, Daystar, UEAB & CUEA, 2000.

In response to a question on the three priority recurrent expenditure items for their universities, the Deputy Vice-Chancellors (Finance) in the four universities all said that salaries were the largest single item. The analysis of financial (secondary) data on operations expenses (Table II.18) confirmed their observation.

USIU kept its share of recurrent expenditure on salaries at or below 40 per cent over the study period 1994/5–1999/2000. On average, personal emoluments consumed 35 per cent of the operations budget every year during that period. The university's second most important recurrent expenditure item was books and journals. This item accounted for an average 5 per cent of the annual recurrent expenditure between 1994 and 2000.

Daystar University's expenditure on salaries has been growing. Whereas it was a modest 32 per cent in 1995, it shot up to a staggering 80 per cent in 1997. On average, Daystar's salaries bill accounted for 56 per cent of its recurrent budget between 1995 and 2000. The other two priority recurrent expenditure items for Daystar were cafeteria and administrative costs. These consumed 11 and 7 per cent of the recurrent expenditure respectively in 1999/2000.

UEAB spent the least on salaries of the four universities studied. Its average expenditure on emoluments between 1995 and 2000 was 32.7 per cent, about 2.5 percentage points lower than at USIU. In the 1999/2000 academic year, salaries and allowances took up 42.9 per cent of the total annual recurrent expenditure at UEAB, up from 30.5 per cent in 1995/6.

At CUEA, an average 50.8 per cent of the recurrent expenditure (1995–2000) went on payment of salaries, but the trend was unsteady. For instance in 1995, CUEA spent 48 per cent of its recurrent expenditure on salaries, but this rose to 56 per cent in 1999 and then fell to 53 per cent and 45 per cent in 2000 and 2001 respectively. As with USIU, CUEA reported that expenditure on books and journals was its second most important recurrent expense after salaries. The university voted a significant portion of its recurrent budget for the acquisition of pedagogical materials, in itself an important indicator of commitment to academic quality. CUEA spent 3 per cent of its recurrent expenditure on books and journals in 1995 but increased it rapidly to 25 per cent in the subsequent year, making an average 13 per cent of recurrent expenditure between 1994/5 and 1999/2000.

Expenditure on research in all four private universities is negligible, except at CUEA where it is being revamped and institutionalized. On average, the private universities allocate less than 1 per cent of

185

their recurrent budgets to research. The same situation prevails in the public universities in Kenya, even though research is often identified as one of their core missions. The revitalization of research activities through the provision of research funding and the improvement of research training for faculty then becomes a critical challenge for higher education in Kenya in general. Overall, the private universities under study had managed to keep their salary and wage bills within reason and thus managed to release resources for other critical pedagogical requirements. The share of instructional expenditures in the total recurrent fund expenditures (a measure of an institution's emphasis on academic vis-à-vis non-academic pursuits) is high, showing that the private universities are striving to preserve their academic core. Academic support expenditure in the private universities through such key services as libraries and computers receives serious attention in budgetary allocation.

The cost of private university education

The general perception of private university education in Kenya is that it is expensive and beyond the reach of the majority of Kenyans. This view may be true from the onset, given that 56 per cent of Kenyans live below the poverty line. The analysis of the cost of education through unit-cost computation and its comparison with the tuition charges prevailing in the private universities were therefore two of the objectives of this study.

One of the challenges facing educational policy-makers in Kenya today is determination of the unit (per student) cost of education. This study established that the determination/computation of unit costs has not been undertaken in either the private or the public universities in Kenya. Officials of the private universities indicated that they used cost estimates based on experience and/or anticipated expenditure and student enrolments to determine tuition charges. They also compare their fees with what their competitors charge before making a decision. Although there may be some danger of these universities acting as cartels in levying charges, this study did not come across such evidence. Initially, the perceived competitors had been the other private universities. Currently, the major market price-setter in the private universities seems to be the self-sponsored public university programmes. For fear of losing students to these programmes, the private universities have tried to hold back on further increases in their charges. Private university unit costs are largely course-based. Students are charged on the basis of a credit

Table II.19: Cost per credit hour/unit for undergraduate programmes

University	Cost in Kshs.	Cost in US$
USIU	3,305 per unit	46
Daystar	4,100 per credit hour	57
CUEA	2,325 per credit hour	32
UEAB	2,500 per credit hour	35

Source: Field data, 2001.

Table II.20: Tuition charges per year for undergraduate programmes

University	Cost in Kshs.	Cost in US$
USIU	171,540	2,383
Daystar	131,200	1,822
CUEA	117,760	1,636
UEAB	154,800	2,150

Source: Field data, 2001; Otieno, 2002.

hour or course. These charges vary from university to university with the total credit hour requirements eventually determining the cost per year for the respective universities (see Table II.19).

On the whole, the cost of university education per student per year (tuition only) for the six chartered private universities and the five with letters of interim authority ranges from a low of Kshs.117,760 (US$1,636) at CUEA to a high of Kshs.171,540 (US$2,383) at USIU. The exception is Scott Theological College, which charges only Kshs.55,000 (US$764), reflecting the heavy subsidy extended to students in connection with the college's goal of training staff for church work. In an attempt to determine whether the cost of private university education in Kenya was realistic, this study made independent computations which showed that the charges were in fact in line with their annual recurrent unit costs.

Tables II.20 and II.21 confirm that the tuition charges levied by the private universities reflect the prevailing recurrent costs incurred. If development expenses were factored in, the overall unit cost would be much higher. Apart from USIU, the other three universities indicated that they did not rely on tuition fees for development expenses.

The tuition fees charged by Kenyan private universities are modest when compared with those charged by private universities in other

Table II.21: Recurrent unit costs per student (in Kshs.), 1997/98–1999/2000

Year/University	Annual recurrent expenditure ('000s)	Enrolment	Recurrent unit cost per year
1999/2000			
USIU	372,315	2,354	158,163
Daystar	294,404	1,596	184,164
CUEA	110,500	1,492	74,062
UEAB	204,500	1,044	195,881
1998/99			
USIU	318,203	2,430	130,948
Daystar	268,000	1,815	147,658
CUEA	96,600	1,446	66,805
UEAB	173,000	952	181,723
1997/98			
USIU	257,922	2,076	124,240
Daystar	210,000	1,661	126,430
CUEA	52,400	1,350	38,815
UEAB	180,000,	842	213,777

Source: Computed from data obtained from private universities, 2000.

parts of the world. Hughes and Mwiria (1990), for example, established that the annual cost of private university education in India was US$1,675, US$9,450 in the UK/Europe and US$11,000 in the US/Canada, and costs have risen substantially since then. Tuition charges, however, do not reflect transportation and accommodation costs that are quite significant. Students at UEAB, for example, were required to pay an additional Kshs.62,100 (US$863) for housing and meals. In essence, resident students have to bear an additional cost for room and board equivalent to 52 per cent of tuition costs. A number of students (mostly male) opted to rent rooms in the university neighbourhood, despite the fact that the university had just built a new hostel with extra capacity which was therefore underutilized. At USIU, room, board and medical charges for resident students amounted to Kshs.144,525 (US$2,007) per year, while at CUEA accommodation cost Kshs.80,000 (US$1,111) per year. At Daystar, commuting students have to pay Kshs.49,000 (US$681) more for transport.

An intriguing finding was that USIU, which charges the highest tuition fees, also has the highest demand for its programmes. The university has managed to attract more students who could 'afford to pay comfortably and who now stand at 70:30 against those who pay with problems as opposed to 50:50 earlier' (USIU DVC Finance, personal interview, April 2001). USIU administrators also insisted that the university's fees were commensurate with the quality of its service. The chief finance officer summed it up thus: 'People go for quality. Our fees are still 16 per cent higher than our competitors' and yet we are able to attract more [students], and this year we even have a long waiting list!' (personal interview, DVC Finance, 25 April 2001). Students corroborated this view: 'Yes, fees are affordable. It is value for money. At USIU good services and quality education are provided to students, so one feels it is worth paying the money' (focus group discussion with student leaders, April 2001).

The USIU situation where high fee levels still attract more students could be a good argument for the cost-effectiveness of private universities in Kenya as well as an indication of the emergence of elitist private higher education institutions in the country.

The financial status of private universities

The analysis of financial data shows that the four institutions are largely liquid and solvent and that they have been able to post an operating surplus over a number of years. USIU had an operating surplus of Kshs.35.7 million (8.5 per cent) in 2000/01. Daystar's operating surplus in 1999/2000 stood at Kshs.4.7 million (5 per cent), while UEAB realized Kshs.18 million (8.1 per cent). CUEA's operating surplus was much higher: Kshs.100.7 million (47.7 per cent). The operating surplus of the private universities should be a good indicator that they are meeting their budgetary goals by living within their means. It does not, however, reflect the degree to which the universities are meeting their educational goals or the extent to which they are balancing their budgets – perhaps by starving programmes, deferring maintenance or taking actions that may affect their long-term operations (Taylor and Massy, 1996). For example, CUEA posted the highest operating surplus of the four, yet it was paying the lowest salaries. This might have affected its ability to attract and retain high-quality staff.

Despite the operating surpluses generated, it is a paradox that qualitative information obtained through interviews at these universities portrays them as facing financial challenges. The Deputy Vice-

189

Chancellor (Finance) at CUEA, for example, emphasized that 'sources of funds are far from adequate because of the growth experienced. There is need for a new library, a lot of basic infrastructure and a central administration block. We need physical facilities for sports, both indoor and outdoor. There is a dire need for more staff and staff offices' (interview, Deputy Vice-Chancellor (Finance), 2002). His counterpart at USIU also lamented the difficulties the university faced due to inadequate financing: 'We do not have the faculty we would want. We have 40 full-time faculty but we would have wanted 80 of them by now! The student/book ratio is lower than we would want; same with the student/computer ratio. We would want more and better classrooms' (interview, DVC Finance, 25 April 2001). This scenario, where private universities post a high operating surplus, re-ignites the 'for-profit' versus 'not-for-profit' debate in higher education.

Financial management strengths

This study identified five financial management strengths of private universities:

(i) *Sound fund-raising initiatives*: The universities, often led by the Vice-Chancellors as the chief fund-raisers, have initiated innovative fund-raising programmes, some with offices overseas to generate and attract funds for scholarships and capital development. The majority of capital investments are funded by such initiatives.

(i) *Adequate financial planning*: Most private universities have put in place participatory budgeting processes, and subsequent financial allocations have followed clearly stipulated and approved development and strategic plans.

(iii) *Professionalism*: In most of the private universities, officers in charge of finance are qualified accountants or have relevant financial training and experience. All four universities studied also reported high levels of financial discipline on the part of the chief executives.

(iv) *Liquidity and solvency*: Private universities maintained good financial health. They were liquid (could meet their immediate financial obligations) and solvent (with an excess of assets over liabilities). These universities have kept their salary bills within balance and were able to release resources for the purchase of other instructional support materials.

(v) *ICT-based financial management* : The accounting and financial records at the universities were computerized and appropriate packages (such as the CARS information system) employed to monitor fees remission and even enhance accountability and shorten auditing time and costs.

191

7 Recommendations

The private university sector in Kenya still has some distance to cover in providing services to its clientele. In this regard, the following recommendations are suggested:

Accreditation, governance & management

1. The Commission for Higher Education should adopt strategies that allow for easier, more efficient and more transparent evaluation of the accreditation procedures. The Commission should also attempt greater flexibility in allowing affiliated universities to initiate new programmes under a much more timely review process.
2. The CHE should also consider revising its accreditation requirements, some of which seem obsolete. The requirements for substantial campus size, for example, might become less relevant with the further spread of information technology.
3. University administration should be seen as a collegial responsibility, which includes staff participation in decision-making. Democratic processes in the private universities would be enhanced if the heads of faculties (deans) were elected by the faculty under their supervision. Administrative decisions must also be seen to be fair and just and implemented without favouritism.
4. About half of the teaching staff in the private universities are currently part-timers drawn from the public universities. With greater competition for the limited pool of academic staff in areas such as the sciences and ICT, the institutions will have to invest more in staff training if they are to survive.
5. In a competitive academic environment, it would be helpful if the religion-based universities loosened their emphasis on doctrinal issues with particular reference to staff recruitment and management.
6. Student governments represent an important resource in the management of student affairs. The university authorities should regard student leaders as partners in common efforts to improve university conditions and to help shape the next generation of political leaders. There is much more of an open-door management style in most of the private universities than in the public ones (with the exception of UEAB), and further movement in this direction should be encouraged.

7, Key administrators might profitably establish a forum in which
the leaders of the private universities could have an on-going
exchange of ideas, innovations and experiences. A forum such as
the Kenya Private Schools Association could easily be replicated
in higher education.

Access & equity
1. Innovative strategies of widening access to the private universities
are needed, especially for the poor and disabled and marginalized
ethnic groups.
2. The private universities should diversify their courses by introducing more programmes in science and technology.
3. Support systems that encourage non-traditional students to thrive
– such as financial aid programmes and transport facilities –
should be strengthened.
4. Private universities should institute equity monitoring and evaluation systems to assess and improve equity of access to their
institutions.

Curriculum & learning systems
Four sets of measures are needed in this regard:
1. The private universities should develop and sustain partnerships
with the private sector and with the public universities to meet
the demands of learners. Priority areas include curriculum
development, teaching, research and internship.
2. The universities should consider improving the terms and conditions of service for faculty in order to attract and retain full-time
academic staff.
3. The universities should formulate research policies that seek to
mainstream research. Partnerships with industry/the private sector
should also promote research and the dissemination of research
findings.
4. University administrators should strive for a better balance
between market-driven demands and the traditional roles of
higher education when introducing new programmes, being care-
ful not to neglect fundamental issues on which African universities have a special responsibility to provide leadership.

In light of the shortage of highly trained staff, better measures are
needed for staff development at the private universities. These could
include revamping or instituting exchange programmes (national,
regional and international), especially for young scholars and

193

academic apprenticeships, where young scholars are partnered with senior professors in both local public and private universities for research capacity-building. Regional bodies such as the Inter-University Council for East Africa could easily facilitate such capacity-building programmes.

Information & communication technologies

Harnessing information technology is a key ingredient for development in the current age. Consequently, it is recommended that:

1. Institutions of higher learning should develop strategic plans, policies and benchmarks to enable the effective identification and implementation of appropriate technologies.
2. The universities should lobby for tax waivers on ICT-related equipment. This would enable them to acquire hardware at affordable rates and improve the infrastructure necessary for programmes such as e-learning.
3. Sharing information should be encouraged among private and public universities, both locally and globally. Initiatives such as INASP should be encouraged as a way of sharing information resources.
4. Institutions of higher learning urgently require appropriate facilities such as VSATs to circumvent the persistent telecommunications problems associated with wire-based communication, which depends solely on the effectiveness of Telkom Kenya.

Financing

The private universities need to further diversify their revenue sources if they are to offer attractive programmes at affordable costs and expand student financial aid facilities. Alternatives to increases in tuition fees might include enhancing entrepreneurship at the institutional level through leasing of assets, selling faculty expertise or conducting contracted research. Additional assistance could be sought from the government, foundations and other donors. Options include setting up long-term loans or grants for capital development. A soft loan facility for the diversification agenda of both public and private universities would be another alternative.

A country-wide study needs to be carried out to determine the unit cost of private university education in Kenya as a basis for rationalizing charges across courses and universities. The Higher Education Loans Board might consider pegging student loan ceilings to the fees charged in order to enhance the affordability of private university education.

The government should continue to support the establishment of private universities by providing such necessary infrastructure as roads and electricity and offering tax rebates or land grants as a way of encouraging educational ventures in areas that are important to Kenya's future. Finally, it would be helpful for the government to spearhead the formation of a consortium of private universities in Kenya or in East Africa as a way of obtaining development capital.

Appendix

Research methodology

This project had a participatory and interactive methodology. In addition, it included a central focus on building research capacity among young Kenyan researchers by providing a forum in which they could work independently with guidance from established scholars. The project was administered by Women Educational Researchers of Kenya (WERK), which has a philosophy and history of having younger researchers work together with senior ones to strengthen research capabilities. WERK established a project management team to steer the project and guarantee its quality, and an advisory board to review draft reports and participate in the project seminar series.

The project had two main components: the case-study field research and the seminar series. While the seminars were presented by recognized experts in particular areas, the field research was carried out by less experienced, often younger, scholars. The case studies focused on five main themes: management and governance, access and equity, information and communications technology, curriculum and learning systems and financing. Young researchers with a background and interest in the respective themes were identified and put in charge of data collection, analysis and writing of reports for each of the case studies.

Data collection

Research methods included document analysis, questionnaires, oral interviews (both key informant and focus groups) and observation. Document analysis was primarily important in eliciting quantitative data, which were used to corroborate information from other sources, especially those that might have had some qualitative bias. The documents included, *inter alia*, relevant acts of Parliament, statutes, charters, policy documents and the catalogues of the private universities. Records of student finances, staff and ICT use were also analysed. These data sources provided information on such areas as the mission and vision of the private universities, their accessibility and gender dynamics, level of staffing and financing and the use of new information and communication technologies (ICTs).

Questionnaires were distributed to 100 undergraduate students in each of the universities. In total, 400 student questionnaires were administered and response rates (overall, per site and per question item) varied. The same questionnaire was used for all four universities. Open-ended questions generated information on the students' regional origin and socio-economic backgrounds, sources of information on private university education and reasons for enrolling. The questionnaire also sought to determine student satisfaction or dissatisfaction with such variables as the diversity and content of courses offered; the quality of instruction; the methods of student evaluation; university social life; transport, accommodation and communication services; and the relevance of courses to labour market demands.

Both focus group discussions and key informant interviews were widely used in this project. Focus group discussions were held with student leaders at the four universities and generated information on the management of student affairs and student financial aid programmes. Key informants interviewed included Vice-Chancellors (at USIU, Daystar and UEAB); Deputy Vice-Chancellors (academic, finance and administration/student affairs); deans of schools, students and faculties; registrars; chairpersons of academic departments; other senior university administrators and lecturers. Other key informants included the Secretary of the Higher Education Loans Board and the Secretary of the Commission for Higher Education.

These interviews provided pertinent information on the broad themes of governance and management, curricula, financing, access and equity, efficiency, policy frameworks, physical and human resources and infrastructure. In addition, fact sheets were employed to obtain quantitative data on access (enrolment), equity (gender, regional, socio-economic), funding and ICT/library restructuring between 1994 and 2001. The data generated trends that informed the performance assessment of the private universities. In addition, researchers examined aspects of the physical infrastructure, such as computers, libraries, classrooms and co-curricular facilities.

Dissemination seminars

A unique component of the project was the incorporation of 'site dissemination seminars' upon completion of the draft reports. A seminar was held with top administrators at each of the universities studied to report the findings following initial data analysis, before wider public dissemination. This aspect enhanced interaction between the research team and each university's prime stakeholders. The forum also gave the research team a rare opportunity to verify and deepen its understanding of the findings. The site disseminations,

197

which were participatory and interactive, also helped in stimulating and supporting research capacity and scholarship among the young researchers. Moreover, the dissemination seminars helped correct misconceptions and brought to the fore gaps in the case-study reports that needed to be addressed.

References

Abagi, D. and J. Nzomo. 2001. 'Structural Reforms in Higher Education: Private Higher Education in Kenya'. Unpublished research report.

Abagi, O., J. Nzomo and W. Otieno. 2002. 'Structural Reforms in Higher Education: Private Higher Education in Kenya'. Unpublished research report. Nairobi.

Achola, P. 1997. *Access, Equity and Efficiency in Kenyan Public Universities*. Nairobi: Lyceum Education Consultants.

Aduda, D. 1994. 'Varsity Intake System Changed', *Daily Nation*, 24 September. Nairobi.

———. 1997. 'Clear Picture on Varsity Admission', *Daily Nation*, 8 February. Nairobi.

Ajayi, K. 1990. 'Academic Freedom and University Autonomy in Relation to Human Liberty: Nigeria as a Case Study', in B. D. Kaba and L.C.A. Rayapen (eds), *Relevant Education for Africa*. Yaounde: World Peace Academy.

Assie-Lumumba, N.D. 1994. 'Demand, Access and Equity Issues in African Higher Education: Best Policies, Current Practices and Readiness for the 21st Century'. Paper prepared for the Donors in African Education Working Group in Higher Education.

[AAU] Association of African Universities. 1999. *Revitalizing Universities in Africa: Strategies for the 21st Century: Final Report*. Arusha: AAU.

Association of Commonwealth Universities. 2002. *Bulletin* (February). London: ACU.

Barsito, K. 1999. 'Education Body Finding It Difficult To Recover Money from Beneficiaries', *The Standard*, 27 February. Nairobi.

Bokione, I. 2002. 'Alarm Raised over AIDS Toll on Varsity Lecturers', *The Standard*, 31 August. Nairobi.

British Council. 1996. *Report on Socio-economic Study of Access to University Education, Performance, Equity and Gender Issues*. Nairobi: British Council.

Brown, F. A. 2001. 'Challenges Facing Private Universities in Kenya: The Case of United States International University'. Paper presented at Women Educational Researchers of Kenya/Ford Foundation Seminar on the Role of Private Universities in Development in Kenya (29 February). Nairobi.

Catholic University of Eastern Africa. 2001. *Self-Evaluation Report*. Nairobi.

Central African News Agency. (undated). *East and Central* 3, 5. Nairobi.

Chandran, Emil and Booko Omwansa, 1999. *Needs' Assessment of the Kapiti Plain.* Nairobi: Daystar University.

Coombe, T. 1991. *A Consultation on Higher Education in Africa: A Report to the Ford Foundation and the Rockefeller Foundation.* London: Institute of Education, University of London.

Court, D. 1979. 'Education and Social Control: The Response to Inequality in Kenya and Tanzania', in Joel Barkan and John Okumu (eds), *Politics and Public Policy in Kenya and Tanzania.* New York: Praeger.

————. 1999. *Financing Higher Education in Africa: Makerere, the Quiet Revolution.* New York: Rockefeller Foundation and Washington, DC: World Bank.

Court, David and K. Kinyanjui. 1980. *Development Policy and Educational Opportunity: The Experience of Kenya and Tanzania.* Occasional Paper No. 33, Institute of Development Studies, University of Nairobi.

Daily Nation. 1999. 'Moi surprises audience', 30 November.

Darkoh, M.B.K. and K. Wambari. 1994. 'Towards Professional Excellence at Kenyatta University', *Journal of Eastern Africa Research and Development* 24: 78.

Daystar University. 1999. *Development Plan for the period 1999–2004.* Nairobi: Daystar University.

Deloitte and Touche (Kenya), 1994. *The Commission for Higher Education Private Universities Study: Final Report.* Nairobi: Commission for Higher Education.

Eshiwani, G. 1983. *Who Gets into Universities in Kenya: A Study of Social Backgrounds of Kenyan Undergraduate Students.* Nairobi: Bureau of Educational Research.

Galava, D. (1999) 'For the Sake of Our University', *Kenyatta University Tribune 14th Graduation.* Nairobi: Kenyatta University, Vice-Chancellor's Office.

Getao, K. 2001. 'Trends in Information and Communication Technology and Their Significance in Higher Education in Africa'. Paper presented at WERK Seminar on Private Universities, Nairobi.

Gichaga, F. 1999. 'Graduation Speech'. University of Nairobi, 27th Graduation Ceremony. Nairobi.

[GoK] Government of Kenya. 1998. *First Report on Poverty in Kenya: Poverty and Social Indicators,* Vol. II. Nairobi: Government Printer.

————. 1999. *Population and Housing Census.* Vol. II. Nairobi:

Government Printer.

————. 2004. Ministry of Education, Science and Technology. *Development of Education in Kenya*. Nairobi: Government Printer.

Gravenir, F.U. and E.K. Mbuthia. 2000. 'Generating Supplemental Sources of Income by Universities in Kenya: A Case Study of Maseno University'. Paper prepared for Conference on Higher Education at Kenyatta University, Nairobi.

Harman, G. and M. Selim (eds). 1991. *Higher Education and Financial Resource Problems in the Asian and Pacific Region in Funding for Higher Education in Asia and the Pacific*. Bangkok: UNESCO.

[HELB] Higher Education Loans Board. 2001. *HELB Review: Financing Higher Education*. Nairobi: HELB.

Hughes, R. and K. Mwiria. 1990. 'An Essay on the Implications of University Expansion in Kenya', *Higher Education* 19: 215–37.

Indangasi, H. 1991. 'Teaching English at University-level in Kenya'. Paper presented at seminar on the Teaching of English and Literature organized by the British Council, Nairobi.

Kanake, L. 1997. *Gender Disparities among the Academic Staff in Kenyan Public Universities*. Nairobi: Lyceum Education Consultants.

Kashorda, M. 2002. 'Using Information Technology in Higher Education.' in *Proceedings of the First Exhibition by Kenyan Universities*. Nairobi: Kenyatta University.

Kenyatta University, 2001. 'Vice-Chancellor's Report for 2000/2001 Academic Year'. *Kenyatta University Tribune*. Nairobi: Kenyatta University.

Koech, D. 2000. *Totally Integrated Quality Education and Training (TIQET): A Report of the Commission of Inquiry into the Education System of Kenya*. Nairobi: Government Printer.

Looijen, M. 1998. *Information Systems: Management, Control and Maintenance*. Deventer: Kluwer Bedrifsinformatie.

Manuh, T. et al. forthcoming. *Change and Transformation in Ghana's Publicly-Funded Universities: A Study of Experiences, Lessons and Opportunities*. To be published in association with Partnership for Higher Education in Africa. Oxford: James Currey.

Moi University. 1994. *Moi University Six-Year Development Plan 1994/95–1999/2001*. Eldoret: Moi University.

Mudhai, F. 1996. 'Funding Varsities: Budget Cutbacks Affect Facilities', *The Standard*, 12 October. Nairobi.

Mugonyi, D. 1996. 'Students to Blame for Low Academic Levels', *Kenya Times*, 28 September. Nairobi.

Murunga, G. 2001. 'Private Universities in the Kenyan Higher

Education Experience'. *CODESRIA Bulletin* 1 & 2. Dakar.

Mwiria, Kilemi. 2002. *Vocationalization of Secondary Education: Kenya Case Study.* Washington, DC: World Bank.

Mwiria, K. and C. K. Ngome. 1998. *The World of Private Universities: The Experience of Kenya.* Northern Policy Research Review and Advisory Network on Education and Training, University of Edinburgh.

Mugwiria, Stanley. 2001. 'The Long Journey to my MBA'. *Sunday Nation,* 17 June.

Ndiritu, D.W., J.M. Chege and K. Atheru. 1995. 'Self-sustaining Programmes for Kenyatta University'. Paper presented to the Kenyatta University Annual Staff Management Seminar held at Mombasa, 31 October to 4 November.

Ngome, C. K. 2003. 'Kenya', in D. Teferra and P.G. Altbach, (eds), *African Higher Education: An International Reference Handbook.* Bloomington, IN: Indiana University Press.

Odalo, B. 2000. 'Undeserving Students get HELB Loans', *Daily Nation,* 5 March, Nairobi.

Ogot, B.A. 2002. 'The Enterprise University: Real or Pseudo?' Paper prepared for exhibition by Kenyan Universities. Nairobi: Commission for Higher Education.

Okwemba, A. 2002. 'University Course for Herbalist', *Daily Nation,* 25 July. Nairobi.

Ondiek, Gordon. 1997. 'It's a Shs.500 Million Varsity Rip-Off', *The People's Daily,* 7 March. Nairobi.

Onyango, D. 2002. 'Hard Lesson in Varsity Parallel Classes', *Sunday Nation,* 18 August. Nairobi.

Otieno, W. 2002. 'Evening Programmes Changing Varsity Life'. *Sunday Nation,* 4 August. Nairobi.

——— . 2002. *Student Loans in Kenya: Past Experiences, Current Hurdles and Opportunities for the Future.* International Higher Education Finance and Accessibility Project. Buffoalo, NY: Center for Comparative and Global Studies in Education, State University of New York.

Republic of Kenya. 1981. *Second University in Kenya. Report of the Presidential Working Party.* [the MacKay Commission]. Nairobi: Government Printer.

——— . 1988. *Report of the Presidential Working Party on Education and Manpower Training for the Next Decade and Beyond.* [Kamunge Report]. Nairobi: Government Printer.

——— . 1994. *Report of the Auditor General (Corporations) on the Accounts of Kenyatta University for the year ended 30 June 1994.*

Nairobi: Government Printer.

————. 1996. *Report of the Auditor-General (Corporations) on the Accounts of Maseno University College for the year ended 30 June 1996.* Nairobi: Government Printer.

————. 1997. 'The Universities Act 1985'. [reprint]. *Kenya Gazette* 40. Nairobi: Government Printer.

————. 1999. *Report of the Auditor-General (Corporations) on the Accounts of Kenyatta University for the year ended 30 June 1999.* Nairobi: Government Printer.

Rontopoulou, J. 1999. *Evaluating Higher Education.* Paris: UNESCO.

Rosenberg, D. (ed.). 1997. *University Libraries in Africa: A Review of Their Current State and Future Potential.* London: International African Institute.

Saint, W. 1992. *Universities in Africa: Strategies for Stabilization and Revitalization.* Washington, DC: World Bank.

Schuller, T. 1991. *The Future of Higher Education.* Buckingham, UK: SRHE (Society for Research into Higher Education) and Open University Press.

Sifuna, D. N. 1997. 'Crisis in the Public Universities in Kenya', in K. Watson et al. (eds), *Reforms in Higher Education.* London: Cassell.

————. 1998. 'The Governance of Kenyan Public Universities', in *Research in Post-Compulsory Education* 3 (2): 175–211.

Standa, E.M. 2000. *Vice-Chancellor's Report on Causes of Riots and Disturbances in Public Universities.* Nairobi: Jomo Kenyatta Foundation.

Taylor, B. E and W. F. Massy. 1996. *Strategic Indicators for Higher Education: Vital Benchmarks and Information to Help You Evaluate and Improve Your Institutions' Performance.* Princeton, NJ: Petersons.

UNESCO. 1998. *World Declaration and Framework for Priority Action for Change and Development in Higher Education.* Paris: UNESCO.

University of Nairobi. 1999. *Report on Rationalization of Functions and Staff Rightsizing.* Nairobi: University of Nairobi.

[USIU] United States International University. 1998. *USIU Strategic Plan, 1998–2003.* Nairobi: USIU.

Wakabi, M. 1999. 'Probe Launched as Makerere Expels Minister', *The East African,* 15 March.

Wambua, C. 1997. 'Nairobi Is No Longer a Shining Example', *Daily Nation,* 20 July. Nairobi.

Watitu, E .2001. 'KU Disabled Face Tuition Fees Crisis'. *The Standard,* 1 December. Nairobi.

Wesonga, D., C. Ouma, D. Ngome and V. Wawire. 2002. *The Develop-*

ment and Role of Private Universities in Higher Education in Kenya: The Case of United States International University. Ford Foundation Sponsored Project. Nairobi: Women Educational Researchers of Kenya.

Wete, F. N. 1998. 'UNESCO Consultancy Report on a Model Curricula for Communication Training in Africa'. Unpublished report.

Woodward, D. 2000. *Managing Equal Opportunities in Higher Education: A Guide to Understanding and Action.* Buckingham, UK: SRHE (Society for Research into Higher Education) and Open University Press.

World Bank. 1993. *Social Gains from Female Education: A Cross-National Study.* Washington, DC: World Bank.

———. 1994. *World Development Report 1994.* New York: Oxford University Press.

———. 1997. *Primary Education in India.* Washington, DC: World Bank.

———. 2000. *Higher Education in Developing Countries: Peril and Promise.* Washington, DC: World Bank.